THE
SMART
ENTREPRENEUR

HOW TO BUILD FOR A
SUCCESSFUL BUSINESS

Bart Clarysse and Sabrina Kiefer

E&T

First published 2011 by Elliott and Thompson Limited
27 John Street, London WC1N 2BX
www.eandtbooks.com

ISBN: 978-1-9040-2788-1

The publisher is grateful to Ceres Power for permission to reproduce the
following images: the Ceres product journey diagram (page 145) and the
Ceres unit's integration with conventional systems diagram (page 146).

A CIP catalogue record for this book is available from
the British Library.

Typeset by EnvyDesignLtd
Printed in the UK by CPI Group

ACKNOWLEDGEMENTS

Thanks are due to many entrepreneurs, scholars and students, near and far, whose experiences and insights have found their way in some form into our thinking and this book, but who are too many to name here.

Kristien De Wolf was instrumental in co-developing, over the years with Bart Clarysse, a practical and structured method for coaching entrepreneurs which provided the inspiration for this book, and in helping us to deliver the method in its present form at Imperial College Business School. Johan Bruneel, another valued colleague, read early versions of many of the chapters and made useful suggestions.

Jean-Marc de Fety, Wouter Van Roost, Professor Colin Caro and Igor Faletski generously shared their time and enthusiasm in interviews for case studies. We also thank Luc Krolls and Rika Ponnet for consenting to our use of their written materials and video-recorded presentations for the case study in Chapter 4, and thank Bruce Girvan, Chris Thompson, Tom Allason, Frank Gielen, Johan Cardoen, Emma Stanton, Mirjam Knockaert, Mathew Holloway and Matthew Judkins for their contributions to the content and accuracy of case studies elsewhere in the book.

Matthew Dixon, of patent and trade mark attorneys Harrison Goddard Foote, cast an attentive and critical eye over Chapter 6, helping to make certain that our treatment of the ins and outs of intellectual property was precise and reliable. Chris Haley of Imperial Innovations helped us to identify a fitting science commercialisation story for our theme in Chapter 1.

In addition, three teams of students on the Innovation, Entrepreneurship and Design (IE&D) programme at Imperial College Business School created Figures 16 and 17 (Richard Lough, Rosie Illingworth, Howell Wong, Philippa Mothersill, Yann Helle and Lino Vital),

Figure 36 (Stacey Sunderland, Christina Stampfli, Damon Millar, Joel Tomlinson, Prashant Jain and Sebastian Lee), and Figure 37 (Solomon Oniru, Clementine James, Olga Borets, Saravanogiri Manoharan, and Luke Trybula).

We also thank Professors David Begg, Principal of Imperial College Business School, and David Gann, Chair in Technology and Innovation Management, for their support to the activities of the Entrepreneurship Hub at Imperial College, which made the IE&D programme possible.

Finally, we'd like to thank the people at Elliott & Thompson for their support, advice, patience and, finally, gentle nudge to get on with it and complete the book, particularly chairman Lorne Forsyth, former and present publishers Mark Searle and Olivia Bays, project manager Jennie Condell and copy editor Kate O'Leary. We are also grateful to author and friend David Charters for introducing us to this affable publishing firm.

CONTENTS

INTRODUCTION

"When I was in college, guys usually pretended they were in a band.... Now they pretend they are in a start-up. "[1]

The entrepreneurial dream

Over the last 15 or so years, 'entrepreneurship' has become synonymous with 'cool'. Paraphrasing the above quotation, you could say that garage rock has been replaced by garage start-ups.

Enterprise has also become a more accessible option for a larger group of people than previously, thanks to the advent of new technological opportunities. In the 1990s, as the reach of the internet and world wide web spread beyond the academic and governmental space into the civilian and commercial arenas, new business models could be conceived to transfer normally face-to-face commercial interactions into the virtual world. Services could be automated and productised, customers could be reached and products downloaded globally, niche markets could be created and served in an economical and unprecedentedly profitable manner. A venture could be started at little cost by a few people tapping code on some computers. A relatively inexpensive website interface could replace a capital-intensive chain of bricks and mortar shops or branches, and a customer base could be built up quickly and 'virally'.

Hence was born a new generation of technology entrepreneurs, whose celebrity status was achieved in record time and stretched beyond the 'in' community of Silicon Valley to the readership of the broadsheet dailies, not to mention television and films. From a business perspective, things became a little silly at the end of the 1990s, when many investors were willing to fund any revenue-less proposition that involved a website, but after the bubble burst a sobered-up new economy began to materialise in the new millennium.

Perhaps not sober enough, though. Entrepreneurship has turned into something of an industry in its own right, spawning a slew of how-to and how-I-did-it books, fanzine-like websites about the start-up scene, and blogs by entrepreneurs and venture capital investors. European universities have played catch-up with those in the US by setting up entrepreneurship centres, business plan competitions, start-up incubators and student entrepreneurship clubs. Politicians and policymakers sing the praises of technological innovators and entrepreneurs as the seeders of future economic growth, and sometimes create public agencies to promote enterprise culture. 'Entrepreneurial attitude' has also come to be considered a positive attribute in high-level job seekers.

Throughout this quasi-industry runs the inebriatingly romantic and inspirational image of the lone entrepreneur; something of a renegade and iconoclast, a charismatic autodidact with an unconventional dress sense (or perhaps none at all), who knows what people will want to purchase before they know it themselves. The archetypal entrepreneur's start-up company generally begins its life in a shed, garage or student house (probably in California), an impressively contrasting image to that of the minnow firm's subsequent expansion into a multi-billion-dollar company.

Why do we propose to join this industry by producing yet another book on entrepreneurship? First, because we have been coaching entrepreneurs since the mid-nineties and were deeply involved in a number of start-ups ourselves. Over time, we saw that the same sorts of problems were raised, almost repetitively, by the different entrepreneurs who came to us for help. Often, just one or two workshops gave them enough of a grounding to get started and overcome initial barriers to growing their ventures. We turned the vast amount of material accumulated through this experience into a core entrepreneurship programme at Imperial College Business School which, we think, has become rather good. This book is an extension of that programme and reflects our hands-on approach to coaching students through entrepreneurial projects and starting entrepreneurs on their journeys.

Second, because the above-mentioned typecast character and many books on entrepreneurship hail from the US, we think a need exists for a book which offers a European perspective, using European case studies and taking into account some of the challenges faced by European entrepreneurs, including the higher degree of scepticism and risk aversion generally found on this side of the Atlantic. The European entrepreneur does not necessarily fit the mythical American stereotype (and many US entrepreneurs probably don't either). Many of the examples in this book thus provide useful guidance for UK and European entrepreneurs and students interested in entrepreneurship.

Third, because not every entrepreneurial light-bulb moment is destined to become the next Google. A tremendous amount of uncertainty surrounds every venture idea at its conception, and we hope that the structured approach presented here can help the reader to manage that uncertainty, by testing his early assumptions about a business idea and adjusting them, if need be, to end up with a more probable business proposition. We don't want to take the excitement or vision out of entrepreneurship, but we do want to insert a bit of realism.

We also hope to convey some insights from academic research that may be applied in practical ways to the shaping of a business concept and the creation of a company – not as hard and fast rules but as initial aids to face the uncertainty inherent in a new venture with an open and dispassionate mind.

The lowest-common-denominator advice frequently given to novice or aspiring entrepreneurs tends to be construed by its recipients as:
 • Get an idea and set out to write a business plan.
 • Search for information in support of your idea to plug into the business plan (shoehorn it in, if necessary).
 • Pitch the business plan confidently to investors and raise money.

However, we stress that, before you can convince an investor or even a customer, you need to convince yourself, with an argument that's a little more than personal conviction or the citation of some high-level market figures from a generic industry report. That's why we propose a book about putting together a business *case* for a new venture, not a book on how to write a business plan.

A business plan is simply a document describing the business you intend to start – essentially, what it will sell, how it will operate and how it will make money. An entrepreneurial business *case* is the rationale embedded in the business plan, explaining why the business is capable of thriving – the *substance* of your business plan. This book aims to provide the tools to build a credible rationale.

Entrepreneurial reality

Only 45 per cent of businesses started in the UK in 2002 survived the five years to 2007,[2] and the *average* sales turnover for small and medium-sized enterprises (less than 250 employees, accounting for 99.9 per cent of UK businesses) in 2007 was £298,000.[3] To reiterate, not all new businesses become Google. Note that these figures cover a period of relative economic prosperity, not a recession. Furthermore, these are general numbers referring to any type of new firm, including small businesses in mature, stable sectors, such as a local restaurant or corner shop.

What we instead call entrepreneurial 'venturing' – starting innovative businesses with high-growth ambition and subject to considerable uncertainty and risk – cannot rely on such stable sectors and business models, and it is this area of new business creation that we address in this book. Innovative ventures typically deal with a product, market or idea that's so novel that little past data or experience exists from which to generate easy predictions about its success. Such start-up ventures also lack the financial resources, established reputations and staying power of large companies. The venture entrepreneur doesn't yet have a direct line of communication to potential customers; in fact, at the beginning of her entrepreneurial journey she may not even know who the right customers will be, nor how the business should be structured. With no exact statistics for business survival in this unstable environment, a failure rate of some three out of four start-ups is the oft-quoted rule of thumb.

This book is consequently aimed primarily at innovation-and high growth-oriented businesses, usually in the form of technology ventures or businesses with new product and service models. Entrepreneurs in these novel situations may need considerable financial capital to start, thus requiring a plan for high growth to justify the investment, and are likely to have less room for trial and error once capital has been invested. Consequently, they have to proceed in small incremental steps, investing time and money in stages, making use of any information they can obtain, applying some cool judgement and willingly adjusting their plans as they become wiser.

We often apply the analogy of dating and finding a spouse to the process of developing a start-up. When you first meet a potential partner, your information about that person is incomplete. Consequently, you're unlikely to propose a commitment to marriage the next day. Nor can you really undertake meticulous research – you'd have to contact your prospect's friends and former love interests and they're unlikely to be accommodating. So, perhaps you start with a short date for coffee and, if that goes well, follow it with a dinner date and so on. At each meeting you learn a bit more about the person, perhaps eventually meet some of their friends, and at each stage your increased insight helps you decide whether to go further. If you discover a 'deal-breaker' flaw, you eventually wind down the relationship; if your perceptions and experiences continue to be predominantly positive, or more positive than negative, you take the further steps leading to a possible long-term commitment.

The decision to start a venture develops in a similar manner, with gradually increasing degrees of personal and material investment.

Who is this book for?

This book will appeal to the following readers:

Aspiring entrepreneurs. You may be considering taking a break from a career in industry or finance to start a venture of your own. Perhaps you've been turning an idea over in your head for some time, but aren't entirely sure how to make it happen. You may have some technical and business skills and knowledge, but not the entire range needed to incubate a new venture. You want to develop these skills to some extent yourself and, even more importantly, understand enough to identify the right skilled people to complement you in the enterprise.

More specifically, if you've been working in an established business or running your own company in a stable environment, chances are that your acquired management skills haven't equipped you to understand, navigate and mitigate the uncertainty that's typical of a new venture, where the environment in which your business operates – or your knowledge of it – frequently shifts and demands that you reshape your idea.

Students, academics and inventors. If you're a student on a business, engineering or science course, you may have been tasked with developing an entrepreneurial project as part of your coursework. Or you may be thinking of starting a business outside of your studies or after you graduate. Or you're putting a business plan together for a competition.

This isn't a textbook to prepare you for an exam or to write an essay on entrepreneurship; rather, it's a practical manual to help you research and prepare a credible business case. The content is the same as that offered to our MBA students on the Innovation, Entrepreneurship and Design course at Imperial College Business School, and – in amended form – to students in the engineering, medicine and science faculties.

If you're an academic considering commercialising an invention or piece of research, this book will also help you understand important aspects of commercialising new knowledge or technology.

Industry. You may be a manager who aims to stimulate entrepreneurial thinking and innovation in your company, or an employee who'd like to launch an 'intrapreneurship' idea. How can the engineers and technicians who design and build products communicate and work with the marketing people who understand customers and the finance people who run cost–benefit analyses? And how can they co-operatively address the stumbling blocks and avoid the blind spots of habit that arise when you depart from established business activity to pursue new opportunities?

This book addresses these different modes of thinking, and includes exercises we have used with success both in university courses and workshops aimed at students of business and other disciplines – such as engineering, science and design – and in executive education sessions on corporate venturing. It can be used on its own or as a handbook for such sessions, as well as for 'accelerator' courses, aimed at developing career skills, such as those run by universities and company academies.

Investors. Finally, you may be entering the world of new venture investment, either as an angel investor preparing to risk your own money or as an employee of a venture capital fund. This book can just as easily be used as a due diligence tool to help you assess a potential investment.

If you're an experienced investor, you can recommend this book to new or aspiring entrepreneurs so they can understand how to satisfy your investment criteria.

How to use this book

The book is divided into four sections, which we present as stages in an entrepreneurial journey. This construct is somewhat artificial, as the evolution of a new business concept is neither so linear nor so predictable in reality. To aid the reader's understanding, however, the information must be presented in a linear and reasonably logical fashion.

Stage 1: Idea creation and evaluation

Our aim in this section is to look at how business ideas are matched with credible opportunities, whether you're starting from a perceived market or from a technology or competence that you'd like to commercialise. We emphasise the importance of considering a range of possibilities and evaluating each new idea with respect to existing alternatives already on the market, and perhaps modifying or improving it accordingly.

Stage 2: From idea to business proposition

This section looks at the broadening of an initial idea for a product, service or application into a rounded business strategy, by employing preferred witness research (see Chapter 4) to identify and roughly quantify a target market. We show you how to consider the opportunities or limitations of your prospective business environment (Chapter 5), how to protect your ideas and inventions from imitation by competitors (Chapter 6), and how to draw on this information to shape a commercial strategy (Chapter 7).

Stage 3: Proof of concept

This section covers ways to demonstrate and test your business proposition, both technically and commercially, through prototyping and some rough-and-ready market testing.

Stage 4: Marshalling resources

This section describes the resources – primarily human and financial – you need to bring a business to fruition, and discusses how to work out a strategy and roadmap for obtaining the most suitable resources at the right time.

Depending on the current status of your business idea, you may find yourself reading each chapter sequentially from start to finish, or jumping forwards and backwards from one topic to another as you need them – rather like consulting a recipe book. Each chapter is thus structured as a self-contained mini-manual, but also refers to related content in other chapters.

Several chapters contain a structured how-to exercise to help you assess and shape a certain aspect of your business case. While these exercises may at first seem rather formulaic, practising them offers a way to retrain your thinking about issues that every venture must consider. Each new venture has a particular set of objectives and problems, so some activities or exercises will be more relevant to your concept than others. Each chapter also contains case examples to illustrate the real-world relevance of each topic.

The Epilogue aims to tie the pieces together and outlines what we hope you can achieve from using this book. No book is a panacea for all problems and no methodology is fool-proof, but our aim is to get you fairly far along the initial process of 'dating' your business idea.

We wish you well on your entrepreneurial journey.

SECTION I
IDEA CREATION AND EVALUATION

1.UNDERSTANDING THE FIT BETWEEN OPPORTUNITIES AND IDEAS

Fitting opportunities to ideas

New ventures aren't conceived in one sitting. Every new venture starts with a perception of an opportunity and the small seed of an idea. During the entrepreneurial journey that follows, this initial hunch will be investigated and developed, reality-tested, corrected, investigated and developed a bit more, reality-tested again and so on. The process continues until an entrepreneur feels enough certainty about the potential value of the idea to think investing time and money (her own and other people's) in it worthwhile – or else discards it as unfeasible.

Before anything else, your venture will rest on two essential ingredients: the identification of a good opportunity and a solution to exploit that opportunity. This stage of your entrepreneurial journey – the *idea* stage – introduces you to the early building blocks for finding these two ingredients.

The first thing you'll do on your journey – and the first thing an investor will eventually ask you to do when you come to meet one – is to outline your opportunity and your solution. So we devote two chapters to introducing different ways of finding and assessing opportunities and solutions. This isn't a one-off exercise, however; you'll refine your opportunity definition as you move through the subsequent stages of your journey, exploring all the factors that could help or hinder your business.

Most of this book is about testing, elaborating and modifying your initial idea about your opportunity and your solution. This first section is devoted to making a few early and basic decisions about your idea (what the business might sell, or several variations) and why it may be a sellable business proposition (the opportunity), using information you already have or can obtain fairly easily, mixed with a bit of your intuition. Later sections of the book are devoted to gathering more information to test your early assumptions.

Many aspiring entrepreneurs move straight from this early idea stage into writing a business plan, and will selectively seek out information that backs their original idea. We do not recommend this approach. Like the first draft of a document, your first idea is more of a hypothesis than a reality, and likely to need retuning before it becomes a proposal for a viable business. Stage 1 helps you make your idea clear and concrete enough for you to start investigating its value in the next stage.

Sources of opportunity

Your opportunity is the compelling reason why your business idea would appeal to customers, and is usually defined as an unsolved problem, a gap in the market or an unaddressed 'customer pain' with respect to existing products or services. Your solution is the thing you'll sell, which may be a product, service or combination of the two, or possibly a platform technology that will be turned into products by others.

It is important to emphasise that, even if you have already devised a technology or designed a product, you'll need to find a genuinely compelling opportunity to sell into. If you don't find a compelling opportunity, you won't have a viable business.

Starting points for new venture ideas typically fall into two broad categories:

- *The demand–pull idea.* This arises in response to a customer need or problem, whereby the entrepreneur needs to create a profitable, innovative solution to meet a need.
- *The 'knowledge–push' idea.* This typically involves a new technology or competence, whereby an innovative solution itself may seem like an opportunity but the entrepreneur must seek a profitable area of application and market – that is, a problem seeking that solution.

We dedicate one chapter to each type of starting point, containing different thinking tools to aid your first steps. The rest of the present chapter is devoted to outlining the difference between the two.

The demand–pull or 'entrepreneurial' business idea

The most compelling opportunities frequently come from satisfying demands overlooked by your competitors. If you can solve a pressing problem in a way that will suit potential customers or meet a desire that other companies have missed, your product or service has a good starting chance of being adopted.

How are unmet needs discovered? Frequently an entrepreneur happens upon an unsolved problem through personal or professional experience or observation of the experience of a relation or friend. If she subsequently discovers that the experience is not individual but widespread (a market), and can determine the cause of the problem (thus suggesting possible solutions), a business opportunity presents itself. The conception and consideration of potentially promising solutions becomes the basis of the idea stage in a demand–pull situation.

Tom Allason's courier nightmare: the seed of eCourier.co.uk

'Does your courier make you happy?' flashes an animated video on the eCourier.co.uk website. The courier business may not appear to be a fertile bed for innovation, but possibly because no one before Tom Allason felt aggravated enough to see it that way. Like many urban office workers, Allason had already experienced unreliable 'express' courier services but, one day in 2003, a slow and slovenly courier made him so unhappy, while he tried to send last-minute event tickets to a group of friends, that he concluded he could probably do a better job himself.

Repeated phone calls to the culprit courier company revealed to Allason that the company's despatch office never knew exactly where the assigned courier was at a given time – whether near the destination or elsewhere. To track his parcel, the despatcher had to radio the courier to discover his location and then phone Allason to pass on the information. Jobs were assigned to individual couriers based on their workload, not their proximity to a customer's location. As a result of traffic problems and the constant juggling of multiple and geographically scattered jobs by the same courier, accurately predicting location or delivery time was impossible, so a premium-priced service that was meant to be a 'fast solution' could end up being neither. Here was a typical customer problem. Could a set of causes be identified?

After berating the boss at the courier company and being told to try doing a better job himself if he was so dissatisfied, Allason decided to investigate the potential opportunity with a bit of further research. In addition to the problem of real-time information, Allason learned that the £1 billion same-day courier industry was extremely fragmented between many small firms (600 in London alone). In fact, it wasn't profitable for a courier company to become too large. The sector's operational model meant that, as customer volumes increased beyond a certain threshold, the number of control room staff – and hence overhead costs – would rise too much in proportion, reducing profit margins. Heavy price competition between so many courier companies also meant this cost could not be passed to customers. This drove wages down, consequently depressing staff morale and performance, as couriers had to take on more deliveries for less pay.

Allason's idea in response to this situation? He thought that if the order and despatch process could be automated and optimised with the use of technology, including a tracking system to monitor each courier's movement around the city, operating costs would go down while order fulfilment would improve.

The entrepreneurial journey proceeded from there. Along with friend and co-founder Jay Bregman, Allason began to search for an expert who could build such technology. They found a team at two Italian universities to build the system for less than $500,000, which Allason managed to raise from friends, family and individual investors, and persuaded logistics expert Dr Cynthia Barnhart, of MIT, to oversee the project.

Today, the eCourier.co.uk despatch system, dubbed 'Larry' by the company, allows customers to book deliveries online, reducing telephone operator staff and saving money. It uses GPS technology and advanced metaheuristics to locate and book the optimum courier for the job – calculating time needed to reach location rather than just distance, by taking into account the road layout and traffic conditions at different times of day. It tracks the progress of pick-up and delivery, so each customer can view his parcel's movement on a live online map. Finally, the 'smart' system is set up to record successes or delays and to 'learn' from this history, adjusting future despatch decisions accordingly.

Today, eCourier.co.uk's tagline is 'happiness delivered'. According to the company, 98 per cent of its deliveries in central London are completed within an hour, and the average bike collection time is 14 minutes. Couriers drive or ride their own vehicles, but the cost savings on control room staff allow the company to pay better rates than competing firms, driving staff performance and customer service up even further and avoiding the risk of manpower shortages. Furthermore, the online technology makes it possible to hire additional couriers and serve additional cities without increasing operational costs, compared with peers who still employ telephone staff to manage orders. Allason and Bregman succeeded in solving the customer and business problems they had observed when they first set out on their journey, and the company reached sales of £5.9 million in 2008. In 2009, eCourier.co.uk was ranked sixth on Deloitte's list of the UK's fastest-growing technology businesses, registering 5,291 per cent growth since 2004.

In 2008, Allason left the running of eCourier.co.uk – which had by then grown to some 250 staff – in the hands of a professional management team, in order to develop another venture. He had considered the fact that the business market for couriers was declining due to the availability of ever-faster broadband connections that make it possible to send heavy business documents digitally. On the other hand, consumer online shopping had become mainstream, and purchased goods needed to be delivered to people's homes. One of the drawbacks of buying online is that you normally need to wait several days for delivery, and often cannot arrange to be home when the courier arrives; even when the retailer notifies you of the delivery day, they will often give a six-hour window. Research had shown that delivery was often the reason why shoppers abandoned an online purchase. To solve this problem, Allason founded Shutl, a start-up whose technology platform allows shoppers to book either same-day delivery (arriving in as little as 90 minutes) or delivery within a one-hour time slot on a specific day. The Shutl platform is linked to the retailer's website, and then acts as an aggregator of local same-day delivery companies (including, but not limited to, eCourier.co.uk) in order to arrange a delivery to the customer's liking. The service is designed to be of benefit to retailers, courier companies and consumers alike. Shutl launched in the spring of 2010, and soon after began offering its services to London customers of Argos, one of the UK's largest retailers.

The knowledge–push or 'solution-seeks-problem' idea

Like entrepreneurial ideas, scientific research may also be undertaken in response to unmet needs – such as the dream of seeking a successful cure for cancer without side effects. If such a discovery is ever made, demand from patients will be unquestionable (although future chapters will point out that there may be other hurdles to commercialisation). But the pursuit of knowledge and science may also throw up discoveries with unforeseen commercial opportunities, sometimes outside the initial scientific domain. So, the idea stage of an entrepreneurial journey in a knowledge–push context typically amounts to a search for possible and promising markets and applications where a new discovery or technology could be in demand.

Professor Colin Caro: from vascular pathology to oil rigs

Professor Colin Caro of Imperial College London describes the evolution of his personal research interest to the filing of several patents and the creation of two spin-out companies, Veryan Medical and Heliswirl, as a 'long, stumbling process'. A science-based business may have a long incubation period when compared with the immediacy of a demand–pull business opportunity, but the process can throw up unforeseen applications.

Caro began his career as a doctor and physiologist. Several years into his career, the untimely death of his brother from a brain haemorrhage prompted him to switch specialism, from pulmonary to cardiovascular medicine. Thanks to the presence of several engineers in his family, he also took an interest in engineering problems, which led him to form professional relationships with biomechanics experts and to co-found a bioengineering unit at Imperial College.

In his search for the cause of atherosclerosis – the hardening of arteries, mainly from build-up of fatty deposits on artery walls – Caro made two important discoveries. First, he proved that this build-up occurred in areas of stagnation: locations along the artery where the flow of blood slowed or accumulated to form a temporary pool. Until that point (and for some time afterward, since the medical profession was slow to accept his findings), it was believed that damage to arterial walls was actually caused by the attrition of blood flowing through the vessels, not by its slowing down. Afterward, he began to consider whether the structure and geometry of the arteries was a factor in blood flow. With the help of magnetic resonance imaging, he discovered that blood does not normally flow in a straight trajectory through the vessels, but rather swirls in a rotating, three-dimensional spiral, which gives the flow increased momentum. This spiral flow is further helped by the subtly helical shape of arteries themselves. Even subsidiary arteries branch off a main vessel in a spiralling curve, rather than a two-dimensional angle. Static flow, stagnation and damage to artery walls are thus likely to occur in places where this spiral geometry is for some reason not present or defective.

Caro imagined the commercial potential for recreating these naturally occurring flow efficiencies, not just in biomedicine but also in broader industrial applications where efficient flow of liquid through a duct might be important, so he approached Imperial Innovations, the commercialisation arm of Imperial College.

An early science commercialisation process aims to identify 'problem-solving' applications with high potential value, protectability and customer demand. Veryan Medical, an Imperial Innovations spin-out founded in 2002 to commercialise Caro's discoveries, first developed helically-shaped grafts for use in coronary bypass surgery and dialysis, SwirlGraft™. By improving flow, the helical grafts have been found to prevent the thickening of vessel walls, (termed 'intimal hyperplasia'), which is a frequent complication resulting from such procedures. More recently, even more compelling applications have been found within the multi-billion-dollar medical stents industry. Stents are tubular devices inserted into blood vessels (or other conduits in the body) when they have become constricted. The stent widens the vessel and prevents the constriction from recurring. Conventional straight stents, however, typically are also prone to becoming blocked by a thickening of the vessel wall. Veryan developed a second patented invention, the BioMimics 3D™ , which is helical in design and acts to overcome this problem by promoting a more physiological blood flow. As of early 2011, testing in patients is currently underway.

Caro's discoveries were also applied beyond medicine. A second company, Heliswirl, was launched in 2004 to develop engineering applications. The company's patented Small Amplitude Helical Tubing (SMAHT) was designed to improve efficiency in a range of fluid-handling industries, such as chemicals, oil and natural gas.

Tension between an opportunity, your knowledge and your solution

Although categorising an idea as demand–pull or knowledge–push is helpful to orient your thinking, do keep in mind that entrepreneurial opportunities don't always fit neatly into one category; even those that sit fairly clearly in one category may contain some element of the other. For instance, Tom Allason was working as a ship broker when he thought of starting eCourier. It's possible that his work experience and knowledge, not just his anger and frustration on that one day, may have attracted his attention toward a business opportunity in transport logistics rather than a different area, and given him enough confidence to pursue it. Caro wasn't initially considering demand from the medical device or oil and gas industries, but his inclination toward engineering as well as medicine helped him first to discover a structural problem behind a disease, then to perceive its wider implications, leading him to approach the technology transfer executives at Imperial Innovations.

As an aspiring entrepreneur, you may have already decided to start a business that will draw on your existing abilities and experience, rather than walking blindly into a completely new business sector. So you might search for a demand–pull problem where your technical knowledge could provide a solution. Given that you already have a bias, this creates a somewhat hybrid situation: is your idea really motivated by demand, or by your preferences?

We raise this question and point out this ambiguity because your desire to create a business that capitalises on your existing abilities and industry knowledge is a smart choice, on the one hand, but could also make it hard for you to be objective enough about your market to create a product offering that customers truly want, rather than one that you'd simply like selling, on the other. Paying attention to the tools and questions in this book will help you to maintain a realistic, dispassionate and enquiring attitude until you're certain you have something that can sell.

Emma Stanton and CBT4L: knowledge meets demand

Emma Stanton was an established psychiatrist with an interest in entrepreneurship and leadership when she entered the Executive MBA programme at Imperial College Business School in 2009. A registrar at London's prestigious Maudsley Hospital, and later seconded to the chief medical officer's Clinical Advisory Scheme, she was accustomed to studying problems and seeking solutions in the domain of public healthcare delivery. She had also observed that Cognitive Behaviour Therapy (CBT), one of several techniques in which she was trained, was rapidly gaining wide legitimacy in the NHS, as well as popularity with patients and publicity in the media.

Stanton's starting point for an entrepreneurial project on her MBA course was to see if there was some way to use CBT in a new venture in the private sector. She knew that stress was a recurring problem for busy corporate executives, so her initial idea was to create a luxury walk-in centre for stress relief, combining CBT sessions with relaxation therapies – a kind of 'spa for the mind'. CBT would lend itself to a walk-in centre because the approach addresses specific problems in a short series of structured sessions. Essentially, her business would replicate what patients do when they attend an NHS clinic for psychotherapy, only the surroundings would be more plush and pleasurable, the customers would pay handsomely, and they wouldn't need a GP referral. What could be more attractive than starting a business through which you could create a new spin on your existing knowledge, one you'd probably enjoy being a pampered customer of yourself?

However, in the process of researching her idea's potential while studying on Imperial's Innovation, Entrepreneurship and Design programme, Stanton identified a few factors likely to prevent the venture from succeeding. One of these was the fact that her target customers – high-earning executives – experience stress precisely because they're so busy and so often on the move that they'd be unlikely to attend the centre regularly, probably resulting in fluctuating or even low revenues. Furthermore, such high-flyers are often reluctant to admit to negative effects of stress, perceiving them as an admission of weakness or inability to do the job. They'd be more likely to put up with stress until assailed by a full-scale breakdown – by which time they'd need dedicated medical care rather than a walk-in stress spa.

So Stanton had to search for a different problem to address, find a different customer and create a different commercial application for CBT, outside her normal area of work. She also had to consider how customer decision-making differed from patient decisions. A broader perspective came from the other

MBA students on Stanton's project team: these included Jonathan Trayner, an HR consultant, Heather Thompson, who designed employee learning and development programmes, and John Abbot, a psychology graduate and computer scientist.

The team eventually glimpsed an opportunity in the corporate training and coaching market for leadership development skills. Most corporate training cannot boast a scientifically proven methodology, and desktop research revealed that a staggering 50 per cent of attendees on corporate training programmes believed they hadn't gained any lasting benefit from them – a significant waste for the employers paying large sums for company managers to attend such programmes. This situation looked like a clear problem searching for a solution.

Stanton and her team's final business plan was for a company that would design and deliver effective leadership coaching for high-potential young executives (opportunity), acquired as group packages and paid for by their employers (substantial revenue), based on a cognitive method that's underpinned by academic research and clinical literature (a credible way to address the opportunity, and possibly a brand), delivered by a team of qualified CBT practitioners. They named this business 'CBT4Leadership'. During their coaching sessions, executive customers would also be at liberty to raise the subject of stress as a leadership challenge (the opportunity initially explored), but as it wasn't the explicit aim of the training, the clients wouldn't be put off the sessions by a perceived risk to their reputation (thus catering to the customer's viewpoint rather than the entrepreneur's). Furthermore, to address the fact that executives are frequently on the move, the company would design 'homework' materials to reinforce the coaching, downloadable as IT applications for an iPhone or other mobile device, for use during a commute to work or business travel (further catering to the customer).

CBT4L didn't ultimately start up as a company, but it is a fitting example of the tension between knowledge–push and demand–pull issues. Your professional or industry knowledge alone may not give you enough insight to land on the right venture idea for the right customer. Usually, some further investigation and refinement will be needed.

In summary...

New business ideas originate from various sources. Sometimes an entrepreneur hits on a good idea from the start, but even so, most successful entrepreneurs have gone through a thinking process to ascertain if they really have identified an opportunity before making the jump. The key is not only to be able to state why your idea or solution is good, but to explain why it compares favourably to alternative solutions on the basis of key criteria.

The next two chapters offer some methods for undertaking that thinking process and assessing an idea. As part of the process, they also demonstrate a refinement process for making adjustments to an initial idea.

2. FINE-TUNING DEMAND-DRIVEN IDEAS AND SOLUTIONS

What?

It all starts with a dream or 'the idea'. But when you get an idea, do you devote time to evaluating it or refining it? The BBC's *Dragons' Den* series often puts on display aspiring entrepreneurs who've spotted a problem but come up with an impractical and unsellable product solution, which consequently does not attract investment. This failure can usually be pinned to two oversights: they do not investigate the problem and characterise the opportunity clearly enough, and they don't stop to consider alternatives or the wider view of the market and industry. They may come up with an idea that would suit them personally, but is not likely to attract a wider customer base.

In order to compare and evaluate several ideas and discern an attractive opportunity, you would benefit from going through a structured idea generation and evaluation exercise, balancing your creativity, intuition and subjective views with some objective facts and considerations. Although it may seem like a formal exercise, the discipline of this process may encourage you to approach business ideas from a broader perspective.

The exercise is based on a simple process: be creative and open-minded in generating many possible ideas, but subsequently be dispassionate and sensible to evaluate and select the best ones. The evaluation is just as important as the generation of creative ideas, and may give you options to fall back on in later stages.

Why?

Should you use this exercise even if you think you already have an excellent new venture idea and are raring to go? At the outset, don't narrow your choices and fix your mind on one idea but consider several possibilities, and the advantages and disadvantages of each option. Why? Because a high chance exists that your idea is based on untested or intuitive assumptions, and it's better to investigate these now rather than when you've already committed your life savings to a new business. For instance, your idea may be great on paper but not technically practicable in real life; it may be something you'd buy yourself but that other people wouldn't; it may not really solve the problem it is intended to or may create other ancillary problems that you didn't consider in your first light-bulb moment of enthusiasm.

For example, very technical people often have ideas that won't satisfy a typical customer. If you're used to dealing with complex machinery or systems, you may be thinking of a gadget that you'd be happy to operate but a technophobe would barely know how to switch on. Engineers famously enjoy fiddling with gadgets and figuring them out; the rest of us usually want to flick a switch and see everything work as if the machine were reading our minds. If you don't build these demand–pull considerations into your idea, you could get so far as developing an expensive product prototype or writing a 50-page business plan before you actually realise that it isn't going to appeal to users. An idea generation and evaluation exercise can help you to broaden your thinking and identify your criteria from the start.

Furthermore, this exercise will help you devise alternative ideas, or modifications to your initial one, so that you may find a better opportunity at the end of it than when you started.

The story that follows, about an entrepreneur developing an idea, demonstrates that the best way to conceive a business is to start by asking a set of questions rather than to base an idea entirely on your personal bias. The story also demonstrates the wisdom of scrapping an idea if you don't find encouraging answers to your questions.

Idea generation through enquiry: Jean-Marc de Fety and mummysworld.co.uk

Jean-Marc de Fety was a second-time entrepreneur when he founded Real Village, the company behind mummysworld.co.uk, in 2009. A former investment banker and vice president at Credit Suisse First Boston, he already had one technology start-up experience under his belt. In the early 1990s, he'd become enchanted by a CD-Rom presenting an animated virtual tour of the Louvre. He decided he wanted to be in the business of digital simulation, so in 1995 co-founded Paris-based Monte Cristo Multimedia, one of the first companies in the world to create educational business simulation games, including Wall Street Trader, a European best-seller with net receipts of around €2 million. The company averaged 100 per cent annual sales growth in its first four years.

After selling out of the business and returning briefly to banking, de Fety caught the entrepreneurship bug again, and began to look for another technology idea, this time using the internet. A graduate of the École des Mines, one of France's most selective engineering schools, he had a stronger interest in sociology than in technology by the time he completed his studies. He now searched for a social problem that might be solved by technology – and found one very close to home. As a divorced father, he faced a single working parent's difficulties with time management whenever his sons, Paul and Thomas, came to stay with him at his home in London.

Since a good deal of business was now conducted over the internet, his first question was: could online content help parents to save time? How?

Indeed, the most time-consuming tasks were those that couldn't be performed online, such as buying children's shoes, a frequent task as children grow, necessitating trying on before purchase. Perhaps the internet could help you find a shop in your neighbourhood that stocked the type of shoes you were looking for at the most attractive price, and perhaps even the size you needed? You could head straight for the right shop instead of wandering all over town. So his first idea was to create a price comparison site devoted to 'real' retail shops located near the user's address, specifically for products that needed to be tried in the shop. He'd start with shoes and then add other products. Revenue would come from the now familiar model of online advertising.

As he researched this idea, he identified some problems. Most shops in London – especially clothes shops – are part of large chains rather than independents, and large companies are slow movers. Getting a company on board – so that it will share its inventory information on a website – would probably take two years. He didn't want to wait this long to collect revenue or prove the soundness of his business concept. So this idea was scrapped.

He then decided it might make more sense to find a specific, attractive group of customers whose expectations could be met fairly easily with a low investment, creating some early revenue and subsequently finding ways to extract additional value (income) by adding other features to the business.

His second question was: where is the money? In other words, to whom could he sell?

Sticking to his basic idea of helping parents, he researched UK national statistics, and discovered that 26,000 mothers lived in nine central London postcodes, with a combined household income of £1.5 billion. This looked like an attractive niche market.

His third question was: how can I extract value from this group? Or in more detail: what do they need? What online content or technology would attract them?

For answers, de Fety turned to his target market – fortunately he knew a few mothers living in this area. He interviewed 20 such women, asking what parenting and time management problems they experienced and what kind of internet content could help. One detail he discovered was that buying children's shoes was indeed a big headache for parents. He also learned that these mothers were an attractive customer group not only because they had high household incomes but were also highly qualified – many had PhD, Masters and MBA degrees and had engaged in full-time motherhood because finding part-time jobs in their professions was difficult. (This actually proved to be a bonus for de Fety, as eight of the women, including a sociologist and a designer, became freelance collaborators in the business.) Furthermore, this was a highly international group, including many expatriates. He could think of many businesses that would like to gain access to this group of customers.

Recognising that if he started a website he'd be up against all the established online business directories and social networking sites, de Fety chose to be distinctive by focusing on a specific location and specialising in mothers and children. His final online business concept, mummysworld.co.uk, isn't so much a social network as an online club for these mothers. This club is exclusive – you need to live within the target postcodes and can only join if you're recommended by an existing member. The content is suggested and created by women from the same target group. The site provides a forum for the women to communicate with each other, but also offers advice and information.

So much for attracting the target group: how will the business make money?

De Fety's plan was to recruit a group of 70 early users to test and rate the site for free. Once improvements were made and interest established, early revenues would come from a combination of display ads, classified ads and membership fees. However, the final challenge would be to derive additional value from this special community, without alienating them. His hypothesis was that the site could offer a specialised service to businesses as a virtual marketing laboratory. Local branches of large businesses could use the site to advertise special promotions or new products and services in the neighbourhood, and then measure the response in the shops to gauge the possible success rate, before rolling their promotions out to other stores.

What makes de Fety a smart entrepreneur in this stage of his journey? Many entrepreneurs start with an answer and don't sufficiently question it before moving to the next step. He started by asking questions, and then used the answers to build up a business concept. After coming up with ideas, de Fety tested them by thinking through the practical implications; he also investigated and verified his customers' needs. He had clear criteria in mind that enabled him to see when an idea should be scrapped.

De Fety's questioning process was fairly intuitive and linear. However, from a commercial viewpoint, his entrepreneurial intuition is honed by previous experience. If you're less practised in commercial idea development, use the structured process below to help you ask useful questions and produce and assess possible solutions.

How?

Depending on how simple or complex your starting idea, you might complete this exercise in a single session, or in several sessions, using any intervals to gather some further information.

While the premise of this exercise may seem simple, it isn't necessarily easy. We recommend it because people favour different thinking styles. Some find it intuitively easy to dream up inspired or even outlandish innovative ideas, and fashion those ideas into an imagined scenario, yet find it difficult to think about the practicalities or suitability of an idea as a viable business. Others are good at analysing, evaluating and judging, but find generating ideas difficult because they judge themselves a bit too quickly. Some, on the other hand, can immediately envision the practical steps needed to implement an idea but don't question whether a real opportunity exists, such as a group of customers who truly want or need to buy the product or service.

An entrepreneurial venture must draw on all of these thinking styles to succeed: the creative and visionary outlook, the practical, action-focused approach, the evaluative or judgemental capability, and the empathic, social mindset that makes understanding the motivations of a real customer possible. Ideally, the founding team of a new venture will involve a range of people who can offer different ways of thinking and approaching a problem, without falling into decision paralysis.

Try to follow the exercise below with several individuals with diverse backgrounds and thinking styles, rather than alone. With time and practice, it's even possible for you to learn and acquire other thinking styles, though you'll always benefit from the contribution of other people with different points of view.

This exercise is a six-stage process based on the work of Edward Lumsdaine and Martin Binks, two academics from the Universities of Michigan and Nottingham, respectively, who specialise in entrepreneurial creativity, and of Ned Herrmann (1922–1999), a human resources expert at General Electric who created a model for different thinking styles. We offer a simplified version of their method here, for the purpose of defining your entrepreneurial opportunity, but recommend reading the work of these authors to investigate further.[4]

Because it begins by identifying a problem, this exercise is especially relevant if you're looking for a demand–pull business idea. (Chapter 3 describes an exercise for knowledge–push ideas.) First, assemble several people for this exercise. If you're already planning to start a venture with another or several individuals, begin with these people. Also consider inviting additional participants (such as friends, colleagues or mentors) who can add a variety of thinking styles and mindsets to the group – call it a preliminary brain trust. Ideally, you should have at least one of each type of person in your brain trust, displaying: creative imagination; strong analytical and evaluative skills; practical hands-on abilities; and empathy with others' needs or wishes.

It doesn't matter, at this stage, whether you expect these specific individuals to join your venture; they are acting as assistants to your thinking process. Each person will contribute the most to that part of the exercise most suited to their thinking style, but everyone should be allowed to have their say, and no single person should dominate the session. The objective is to look at problems and possible solutions from several angles.

The six phases of your idea generation exercise are:
1. Seek and observe unsolved problems.
2. Explain and define problems.
3. Brainstorm ideas and solutions.
4. Organise and synthesise your ideas.
5. Evaluate and select ideas.
6. Plan how to implement selected ideas.

You could conduct the session as an open, free-flowing discussion, recording everyone's comments on a flip chart, or ask people to write ideas down on paper or post-it notes that you'll subsequently share.

1. Seek and observe unsolved problems

In a demand–pull case, a strong business opportunity is based on a compelling problem or desire, experienced by a potential customer, which current offerings have not yet solved. The first step in the exercise is to find and choose a problem.

You may have come to this book with a particular problem in mind and an entrepreneurial ambition to solve it, in which case you can skip the first step in this exercise. On the other hand, you might find this step useful to help you think about related or similar problems that you could also explore as part of your business idea.

You can identify problems in a number of ways:
• Analyse current trends in the social and business environments.
• Consider conducting a PEST analysis (you can easily find simple information on this technique on the internet).

- Consider a problem experienced by you or someone you know.
- Look at business problems experienced by your employer that aren't being solved in-house, where your insider knowledge could be useful to create a solution.
- Consult experts about problems that affect their domain or industry.

Write down your problem ideas. Then, for each one, note down what would improve for the parties affected if the problem were dealt with. In other words, how important is the problem? Which of these problems seems the most compelling?

2. Explain and define problems

Looking beyond the surface of the problems and understanding their root causes will help you to think of realistic solutions. Here, the team needs to take an investigative attitude to understanding problems.

Choose one problem to look at in further depth:

- Use the five Ws to start exploring the full context of the problem: **w**ho suffers from the problem, **w**hat happens when the problem arises, **w**hen does it happen, **w**here and **w**hy?
- Look at the chain of causes: when you come to the 'why' question and identify one cause, keep asking what causes that cause and so on. For example, pollution is caused by heavy traffic. Why do we have heavy traffic? Because too many people drive cars; why? Explanations may include the fact that people don't share cars, lack of public transport, low availability of alternatives (such as employers allowing teleworking), dangers of cycling, bad weather or a shortage of places to lock up a bicycle. Each partial explanation may reveal a series of causes, any of which might yield opportunities for solutions that could be offered by a new venture.

In the end, you should arrive at a final *problem definition*, which, in the next step, will lead to a brainstorming session.

To encourage creativity and an open mind, make your problem definition short and simple, and phrase it as a question rather than a statement. For example: 'How could cycling be made more appealing?'

3. Brainstorm ideas and solutions

This is the most creative part of the exercise. The key to successful brainstorming is *making no judgements* about whether an idea is good or not. No one should feel shy about expressing an idea; even silly, wild ideas can be springboards for thinking of ingenious, practical solutions to problems. The point is to think up and record as many proposed solutions as possible, from the obvious to the unusual or even outlandish – from better cycling helmets or wider cycle lanes to cycling overpasses … or flying bicycles.

Brainstorming is best done out loud in a group discussion, because each idea may stimulate more ideas in the minds of other group members: thus 'hitch-hiking' on the back of each other's ideas should be encouraged, and no one should be bashful.

Record all of the group's ideas in brief form – detail isn't necessary at this stage. Write enough to fit on a post-it note. Laugh if the ideas are funny – mirth stimulates more ideas – but avoid sarcasm. Don't shoot down anyone's idea, and write *all* ideas down, regardless of how strange. Use post-it notes because they allow you to easily re-organise ideas in the next stage.

Even if you start with a clear product or business idea in mind, we still recommend a brainstorming session to think of alternatives; the results will make for a better evaluation of your idea later in this exercise.

4. Organise and synthesise your ideas

Following the brainstorming session, your team needs to sit back and look over all the ideas with a more practical eye. However, still maintain a positive outlook and avoid judgement at this stage.

The group will notice that some ideas are similar or related in some way, and can be grouped into *categories*. To refer to the cycling example again, you may find that some ideas involve better safety gear for cyclists to wear, others focus on re-designing the bicycle itself and some consider changes to the cyclist's environment, such as the roads. There may also be various other ways to categorise ideas. Decide on a set of categories that make most sense to the group. Group 'stray' ideas that don't fit anywhere into a 'miscellaneous' category.

Next the group further elaborates on ideas to work them into more detailed, practical solutions. Create a smaller number of more fully explained ideas with a clear purpose.

One reason for organising the ideas into categories is that you might find that a combination of two or more ideas can provide a more appealing solution than one of those ideas by itself. Also consider whether:

- The stranger ideas can also be worked into something more realistic and practical.
- Any relevant technologies, or combinations of technologies, exist that might make an idea feasible.
- A similar product or solution already exists in another business sector, and might be adapted and applied to your problem as well.

5. Evaluate and select ideas

Now you need to judge the merits of each idea against a set of criteria.

Go back to the way you first defined the problem, and look again at all aspects and causes of the problem, as well as the benefits of removing the problem.

Use your understanding of the problem to identify a set of criteria that must be met for the problem to be solved in a satisfactory manner. The criteria may be relevant to the people experiencing the problem (e.g. cyclists), but also the parties who may be involved in providing solutions (e.g. equipment makers, bicycle shops, traffic police, pedestrians), and even to you as a solutions provider (do you have the skills and contacts to provide such a solution?). What is most important to these stakeholders? Depending on the problem and solutions you're considering, criteria could include things like affordability of the product, the cost to produce it, ease of use, barriers or hurdles (such as regulatory approval for a safety device), or compatible infrastructure to support the use of a product (such as places to lock a bicycle securely).

Your group may need to suspend the session at this point as you may need to do some research or talk to industry experts in order to determine the most relevant criteria for the situation you're attempting to address.

Once you've identified a set of criteria, you can use a set of **decision matrices** to score the advantages and disadvantages of your proposed solutions or concepts.

Using the matrix in Figure 1, start with a set of general criteria to score several product concepts, using a plus (+) when a concept enjoys an advantage with respect to a criterion, and a minus (-) for a disadvantage.

Criteria	Concept 1	Concept 2	Concept 3
Effectiveness	−	−	+
Cost	−	+	−
Compatibility with infrastructure and other products	−	+	−

Figure 1 **Matrix 1**

Next, eliminate concepts that score very low, such as Concept 1 in Figure 1. As you narrow down the concepts, you can also introduce more detailed criteria, as shown in Figure 2. At this stage, you may find that one

Revised criteria	Concept 2	Concept 3
Effectiveness in solving the problem	−	+
Effectiveness in ease of use	−	−
Cost	−	−
Compatibility with infrastructure and other products	−	−

Figure 2 **Matrix 2**

concept scores highest relative to others, as Concept 3 in Figure 2, but that it is still not a high overall scorer. Your team may need to think of some possible modifications to the idea that would make it more advantageous, and elaborate in further detail, until you find a satisfactory solution, as shown in Figure 3. As a variation, if

Revised criteria	Modified concept 3
Effectiveness in solving the problem	+
Effectiveness in ease of use	+
Cost to design and produce	+?
Cost to customers	+
Compatibility with infrastructure	+?
Compatibility with other products	+

Figure 3 **Matrix 3 (question marks indicate possible improvements to original idea)**

similar or comparable solutions for your problem already exist on the market, you can also *benchmark* your ideas against the existing

Criteria	Existing Concept	New concept 1	New concept 2	New concept 3
Effectiveness	0	–	+	+
Cost to produce	0	+	–	+
Ease of installation / compatibility	0	+	–	–

Figure 4 **Matrix 4**

competition, scoring them against the status quo product, as shown in Figure 4.

If a crucial criterion isn't satisfied by any of your new concepts, as shown in Figure 5, you may need to scrap this idea and find a better solution.

Criteria	Existing Concept	New concept 1	New concept 2	New concept 3
Effectiveness	0	–	+	+
Cost to produce	0	+	–	+
Ease of installation / compatibility	0	–	–	–

Figure 5 **Matrix 5**

6. Plan how to implement selected ideas

As a final step, you now need to draw up an action plan setting out how your concept would be implemented. Essentially, this refers to what your business will produce and sell, and to whom, and is the basic business idea that you'll investigate further, using other chapters in this book.

It's worth noting down any potential challenges to the product or service, and ways to overcome possible resistance. Will you need the co-operation of other parties to make this product work or sell, and how will you obtain this buy-in? Who might resist your solution, and why?

Could any action or change on your part make resistant parties change their mind and accept the solution?

In summary...

A good idea needs to withstand a testing and questioning process like the one in this chapter, as well as the challenges raised in the rest of this book. At this stage, the key is not only to be able to state why your idea or solution is good, but also to explain why it compares favourably to alternative solutions based on key criteria.

The main value of this exercise is that it allows you to judge several ideas against a single yardstick. Most people find it more intuitive to compare several ideas by listing the pros and cons that come to mind for each. The problem with this approach is that the pros and cons will usually vary and be unrelated to each other, thus making comparison or weighting difficult. This exercise forces you to identify a core set of criteria that would optimally solve the problem (and could be delivered realistically), and then compare each idea against the same set of criteria.

As you move through successive stages of business idea development, and discover more about your opportunity, your market, your industry, and potential risks, you can come back to this process to test and improve your idea again.

Finally, at some point you're likely to discuss your idea with people who'll challenge it. Some of these may be people whose support and co-operation you'll need. If you've devoted a bit of effort to challenging and evaluating the idea in an objective manner, you can make a more persuasive argument, combining your enthusiasm with more dispassionate considerations. One of the most persuasive responses you can make to a challenging question or objection is to show that you've considered the same issue yourself and come up with a credible solution.

3. SHAPING APPLICATIONS FROM KNOWLEDGE-DRIVEN IDEAS

What?

In Chapter 2 we discuss a way to generate and evaluate potential business ideas in response to a need or problem, in a demand–pull context.

This chapter supposes you're in the opposite, knowledge–push situation: you have a new platform technology or a body of knowledge and expertise, and you need to find a way to build a business around it. Essentially, you need to find a problem that can be solved compellingly and profitably through *applying* your technology or your specialist knowledge, in other words, creating a promising *application*.

One typical way to do this is to start a consulting business, delivering customised projects to clients, employing your technology or know-how to meet each client's specific need. This is frequently the way that new technologies are tested in a very early marketplace, but consulting by itself isn't a recipe for business growth. A consulting business is easy to start, requiring less early investment than a product business, but revenue is limited to the number of hours that your consultants work. To make more money, you have to hire more consultants, and people are usually the most expensive cost of a business. Consequently, we generally say that you can build a good 'lifestyle' business around consulting (until your technology becomes obsolete), but to build a scalable or growth business, your goal must be to find a product, application or service that can be replicated many times at low cost – in other words, things that you aim to sell off the shelf.

Consulting may be a way to get to know the market, so that you can identify an application which could be built into a scalable product or service. However, businesses that start in this way can also become stuck in consulting mode, because the bespoke demands and urgent deadlines of each consulting project and client take precedence over longer-term product development.

Plenty of examples of platform technologies that have led to diverse applications in different industrial and business sectors exist. Digital microchips were first used in the aerospace industry in the 1960s, but today they're in nearly every machine we use: computers, phones, televisions, industrial equipment, medical equipment and cars, among others. Light-emitting diodes (LEDs) were first used in expensive laboratory equipment, but then spread to traffic lights, rear lights on cars, bicycle lights, torches, televisions and, increasingly, architectural lighting in commercial and residential buildings. The internet began life as a communication tool for research academics and government, but its commercial and civilian applications have multiplied, not only for sales but also for customer service, publicity, information, tax filing and so on. The internet has even transformed business models in certain sectors – where once you needed to consult the expertise of a financial consultant, today it's possible to locate information, compare prices and choose savings accounts, investments or insurance policies directly online.

The important point, however, is that these technologies didn't enter all these application markets at the same time, but in phases, and the same will undoubtedly be true for the technology or competence you are hoping to commercialise as you read this book. In some cases, this is because other complementary technologies and components need to be developed before a whole product or solution can be offered; a novel product is frequently created from a combination of technologies. However, there are also important commercial considerations to take into account when selecting an application, such as: the financial cost of developing it compared with the price a customer would pay; the amount of time needed to develop the application for market readiness; the risks involved in introducing an unproven product in certain sectors; and, most important of all, the technology's real attractiveness to potential customers and industrial partners – what's also known as a 'problem to solve', the 'compelling reason to buy' or 'customer pain'. That's why venture entrepreneurs and investors are always looking for the 'killer application' that will hook a captive and sizable market.

Finding the 'killer app' often takes time and a certain amount of trial and error. In this early stage, we recommned you map out the possibilities in terms of potential industries and products, and begin to analyse some of the technical and practical advantages and disadvantages compared with competing solutions. In Stage 2 of your journey, you use this information as the basis for investigating more thoroughly the market attractiveness of certain applications.

Why?

According to technology marketing experts, trying to enter several application markets at once can be counter-productive; it confuses potential customers rather than creating a clear and credible image for the technology, and you're unlikely to have enough staff and money in an early start-up to work on several product launches at once. A more successful strategy is to focus effort on proving the technology in one application market. Success with one application creates interest in other markets, because prospective customers are more attracted to replicating success than to taking risks on an unproven idea. As customers in other markets take notice of your technology's achievements and ask whether it can be applied in their industry as well, your knowledge–push business becomes a demand–pull business.

Too frequently, companies and businesses waste time and money developing applications and products that generate low demand or are unprofitable. Customers and markets may not respond in the way entrepreneurs assumed they would, while the route to market can be littered with other obstructions, such as industry resistance, regulatory hurdles, competitors, changing trends or simply the prohibitive cost and effort involved in customers switching from the products they already use. Therefore, what may appear to an inventor as the hottest product or application – from a technical or creative point of view – may not be the most likely to succeed on the market. If you don't consider a variety of factors and keep your ear to the ground, you could waste time and resources trying to enter the wrong market, possibly while a smarter competitor overtakes you.

CropDesign: anticipating the market for high-yield crops

Let's look at an example of the difficulty of selecting a good commercial application. CropDesign, a plant genetics start-up ultimately acquired by German chemicals giant BASF, was founded in 1998 in Belgium to develop and commercialise genetically modified (GM) traits in plants, based on research into cell cycle genes and a number of patents on effects of gene modification held by the University of Ghent, the Flanders Institute of Biotechnology and several other world institutes. When the company was founded, the technology was still in development, an application hadn't yet been chosen and the business plan was vague and rather broad, aiming simply to build a proprietary technology platform in the area of plant cell cycles, related to growth, crop yields or crop protection. However, these were the heady days of late 1990s venture capital, so CropDesign was able to raise an initial €4.5 million from early-stage investors, purely on the basis of technological promise, even though a clear market opportunity had not yet been identified.

By 2000, the business plan was more defined, as the company began to identify value-creating opportunities. Genomics was now a booming field in scientific research, with many institutes and companies investing in creating new gene sequences. What was missing was a technology platform that would help translate pure research for industrial use. CropDesign embarked on the development of a trademarked screening and bioinformatics platform, Traitmill™, capable of reliably determining the key genes responsible for specific traits in a plant. The company raised another investment of €25.7 million for this initiative, and subsequently pursued a dual route of both technological and product development.

In the first instance, to help develop and test the platform, in 2000 CropDesign entered an alliance with Grain Biotech Australia in a joint programme to develop transgenic varieties of wheat. Several other partnerships followed in subsequent years. At the same time, CropDesign also embarked on a programme to develop its first proprietary commercial application: a GM variety of rice with a radically increased crop yield. Rice was chosen in response to the global population's increasing food requirements, particularly in developing countries in Asia. Thanks to the R&D that resulted from these investments, by 2003 CropDesign had developed Traitmill™ to the point where the company claimed it could increase crop yields by an impressive 50 per cent. The value of this technology was underpinned by a research collaboration deal that CropDesign entered in the same year with DuPont's subsidiary, Pioneer Hi-Bred, one of the world's largest corn seed companies, to test genes discovered by Pioneer using the Traitmill™ platform.

Then, in 2004, a change of commercial direction occurred – the company scaled back its rice programme and announced that now it would develop GM corn instead. CropDesign had by this time used much of its funds on its rice project, and while much of the knowledge gained was transferable (as the collaboration with Pioneer Hi-Bred testified), the company had to raise another €11 million from investors to develop the new application.

In 2005, CropDesign entered a €25 million partnership in corn development with BASF Plant Science, initially intended to raise the start-up's profile in preparation for an initial public offering (IPO) and stock market listing. However, the news prompted interest and offers from potential corporate acquirers, which led to a buy-out by BASF in 2006. CropDesign's early investors preferred the trade sale to BASF as an opportunity to cash in more quickly on their investment than would be possible with an IPO. This isn't surprising, as venture capitalists typically aim to exit an investment after five years, and the company was now eight years old. Unconfirmed press reports put the sale price at a rumoured €100 million or so. However, CropDesign had by that time absorbed around €40 million from its investors – meaning that a sale at the rumoured price would've provided a general overall return of a little over double the money invested. As each tranche of investment would have been agreed at a different valuation, it's not possible to know the return realised by early, as opposed to later-stage, investors. However, venture capitalists who invest in a venture's later funding rounds (presumably at a higher share price than earlier investors) are normally looking for a return of three to five times their invested capital. Thus, in a world where most start-ups go out of business, CropDesign was certainly not a failure, but perhaps the company could have found a way to use less money and realise a higher return for investors at an earlier date.

Why did CropDesign choose rice in the first place, and then change application? To begin with, there was a technical reason: rice is a less complex plant than corn so is easier to modify, meaning the development time would be shorter. More importantly, the company took the brave line that it would become an independent seed producer, rather than simply licensing its technology to existing product companies or entering into product development partnerships. This is an expensive and risky decision, but going it alone (if you have a sure thing) usually leads to higher profits and a better return on investment than licensing or even partnering. Since the market for rice was fragmented, with many small producers, CropDesign thought there was a chance to become an innovative market leader. On the other hand, a number of large companies such as Monsanto, ICI Seeds and Syngenta were already established in the seed market for corn and maize, and had direct customer relationships. CropDesign would find elbowing its way into that market difficult, and might be forced to trade through the incumbents, who would be expensive distribution intermediaries between the start-up and end customers. CropDesign preferred to avoid this competition.

While the choice may initially seem astute, CropDesign's decision meant that it would have to single-handedly create demand and capture customers for GM rice, whereas the presence in the corn market of large companies – which are typically conservative investors – was an indication that market demand already existed, and success was just a matter of gaining market share. By avoiding contact or competition with the incumbents, CropDesign in fact chose the riskier route to market, replacing competition risk with market risk. Various factors contributed to the interruption of the rice programme, not the least of which was lack of interest from seed buyers. CropDesign was not intrinsically wrong in identifying increased food crop yield as a business opportunity, at a time when other GM developers were focusing on pest resistance, but the company was too far ahead of market demand. Popular sentiment regarding GM food, based on concerns in relation to its safety, was mounting, leading both food producers and politicians to drag their feet, consequently slowing down regulatory approval of many GM crops and drawing out the debate in many western countries. Even a small start-up like CropDesign found 30 demonstrators on its doorstep one day in 2002. At the same time, corn-based biodiesel was gaining a strong foothold, especially in the US market, so the switch to corn products allowed CropDesign to escape negative publicity tied to so-called 'Frankenstein foods'.

Were CropDesign's founders at the mercy of unpredictable events and bad luck, or could the company have planned its strategy differently? Let's look at the historical context. Widespread controversy relating to genetically modified organisms (GMOs) existed by 2003 (and continues today), but the public and press had already begun to voice concerns in the late 1990s, when CropDesign was founded. Research by agricultural giant Monsanto – which was reported in the financial press – uncovered public hostility to GMOs in 1998, while the US Environmental Protection Agency faced a lawsuit over approval of GM crops, filed by a consortium of farmers and environmentalists, as early as 1999. CropDesign might have guessed that regulatory approval could turn out to be a stumbling block for food crops – at least until proof of safety could be obtained – and built contingency plans into its decisions. As for the biofuels market, the Kyoto international conference in 1997 put environmental issues visibly on the international political and media agenda, including the prospect of green fuel technologies. By 1998, the year CropDesign was founded, some 20 countries around the world had commercial biodiesel projects underway, and corn biofuels enjoyed substantial support in the US, the world's largest energy market. So there was a clear technical application and market opportunity for high-yield GM corn at an early date.

While it's easy to make judgements with hindsight, it seems that CropDesign's founders and managers had an opportunity to spot trends and make alternative plans sooner than they did, saving several years and some of their investors' money, to create more value from the business.

In December 2009, the Chinese government issued approval for two strains of (domestically developed) GM rice, indicating that Asia's vast market was finally opening up. From CropDesign's perspective, the investor that stands to benefit from this development now is BASF PlantScience, not the company's early founders and investors.

Predicting the future for a radically new technology is always difficult, but an entrepreneur should nonetheless try to survey the landscape and make the best educated guesses possible.

How?

So, how do you search for the 'killer app'? It takes time, investigation and reflection. You may have to draw on your own professional knowledge, but also talk to experts in various industries (we describe 'preferred witness research' in Chapter 4) to understand whether there's a need for or interest in a new product, or resistance to change.

When you've done your research and talked to experts, you will need a way to organise and analyse your collected data. To make the best use of your investigation and analysis, you can draw up a knowledge/application matrix, an evaluation tool to help you map out and compare the possibilities of your application.

Step 1: What does your technology do?

List the new functionalities of your technology and brainstorm the possible applications for which it may be used.

Step 2: What are the alternatives?

For each application you've identified, list the alternative technologies or methods that also deliver these or similar results. These may be clear competitors but be aware that, in some cases, an alternative may also be a substitute solution – such as finding a different way to solve a problem (possibly without technology), preventing the problem or even doing nothing. To give a simple example, a commuter could have a choice between buying two different brands of car, buying a small run-around or large saloon car, or choosing to ride a bicycle or use public transport. All of these could be considered as competing methods for satisfying the same need to travel.

Step 3: Map out the alternatives, the industries and possible markets

Normally we assume that customers for a new technology will be businesses within an industry (as opposed to consumers), who will use the technology in new products, services or production processes. Make a list of the industries that might make use of your technology in these ways. There may be several possible applications within each industry.

For each industry that seems promising, arrange the information in a **knowledge/application matrix** that shows, for each industry, both your technology and alternative methods in use (see Figure 6 for an example).

Step 4: Compare advantages for the customer

For any application, each alternative solution or product offers advantages and disadvantages for potential customers and users. Determine the relative advantage of your solution. Choose one or a few applications or

Alternative technologies/methods	Target Industry A (eg, automotive)		Target Industry B (eg, aerospace)	
	Market app 1 — eg, consumer vehicles	Market app 2 — eg, commercial vehicles	Market app 3 — eg, civil aviation	Market app 4 — eg, military
Your technology / knowledge	App example 1	App example 3	App example 8	App example 10
	App example 2	–	–	App example 11
Alternative 1	–	App example 4		App example 12
	–	–	–	–
Alternative 2	App example 5	–	App example 9	–
	App example 6	–	–	–
Alternative 3	–	App example 7	–	App example 13
	–	–	–	–

Figure 6 **Sample knowledge/application matrix**

industries to further research. For each potential application, identify the most important criteria that would make a product feasible:

- In which industry or application domain does your technology seem to offer the most added value to customers?
- How does your technology compare with other alternatives based on apparent user needs (which you'll verify in future research) and practical feasibility?

For instance, cost, performance, ease of use, ease of installation, compatibility with other products or components, durability or aesthetics could all be criteria of varying importance for different markets. If you don't have direct insight about the most important criteria in a certain market, you may need to speak to a technology or industry expert.

Criteria	Market application 1			
	App 1	App 2	App 5	App 6
Cost	++	–	0	–
Ease of use	+	0	0	+
Accuracy	+	– –	++	+
Durability	+	+	– –	+
Compatibility with complementary products	++	+	+	+
Regulatory compliance/approval	–	–	+	+
Does a market already exist?	+	+	–	–
Total scores	**7**	**–1**	**1**	**3**

Figure 7 **Evaluation matrix for applications in first column of Figure 6**

Once you've identified a set of key criteria, create an individual **evaluation matrix**, as shown in Figure 7, to score your proposed product against the alternatives. The goal is to find industries in which your technology will have the highest overall advantage compared with competitors or alternatives. Some of the criteria may have to do with technical needs, such as cost or performance, while others may be related to the business or legal environment, such as regulations and safety testing. Another important criterion could be compatibility or interoperability with other products or services that would be used alongside yours – the harder the fit, the harder the sell.

Test your added value for other applications in the same manner: set the criteria, and then score the alternatives.

As we said in the last chapter, the advantage of using a matrix like this is that it forces you to compare all possibilities against the same criteria, rather than compiling a random list of 'pros and cons'.

Step 5: Compare the advantages for your business
You also need to consider which applications are most interesting for you as a business.

Consider the following points:

- Is there already a market for a similar technical solution in the target industries you're considering? Is the existing technology currently used by these potential customers nearing its performance limit? Are any of these industries experiencing a critical need for higher performance, making them willing to consider an expensive new technology?
- Do you already have a relationship with a particular industry or market? For instance, access to distribution channels or customers in this market, or industry relationships that would help you to enter this market?
- Is an industry likely to invest in new technology at this time in the economic cycle? Some industries are cyclical and only invest when economic conditions are strong.
- Is this industry subject to long certification and regulatory procedures that could slow down commercial roll-out of innovations?
- How much further work is required to develop this application? How long would it take and how much would it cost?

Many of the questions in Step 5 can be answered by using the advice in the next section of this book.

In summary...

Finding a market for a new technology, or a new way of commercialising a body of knowledge, can be a difficult challenge. It's hard to know today where a brand new technology will be most in demand in a few years' time.

Many new ventures make a selection by trial and error, and sometimes this is the only way to test assumptions and find the most commercially feasible application. However, this can be a time-consuming and costly process. In the early stages of developing a business rationale, it's a good idea to do some basic investigation and evaluation of several potential routes to market. Think carefully about the criteria that would determine the adoption of your technology in a certain industry, and identify early signs of interest or possible barriers that need to be monitored. In addition to helping you make a decision based on a more solid rationale, this exercise may also throw up some fallback options if the path you initially choose proves unfeasible at a later date.

SECTION II
FROM IDEA TO BUSINESS PROPOSITION

4. SEGMENTING YOUR MARKET AND USING PREFERRED WITNESSES

Once you have come up with an idea and tested its merits against alternatives, as discussed in Chapters 1 to 3, this second part of the book helps you to look at how your initial business idea is likely to fare in your industry environment, your ability to protect your ideas from imitation and the possible market demand for your offering. The present chapter focuses specifically on market demand, but also describes how to carry out preferred witness research – a tool that you can also use to research your industry environment, as outlined in Chapter 5.

What?

We've heard this type of argument many times: 'The potential global market for this product amounts to 100 million customers, for a total value of £2 billion. All we have to do is capture 2 per cent of this market, and we can realise sales of £100 million. So, even with this *conservative* estimate, the market for our product is attractive.'

The exact numbers may change from case to case, but the premise is the same: blind, shoot-from-the-hip market estimation; the untested belief that a random, unspecified 2 per cent of the market ('surely not an unreasonable target,' thinks the entrepreneur) will buy the venture's product or service. Many novice entrepreneurs present their opportunity in this way, perhaps citing a collection of high-level market reports to show that they've done some homework. But any seasoned investor who may be listening is likely to switch off at this point.

Let's assume that this 2 per cent figure chances to be accurate, even if it's been plucked from the air. Which 2 per cent of the market are we talking about? What characterises this 2 per cent of potential customers from the other 98 per cent and prompts them, specifically, to buy your product? And why might the other 98 per cent *not* buy your product?

If you don't know who your customers are and can't identify their defining characteristics, you won't know how to reach them, whether you're creating a product that's adequately tailored to their needs or through what channel you can sell it to them. And, more importantly at this stage, you cannot begin to quantify the realistic size of your market to make a credible business case.

The question, in the typical parlance of venture investors and experienced entrepreneurs, is: what is your *addressable* market? Or, more simply, how have you *segmented* the broader potential market, and which market segment do you expect your business to serve? An addressable segment usually possesses a combination of characteristics that fit a given product; these may vary in complexity, from simple differentiators, such as age or geographic location, to more complex ones, such as a particular lifestyle, taste or unsolved problem.

If you want to do your homework, market reports and newspaper articles can only provide a starting point for qualifying and quantifying your market. They won't provide sufficient information about your addressable market because they usually offer only bird's eye views of broad markets. In the case of an innovative new venture, with which you're aiming to address an unmet and sometimes unrecognised market need, you're unlikely to find a market report from Mintel, Datamonitor or the like that analyses the unusual or novel customer group that you're hoping to serve.

On the other hand, if you're building a business case to start a new venture, you won't have access to the fully-fledged research team or budget that large companies use to conduct extensive research on customer samples. How, then, can you obtain some credible information about your addressable market segments?

Enter the 'preferred witness'. Put simply, she's a person who has enough experience and knowledge of a market or industry to be able to give you an insider's view of what concerns, motivates or deters a potential customer or partner. Conducting a series of preferred witness interviews should help you determine what your most promising customer group will be, estimate the size of this group to some extent, and predict their needs and how they'll react to your offering. Once you gather this qualitative information, you can review the quantitative data in the conventional market research reports, and make some informed and intelligent guesses about your specific market area.

Preferred witnesses aren't just useful for customer and market research – you can and should find preferred witnesses who can inform the other areas mentioned in this book by offering insights on the industry, competitive landscape and technology issues. The more your business case is based on ground-level information rather than high-level assumptions, the more credible it will be.

Why?

Part of what defines the attractiveness of a business is the potential size and eagerness of its target market. Yet, put simply, the market-size argument made in the opening paragraph of this chapter is too random, and consequently too risky for most business start-ups and their investors.

Novice entrepreneurs also frequently assume that they can approach and sell to several market segments at the same time. In practice, however, this proves very difficult, if not impossible. Trying to be all things to all people usually satisfies no one, and it reduces the differentiation factor that marks out a new company and gives it an identity and relationship with customers that is distinct from those of its competitors. A new product or business often *is* potentially appealing to several different target markets, but start-ups with limited resources can better employ their effort and money to solidly address and acquire one market segment at a time, building up reputation and business momentum at each step, rather than spreading their resources too widely and thinly from the start. Therefore, your business case needs to include an understanding of different approachable market segments, and the reasons why some are more attractive to start with than others.

GenAppeal: seeking the target market's unique code

Luc Krols wanted to turn genetics into true love ... and money. Drawing on his PhD in genetics and his MBA, Krols came up with an idea to capitalise on scientific research revealing that sexual attraction between men and women is greatly influenced by the genetic make-up of their immune systems, which is signalled through pheromones and subtly detected through sense of smell.

Krols' business proposition, GenAppeal, was based on a famed 1995 scientific study that asked a group of women subjects to sniff several t-shirts, each of which had been worn for three days by a different man, then rank the different t-shirts' odours for attractiveness. As it turned out, each woman consistently preferred the smell of a man whose immune system was genetically different from her own. This and subsequent studies confirmed that, in humans as well as other animals, a correlation exists between sexual attraction through sense of smell and different immune systems. This diversity has an evolutionary benefit: the offspring of mates with differing immune systems will have a genetic resistance to a wider variety of diseases, and thus a better chance of survival.

What interested Krols, however, was that studies appeared to reveal that this genetically determined attraction also leads to more satisfying physical relationships, lower levels of infidelity and higher fertility, leading to potentially better long-term relationships. Krols thought this finding could be of use in the dating industry, helping people seeking love to find compatible partners.

The core business idea behind GenAppeal was therefore to offer genetic testing and analysis of these immune-system genes for people on the dating market and then feed the results into a database capable of matching genetically compatible members. This matching would offer a new – and possibly more compelling – way for daters to pinpoint potential partners to whom they'd feel strongly attracted, before actually meeting them. Krols thought the test could complement conventional tools found on dating websites, such as chatting, personality profiles, and the like.

However, when Krols wrote the business plan for GenAppeal with a view to seeking investment, he made very broad assumptions about his addressable market, which meant that the suitability of his business model was questionable.

Qualitatively, Krols characterised the expected users of his service as: singles with busy professional schedules; divorced people looking for a new start; people familiar with the internet and comfortable with online dating; and people who use marriage agencies. He assumed users could be aged anywhere from 25 to 50. This gave him a wide range of putative customers to cater to.

From quantitative research conducted on the internet and taken from statistics agency data, Krols learned that singles account for 14 per cent of the population in his native Belgium and in the Netherlands, while the average among northern, mid- and southern European countries was 12 per cent, amounting to 45.7 million people across these regions.

Data from the Netherlands statistics agency indicated that 65 per cent of Dutch singles are actively looking for a partner. By extrapolating this figure to the rest of Europe, Krols estimated that GenAppeal would have a potential customer base of 29.3 million individuals.

However, his research didn't confirm whether these statistics fit the qualitative profile that he imagined for his customers. For instance, it wasn't clear to which age groups the 65 per cent of people actively searching for partners belonged. Krols believed in any case that his service would interest singles in all age groups.

Krols' chosen business model would see GenAppeal set up its own dating website, which would include all the other features already found in incumbent dating sites, and sell the genetic tests primarily through this channel. Customers would perform the genetic test at home, taking a swab from their inner cheek; they'd then send the swab to GenAppeal for analysis. In addition to determining compatibility, the swab would also be used to confirm a person's gender and provide a 'genetic fingerprint' to prevent people from registering on the site multiple times using different identities, presumably giving GenAppeal some additional differentiation from other sites, where such practices can pass unnoticed.

As a secondary market, Krols proposed that the testing service could also be sold through marriage agencies. These businesses would make the test available to their clients in the form of a voucher, and the clients would have to access the GenAppeal site to utilise the results. The marriage agency would take a commission, but the GenAppeal service would be positioned as a third-party product.

Krols anticipated charging end users a one-time payment of €125. His informal research suggested that older singles would be willing to pay far more than this amount, but as he wanted to serve a large age group he chose a price comparable to other types of DNA analysis, such as paternity testing, even though the latter is aimed at a completely different type of customer.

At this point, when Krols came to make his financial projections, his research reports couldn't provide him with a clear picture of where customer demand was most concentrated. So he outlined three financial scenarios, in which the company might acquire 0.5, 1 or 2 per cent of the broad singles market, with 1 per cent being the 'realistic' scenario and the other two figures being 'pessimistic' and 'optimistic', respectively. How he chose these figures isn't clear. He also calculated a target market of a random 1 per cent of all singles in each country, without considering the percentage of singles who might be actively looking for partners (which he'd extrapolated from Dutch figures as being 65 per cent). Although he'd presented some basic demographic information about singles (age groups, divorce rates, active daters) in a section of his business plan, he didn't build these distinctions into his sales forecasts, probably because he only had patchy information. Because 1 per cent doesn't intuitively appear a large share of the market, this projection must have seemed plausible to him, as long as it was enough to turn a profit on paper.

While it's understandable that, in the absence of available information, an entrepreneur might resort to a seemingly conservative percentage, this isn't the only nor is it the most desired option when defining a market.

Krols was asked to present the GenAppeal business plan as a teaching case to a group of students at Vlerick Leuven Gent Management School in Belgium, and a preferred witness was also invited to present her knowledge of the singles market. The witness was Rika Ponnet, co-founder and owner of Belgian marriage agency Duet, sexologist and author of *My Life as a Matchmaker*[5], with 13 years of matchmaking experience behind her. Ponnet was able to offer a close-up view of the singles market (in Belgium), some insight into how it was segmented, the motivations of customers, and how different dating businesses catered to different customers.

First, she noted that statistics don't always confirm current popular and media perceptions of single people – typically young high-earners, living a partying city lifestyle. While it was true that a major proportion of singles lived in urban areas, they were considerably older than popularly thought: 40 per cent of all singles belonged to the Baby Boomer generation (born 1945–1963) and 30 per cent to Generation X (born 1964–1980). Only 20 per cent were in the younger Generation Y. These results were partly explained by the difference in size between these generations.

A 2004 study also showed that Belgian singles had less disposable income than was popularly assumed. Some were single or divorced parents, some were young people in entry-level jobs; all were living within the constraints of a single income. Often they had to make important choices about how to spend their money. These singles were also found to spend less time on the internet than couples or families, to eat fewer takeaways, to take fewer holidays and to have less sex than couples.

Economic and lifestyle factors are important when considering the different motivations of people in the dating market. While a large proportion of singles (65 per cent according to Krols' research) may appear to be looking for a partner by being on the dating scene, Ponnet categorised these daters as either 'seekers' or 'players'. Seekers have a strong desire to be in a long-term relationship and are willing to put considerable effort into finding a life partner, while players usually have less focused motives: sometimes they simply want to meet new people and expand their social circle, or they may wish to have brief relationships or flings. Some players, according to Ponnet, even use internet dating sites as proxy therapy, chatting online about their personal lives – such as a recent break-up or divorce – without actually meeting anyone in person. And finally, some people switch between playing and seeking at different times in their lives.

Not surprisingly, players are more likely to use inexpensive, easy and flexible methods to meet people, such as dating sites, whereas seekers are more likely to spend a larger amount of money using a personalised, results-driven service, such as a matchmaking agency, or a matchmaking website that employs psychometric tests. Seekers, especially women, also appreciate the vetting and identity checks offered by a matchmaker. The difference in cost is considerable: one-year membership of a matchmaking agency could cost from €500 to €1,500; membership of an ordinary dating site could cost from a few euros a month to perhaps €250 a year.

According to Ponnet, 10 per cent of people who joined one of Belgium's largest dating websites typically found a partner by the end of one year (compared with 50 per cent of her agency's clients). From that data she estimated that only about 10 per cent of internet daters are likely to be serious seekers. She also noted that most seekers are in their thirties and forties.

Having presented her view of the singles market, Ponnet recommended that Krols only target the seekers segment for his genetic test, because players were unlikely to pay an extra fee or make an effort to find Mr or Miss Right.

This segment choice had implications not only for the size of GenAppeal's market, but also for the way in which Krols should sell his core offering. Ponnet pointed out that seekers had a whole range of requirements when searching for a partner, not limited to sexual attraction alone. Therefore, she recommended that the GenAppeal test be offered as part of a package of personalised vetting and matching services, not as a stand-alone.

Finally, Ponnet noted that many singles were still biased against using scientific matchmaking techniques and services, including the psychometric tests already offered by agencies. Since the public still adheres to romantic notions that love should happen spontaneously, she said, care should be taken to present the GenAppeal test in a positive way, as an empowering tool, not as a remedy for people who've failed to find a partner by other means. Consequently, she recommended a public relations campaign rather than internet marketing.

How?

Secondary, or top-down, research is information gleaned from market reports, statistics agencies, the media and similar sources. Preferred witness testimony is a form of bottom-up or primary research.

In order to carry out an entrepreneurial market assessment on a low entrepreneurial budget, you can combine top-down and preferred witness research to gain an approximate picture.

Performing top-down or 'desk' research

There are plenty of market and industry reports created by market research or financial information companies, often available from online databases that aggregate reports from several providers. In addition, databases such as Amadeus in Europe provide company information. However, these professional sources may be expensive to access.

You may be able to access these reports inexpensively through a library, possibly a public library with a commercial section, such as the British Library's Business and IP Centre in London, a university library, or perhaps your current employer's library if you work for a large organisation.

Government bodies, such as a national statistics agency, a government department for a specific sector, or a specialised agency, can offer demographic or more specific sector information. The

UK's Office of National Statistics, for instance, makes many reports available online.

Industry trade associations may be another source of specialised information. Some associations create reports that are publicly available, while others may be able to provide specific information in response to a direct request.

The national and financial press are another source of searchable information, as are trade journals. Newspaper and magazine articles can be searched online through a search engine, such as Google, or through the websites of individual publications. Access to some information might require payment. There are also useful online databases of press articles, such as Factiva, that do require a subscription but might also be accessible through a library.

The websites of companies in your target sector will contain a good deal of information including product descriptions, company news and history, financial information, datasheets and annual reports. Further information about an individual company's history and finances may be found through the relevant country's national register of companies, such as Companies House in the UK, or through international databases such as Amadeus.

Doing desk research also requires some judgement about the reliability of information. Not all sources are equally reliable; reputable publications and organisations are generally likely to be more reliable than lesser-known ones, but in any case, it is advisable to cross-check information from two or three sources where possible, and note any anomalies. Whenever you use information from desk research in a business case, business plan or pitch for investment, you should clearly reference the source.

In his business plan, Krols offered the following information gathered from his top-down research:

- On average, European singles amounted to 12 per cent of the population.
- In the Netherlands, 65 per cent of singles were reportedly trying to meet someone.
- In the Netherlands, 40 per cent of 25-year-old men were single, decreasing to 15 per cent by age 50; while 25 per cent of 25-year-old women were single, decreasing to 10 per cent at 50.
- Dutch people were also marrying later in life, implying a future increase in the singles population, particularly in the over-30 age category.

- In Belgium, there were as many divorces as marriages, implying that the quantity of singles at least remained constant.
- Google Trends showed a steep increase in queries for online dating from 2006 onwards, particularly English- and Dutch-speaking searches, implying increasing demand.

This data shows how difficult it is to assess the target market for a new product using widely available top-down research and statistics because very little qualitative information about potential customers' motivations exists.

Figure 8 **Luc Krolls' initial 'realistic' market share assessment for GenAppeal**

	Country	Population	% singles	Number of singles	%	Expected GenAppeal customers
Mid Europe	Netherlands	16,491,461	14	2,374,770	1	23,748
	Belgium	10,379,067	14	1,453,069	1	14,531
	Germany	82,422,299	17	13,682,102	1	136,821
	France	60,876,136	12	7,244,260	1	72,443
	UK	60,609,153	13	7,636,753	1	76,368
	Austria	8,192,880	14	1,138,810	1	11,388
	Switzerland	7,523,934	15	1,158,686	1	11,587
	Luxembourg	474,413	12	56,455	1	565
	Ireland	4,062,235	12	483,406	1	4,834
	TOTAL	**251,031,578**				
Southern Europe	Spain	40,397,842	12	4,807,343	1	48,073
	Italy	58,133,509	12	6,917,888	1	69,179
	Portugal	10,605,870	12	1,262,099	1	12,621
	TOTAL	**109,137,221**				
Northern Europe	Norway	4,610,820	16	756,174	1	7,562
	Sweden	9,016,596	12	1,072,975	1	10,730
	Finland	5,231,372	12	622,533	1	6,225
	Denmark	5,450,661	12	648,629	1	6,486
	TOTAL	**24,309,449**				

Krols decided to assume a 1 per cent take-up, making his market assessment essentially that shown in Figure 8. However, Ponnet's testimony showed that these assumptions overlooked qualitative differences between types of singles. Top-down research can nonetheless provide some of the high-level numbers against which you can compare your bottom-up research, as we'll see in the following sections.

Performing bottom-up research

Now that we've shown, with GenAppeal, the kind of information that can be gleaned from bottom-up research using preferred witnesses, let's look at how you can obtain this information.

SELECTING AND BUILDING A SAMPLE OF PREFERRED WITNESSES

Direct and indirect witnesses. When doing witness research, you may talk to *direct witnesses*, who represent firms or customer groups to which you already hope to sell or with which you hope to work, or *indirect witnesses*, who have regular contact with and knowledge of your target customers, such as vendors (retail or wholesale), consultants, technical experts, people from government bodies or trade federations, and the like.

Different buying influences. In their book *The New Strategic Selling*[6] Robert B. Miller and Stephen E. Heiman qualify most business to business (B2B) sales situations as 'complex sales', meaning that several people in a target client company, each with different interests and degrees of influence, will be involved in the decision to purchase a product. They argue that, to obtain a satisfactory sale and build a mutually satisfying and lasting client relationship, all four of the *buying influences* described below should be consulted, catered to and persuaded. Buying influences are also useful to bear in mind during preferred witness research, when building the value proposition of your business case. (They may also be useful to create future sales leads.)

> *The economic buyer.* This person controls the company or departmental purse, directly signs off important purchases and decides on procurement policies in general. For large or expensive purchases, he may be the company's general manager, finance director or similar; for smaller purchases, someone with divisional authority may have

discretion within the confines of a departmental budget. The economic buyer's purchasing criteria will focus on the business impact of a purchase, such as return on investment in a new product, cost-saving, revenue enhancement and switching costs, as well as the relative size and importance or critical nature of any such impacts compared with other spending decisions. This person may be the most difficult to obtain an interview from, but his viewpoint cannot be ignored.

The technical buyer. This person's job includes screening out suppliers on the basis of technical specifications. A company technology manager may be the first person we imagine as a technical buyer, but in truth, technical specifications could include any aspect of a purchasing relationship, from a product's technical features to any legal, contractual or regulatory requirements, logistics, credit terms and so on. Thus, depending on the nature of your offering, technical buyers could include purchasing agents, production managers, technology managers, legal counsels, accountants, facilities managers and so on. A technical buyer will want to know the measurable, quantifiable benefits that would be derived from adopting your product. He may also, however, veto a purchase simply because the innovation 'wasn't invented here' and the product could thus overshadow his own competences. If a technical buyer opposes a new purchase on the basis of technicalities, an economic buyer will frequently take his advice.

The user buyer. This person will have to use your product herself or supervise its use by other employees. Her role will be to judge the day-to-day impact of your product on operations, or more specifically on the job she and her colleagues perform. Does she perceive your product as a tool that will enhance or hinder her personal success in getting the job done? Although user buyers may seem lower in the company hierarchy than other buying influences, they cannot be ignored: the way in which they use your product – successfully or not – will affect how the rest of the company perceives your product's benefits or faults. They have considerable power to sabotage your offering if you don't consult them and consider their needs and interests.

The coach. This person is on your side and wants your product to succeed, often because he sees your success as tied to his own. A coach may already inhabit one of the other buying influence roles, or he may be someone in your network who's external to the situation but possesses knowledge of and credibility with one of the other buyers, such as an indirect witness. He can offer advice on how to approach other players, and may also offer to introduce you to them and, in the best circumstances, put in a favourable word.

FINDING AND APPROACHING WITNESSES

You need to rely as much as possible on personal and professional networks to gain access to preferred witnesses. People will be quicker to respond and offer their time if you're referred by someone they know rather than make a cold call, but if the latter is your only option, it's still worth a try. Through proactive networking, you should be able to find some suitable initial witnesses. If an interview goes well, your witness may also be willing to refer you on to other suitable candidates.

At this stage of your business case, when you're merely trying to understand your potential market, the key to securing an interview is to make clear that you are not trying to sell anything to your witness, only trying to form an accurate picture of their perspective, needs and preferences, and to fill gaps in your current knowledge. When you set interviews in this context, you usually find that people enjoy being asked for a candid 'expert' opinion, appreciate your aim of developing a good product offering, and may also provide you with much useful background information.

When approaching preferred witnesses, determine which type of buying influence you're talking to and, ideally, try to speak to a selection of people covering each buying influence in an industry or company to understand the perspective of each.

In small companies, such as Rika Ponnet's matchmaking agency, the economic and technical buyers could well be the same person, which could make adoption of your proposal simpler. The user buyer could also be Ponnet herself, one of her clients or even another matchmaking consultant who has face-to-face contact with the agency's clients and would need to explain and sell a new product or service. In large companies, on the other hand, there could be several economic, technical and user buyers who would have a say in the matter.

Although the *Strategic Selling* format is based on B2B situations, you may find that you would apply similar thinking about different buyers' criteria in consumer purchases; for example, when different members of a household have different viewpoints on purchasing decisions. A child may want to own a certain toy or game because it is fun or enhances his status with friends at school, while parents may be concerned about the toy's educational value, safety, price/quality relationship, or other factors that you may discover through your research.

You can also use indirect witnesses, such as vendors, to begin to understand different consumer types: for instance, Ponnet is a direct witness when considering how to sell GenAppeal to matchmaking agencies, but an expert indirect witness with respect to consumers in the singles market.

STRUCTURING AND CONDUCTING WITNESS INTERVIEWS
What you should aim to find out. Use the answers to the questions below to form a picture of your target market segment:

1. Most importantly, is there any desire, need or urgency for your offering in this market segment? Why or why not? *Strategic Selling* posits several prospective customer scenarios, which we paraphrase for market segmentation purposes here:
    *   Is there a problem which needs urgent attention? This could be a very promising market segment if you can offer a solution.
    *   Do witnesses indicate that they're not in urgent trouble, but are ambitious for business growth or competitive advantage? This is a promising segment if your offering can help realise those ambitions, but one where prospective customers may also be shopping around for other solutions, so you may have to contend with competitors.
    *   Do witnesses see a future possibility for growth or a potential problem arising, but do not yet see it as urgent? This may indicate a segment to approach, but one that will not develop quickly or soon. Perhaps it could be a second or third market segment to enter later.
    *   If witnesses in a segment experience no problem or need for your product, even if you see one, or they have already found

another solution, this segment is probably not worth pursuing. At best, it might become a late adopter of your product if its value becomes proven elsewhere.

2. Once you have gauged the level of interest, how would you need to design or package your product, pricing and revenue model to attract this particular market segment?

3. If a witness is critical or dismissive, ask him to explain why he would reject your product or business. Could you design your offering to eliminate these objections (or would other, more lucrative market segments be easier and less costly to acquire)?
   Note that there may be some forms of resistance that cannot be overcome. For instance, some large companies will not sign a small start-up company as a supplier, because there is too much risk that the start-up could fold, leaving its clients uncovered. If you are selling a mission-critical product and this answer comes up frequently, it may suggest that you should approach small and medium enterprises (SMEs) instead to see if they are more receptive, or you may have to team up with a larger delivery partner and share revenue.

4. If a witness is receptive to your idea, also ask him to explain the specific benefits he sees in it. How could you design your offering to maximise these strengths, reduce or eliminate any negative factors, and make it *easy* for this segment to adopt the product?

5. What are competing solutions to your own offering? What is preferable, satisfying or dissatisfying to the witness about these alternatives? This is a chance to test your own assumptions about what gives your product competitive advantage over current offerings.

6. How does a member of a market segment make a decision to buy? Who is involved in the decision process? How long does a decision take?

7. In a B2B situation, can you come up with a proposition that would satisfy all the likely individual buying influences and also benefit the company as a whole?

8. How much does the witness already spend on this area or problem today? Would they prefer to spend less, or spend more for a better result? If the response to your proposed product is positive, what might be an approximate volume of purchases? Would a trial be required?

9. What are the witness's typical criteria and standards for making a similar purchase? Consider, for example, price, quality, features (which ones), compatibility, an established and known supplier.

10. Can the witness give you any information on competitors or other players; or insider quantitative information about the market segment? Witnesses can often provide trade sector reports and figures that are not widely available on general information databases.

The question format. Use a basic questionnaire format for consistency, but remember that the interview is centred on the witness's point of view, not yours, so the conversation is likely to veer in different directions with different witnesses. Some questions may even be irrelevant to certain witnesses, so be prepared to improvise and come up with new questions based on the answers the witness gives you and the stories she tells you. Give the witness the option to reframe the subject and describe her real concerns or knowledge to you. You need to probe and ask 'why' in response to answers, in order to acquire and understand the reasons behind witness viewpoints.

Don't ask leading questions that may condition the witness's answer or sound presumptuous. At most, test previous assumptions or information sourced from other witnesses by opening a question with 'Is it true that…?' or 'I have been told that …'. Give the witness the option to correct you (and find out why they are doing so).

Making best use of interview outcomes. Be open to any information that is offered to you (including the unexpected) and ask yourself what it may mean for your product and business model. Rather than assembling a checklist of yes/no answers, your aim should be to interpret what you're told and use it for further inquiry. Below are some theoretical scenarios to illustrate possible interpretations of witness answers.

> Great market scenario: *We've been asked to produce more work with less staff. Your software solution would help me realise my productivity targets and also satisfy the company's profitability targets.*

If one witness answers this way, you may have found a customer. If several do, you may have found a good segment to launch in.

> Poor scenario, but which may suggest a different version or packaging of your offering: *Your software solution might benefit the company, but it could create a risk of redundancies on my team. (Subtext: this would damage me personally by lowering my status as a manager in the company.)*

In our own work, we found a similar situation when performing research on a concept for a software tool aimed at improving a particular aspect of web design and development. Marketing managers and owner/managers of web design agencies showed some interest in the tool's possibilities as a quality control and marketing aid. However, employee web designer/developers – as well as team managers of in-house web departments – were more sceptical. Designers claimed that they already kept abreast of the issues that the tool was meant to address, and that similar if less sophisticated tools were already available for free. They also said that using the tool could take up too much extra work time for little added benefit. Team managers said that their staff were already well-trained in these design issues and were addressing them effectively. The apparent subtext was that they did not like the idea of a software tool replacing or dumbing down the judgement and creative ability of a skilled worker.

This feedback suggested that the entrepreneur either needed to prove that there was an unaddressed quality problem – at risk of alienating some target users – or that the product offering should be re-designed or packaged to enhance rather than replace skills. This could perhaps be done by broadening its scope to offer added features. Alternatively, it might be targeted at a segment of amateur or inexperienced designers, or repackaged as a training tool for design students. Witness research on these alternative segments would be needed to examine these possibilities.

No-go scenario: *I just bought something like this* or *I already have a preferable way of addressing this problem.*

If this answer surprises you, you may not have done your competitor research thoroughly enough, but this witness is offering you a useful chance to ask and find out more about competing solutions.

Be aware that the witness research may suggest different market segmentations that you hadn't thought of before, because you learn new facts about the market. Therefore, you need to be flexible in your segmentation.

How far to go? One of the first questions people ask is: how many interviews will I need, and how long should I keep going? As every business faces different challenges, there is no standard quantity. The ideal cut-off point is:

- When a new conversation no longer yields important new information (provided that you have already interviewed a spread of different witness types).
- When you can explain the reasons behind discrepancies or contradictory information received from different witnesses in a market segment.

Combining top-down and bottom-up research

IDENTIFYING PRODUCT AND MARKET SEGMENTS FOR YOUR BUSINESS

There are many ways to segment a potential market; each business will adopt a different approach. Figure 9 provides a list of common criteria.

Factor	Consumer markets	Industrial markets
What are the customer's characteristics?	Age, gender, ethnicity Income Family size Life cycle stage Location/nationality Lifestyle	Vertical industry Geographical location Size of company Technology Profitability Style/culture of management
How will the customer purchase/use the product?	Size/frequency of purchase Issues with brand loyalty Purpose of use Purchasing behaviour Importance of purchase Source of purchase	Application of product Importance of purchase Volume of purchases Frequency of purchase Purchasing procedure Distribution channel
What are the customers' specific needs, and preferences?	Solution to a problem Similarity to or improvement on existing purchases Price elasticity Brand preferences Desired features Quality Importance of switching costs	Solution to a problem Performance requirements Cost saving or revenue enhancement Assistance from suppliers Brand preferences Desired features Quality Service requirements

Figure 9 **Possible market segmentation criteria**

There are also different ways to segment and package your core product offering. Possibilities may include, for example:

- Large/small size or quantity
- Core product only, or product sold with supporting services
- Different versions for different uses
- Integrated or modular system
- Components
- Stand-alone offering or co-packaged/bundled with other products or services
- Core technology or specific applications

- Service as pay-per-use or subscription
- Service sold directly or offered through third parties

As a visualisation tool, before starting your bottom-up research, map the relationship between the various ways in which you could package your core offering and different perceived customer groups on a **product/market (P/M) matrix**, as shown in Figure 10. List your offerings in the left-hand column and your apparent market segments along the top.

	Market segment 1	Market segment 2	Market segment 3
Product offering 1			
Product offering 2			
Product offering 3			

Figure 10 **Product/market matrix**

As you undertake your preferred witness research and combine it with top-down information, you'll begin to both qualify and quantify the

	Market segment 1	Market segment 2	Market segment 3
Product offering 1	No demand	Big market but low demand	No benefit to customer
Product offering 2	Demand exists, small market size	Not applicable	Large market, high demand for product
Product offering 3	Not applicable	Customers cannot afford this product	TBD

Figure 11 **Evaluating product/market combinations; the circled option shows the most attractive market**

suitability and attractiveness of different product/market combinations, as shown in Figure 11.

KEEP IT FLEXIBLE AND REFINE YOUR SEGMENTATIONS

As you carry out your preferred witness research, your assumptions about your product and market segments are very likely to change and become more varied.

GenAppeal's initial business plan, based on top-down research, suggested the segmentations shown in Figure 12. However, after hearing Rika Ponnet's commentary, the market landscape looked more like that shown in Figure 13.

	Market: consumer or end user	Market: business to business	
	Singles 20–50	Marriage/dating agencies	Other dating websites
Offering: GenAppeal website	✔	✔	?

Figure 12 **GenAppeal's initial segmentation**

	Market: business to business		Market: consumer or end user			
	Other dating websites	Marriage or match-making agencies	Singles 20–30	Singles 30–40	Singles 40–50	Singles 50+
Offering: GenAppeal website	✖	✖	✖	✖	✖	✖
Genetic testing service through third parties	? Rika thinks not: need to ask websites	✔ as part of a package of services	✖	✔ 'Seekers' only = 10%	✔ 'Seekers' only = 10%	✖

Product/service offerings

Figure 13 **A revised segmentation for GenAppeal**

PUTTING IT ALL TOGETHER

Let's pretend that Krols were to pursue further market segment research (in real life, he became less convinced about the scientific claims behind his idea).

When combining top-down and bottom-up research, Krols might decide to assume that 10 per cent of all singles are seekers. If he could find a more specific figure for singles who are doing some form of dating compared with those who remain celibate (65 per cent according to statistics from the Netherlands, but we cannot be certain it's the same elsewhere), Krols could make an even more targeted assessment of the number of seekers within this dating group (10 per cent of 65 per cent = 6.5 per cent of all singles).

Additional top-down and bottom-up research might include some assessment of internet usage by singles in a certain age group (e.g. 50 per cent in Figure 14). Note that Ponnet pointed out from her research that singles spent less time on the internet than families, indicating that a website may not be the most effective sales channel.

Furthermore, to flesh out the business case, additional witness research would be needed to either back up Ponnet's comments or uncover alternative scenarios. For GenAppeal, further interviews would include conversations with:

• Other matchmaking agencies
• Dating websites
• Some seeker singles – preferably covering both agency customers and website users
• Any other players discovered during the research

If Krols intended to market his product internationally, he would also do well to interview witnesses from target countries to obtain information on cultural differences. The aim, in all cases, would be to obtain, extrapolate or confirm customer segmentations, as well as approximate numbers or percentages based on estimates from expert witnesses or from interviewing a fairly large sample of singles who are customers of matchmaking services.

As a work in progress, Krols' combined top-down and bottom-up market assessment might start to resemble Figure 14 for a product aimed at an internal market segment (for brevity, we only show breakdowns for

Country	Population	% singles	Number of singles	Number of singles of target age	Seekers (approx. 10%)	Internet users (here estimated at 50%)
Netherlands	16,491,461	14	2,374,770	1,899,816	189,982	94,991
Belgium	10,379,067	14	1,453,069	1,162,456	116,246	58,123
Germany	82,422,299	17	13,682,102	10,945,681	1,094,568	547,284
France	60,876,136	12	7,244,260	5,795,408	579,541	289,770
UK	60,609,153	13	7,636,753	6,109,403	610,940	305,470
Austria	8,192,880	14	1,138,810	911,048	91,105	45,552
Switzerland	7,523,934	15	1,158,686	926,949	92,695	46,347
Luxembourg	474,413	12	56,455	45,164	4,516	2,258
Ireland	4,062,235	12	483,406	386,725	38,672	19,336
TOTAL					2,818,265	1,409,132

Mild Europe

Figure 14 New estimates elaborated from combined top-down and bottom-up research

Country	Number of singles of target age	Seekers (approx 10%)	Number of marriage agencies	Likely take-up by marriage agencies (%)	Total number of agency customers	% agency customers likely to want test	Likely price per test	Market value
Netherlands	1,899,816	189,982	?	?	?	?	?	?
Belgium	1,162,456	116,246	?	?	eg 100,000	eg 40%	eg €150	eg €6 million
Germany	10,945,681	1,094,568	?	?	?	?	?	?
France	5,795,408	579,541	?	?	?	?	?	?
UK	6,109,403	610,940	?	?	?	?	?	?
Austria	911,048	91,105	?	?	?	?	?	?
Switzerland	926,949	92,695	?	?	?	?	?	?
Luxembourg	45,164	4,516	?	?	?	?	?	?
Ireland	386,725	38,672	?	?	?	?	?	?
TOTAL		2,818,265	?	?	?	?	?	?

Central Europe

Figure 15 Estimates on pricing and likely take-up

Mid Europe here). If Krols were to pursue the suggestion of selling the test through marriage agencies, and seek further opinions on pricing and likely take-up, he might work out an estimate like that shown in Figure 15. Suppose that Krols decided to charge different prices for the service. For instance, with a low price for the test but an additional charge for database searches and matches, or a subscription fee, he could adjust the estimates and market value according to information he might acquire on how long it typically takes to find a partner or how frequently clients return (repeat business).

The method above is *not* an exact science and certainly isn't fool-proof. Educated guesses and assumptions will still need to be made. There will be limits to how far an entrepreneur can pursue such research and how much detail he can obtain. Yet it is still more insightful than generalised top-down research, allowing Krols to explain some pertinent reasoning behind his assumptions, understand where some risk might be involved, and improve the assumptions as he acquires more information. The witness research also offers insights regarding other aspects of Krols' business case, such as his value chain (marriage agencies now replace dating sites as likely competitors or primary distribution channels, for example), his business model and how he might tailor his offering to seekers of a certain age who are more likely to buy.

Preferred witnesses for all types of research

Preferred witnesses are always useful to inform any aspect of your business case, including your industry environment.

Figures 16 and 17 provide an example of a student project seeking marketable applications for an engineering technology patented by Imperial College – a flexible aerofoil with a smart core, capable of changing shape in response to wind conditions or other requirements. The students considered whether to sell the technology outright, license it to other companies for various uses or start a company that would manufacture products using the patent. They were also unsure where a business using this patent might sit in the industry value chain. Consequently, they qualified preferred witnesses and potential customers or partners according to the interviewee's position in the value chain (explained in Chapter 5). Figures 16 and 17 thus illustrate a summary of their research into two potential industries.

Process flow: IP > Technology > Design > Manufacture > Integration / Testing > After sales service

Rolls Royce and BP Energy
SBM Single Buoy Mooring
Pelamis Wave

	BP Energy	Pelamis Wave	SBM (Single Buoy Mooring)	Rolls Royce
Is your industry currently looking to new podct development?	Maybe	Yes	Yes	Yes
When would you think there could be an interest?	?	?	?	When mature
Are you more interested in: Technology platform / Single product provider / Integrated solution 1 / Strategic alliance — Problem solving / Single product provider / Integrated solution 2 / Partners	Integrated solution 2 strategic alliance		Integrated solution 2 (complete supply of product)	Buy IP and intellectual know-how
Are there any applications you could see for the product?	VIV stakes, propellers	Propellers	Propellers	Aerofoil / hydrofoil
Are there any issues you can identify or problem identification you could think of for us to resolve?	Unreliable in seawater application			Technmology readiness
Assuming there is an interest, what volume of products could you see your company requesting, in an optmistic view? As a test sample / As a volume purchase	Test 1 or 2	Test 1 or 2	Test 1 or 2	N/A
What are the most important design characteristics for you? Ease of use / High reliability / Follow-on service / Complex shape morphing / Price	Install it and nver touch it again idea or services	Service reliability	Service reliability	Reliability, price, functionality

Figure 16 Preferred witness research for smart aerofoil technology – energy industry

IP › Technology › Design › Manufacture › Marketing › After sales service

Chartered Surveyor
WilkinsonEyre
Arup

	Chartered Surveyor	WilkinsonEyre	Arup
Is your industry currently looking to new podct development?	No	Yes	TBD
When would you think there could be an interest?	When it is an industry standard		TBD
Are you more interested in: Technology platform Single product provider Integrated solution 1 Strategic alliance Problem solving Single product provider Integrated solution 2 Partners	Integrated solution 2	Integrated solution 2	TBD
Are there any applications you could see for the product?	Earthquake-proof buildings	Potential for anything	TBD
Are there any issues you can identify or problem identification you could think of for us to resolve?			TBD
Assuming there is an interest, what volume of products could you see your company requesting, in an optimistic view? As a test sample As a volume purchase		Simple test sample for mock-up	TBD
What are the most important design characteristics for you? Ease of use Complex shape morphing High reliability Price Follow-on service	High reliability and follow-on service	Follow-on service	TBD

Figure 17 Preferred witness research for smart aerofoil technology – building industry

In summary...

An arm's length assessment of your market won't convince investors because they can see the risk of your product not attracting the intended customers. Use preferred witness research to qualify your customers, segment your market and make approximate estimates of market size.

If you don't know or have a relationship with your market, your business may have to partner with or sell through another business that does. You may also need to acquire a team member with relevant experience of that market.

5. CARVING OUT A PLACE IN YOUR BUSINESS ENVIRONMENT

What?

Although people typically talk about business value in terms of the value created by a business directly for the customer, there are other players outside the boundaries of your venture that will have an impact on this value and on your ability to deliver it. It may be tempting to imagine your venture thriving purely on the intrinsic value created by your product and appreciated by your customers, who will thank you by readily opening their wallets, but most businesses do not exist in and cannot survive on a simple direct relationship with the end customer. There is a system of resources and players surrounding you, with which you will have to interact to deliver a product to the market. The environment will vary from business to business and industry to industry, but may include groups that supply you with raw materials or technology, groups that will produce or manufacture your product or service, those that will package or market it, the 'middlemen' that might be needed to sell the product to your customers (anything from a retail chain to the company that hosts your e-commerce site), those who will deal with after-sales support, and any other functions that are needed for your business not just to exist, but to have value. Each of these players adds some value to your business or product by providing something that your customers want and will pay for, and hence we refer to it as a unit in the *value chain*.

The value chain is the path of business transactions along which your product or service offering travels, from its conception to the final product delivered to the end customer – as shown in Figure 18. Your aim

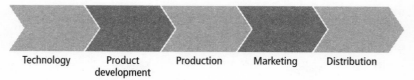

| Technology | Product development | Production | Marketing | Distribution |

Figure 18 **A generic template of a value chain**

should be to find the path of least resistance to the market, with the best possible profit.

Somewhere in this product value chain – or perhaps in several places – sits your venture. However, as a start-up you're unlikely to have all the resources needed to occupy the whole value chain from product invention to customer sale, the way a large corporation frequently does; you're going to have to persuade other players to do business with you. Put simply, who are these players, how will they interact with you and what's in it for them?

The value chain concept was first introduced by Harvard Business School professor Michael Porter[7] as a tool for a firm to survey its industry environment and choose an advantageous position for it to occupy in that environment.

As with a living organism, your venture's survival will depend not only on its internal workings but also on the friendly or threatening conditions of the habitat surrounding it. In order to understand your industry value chain and how this habitat will influence your business, you also need to assess the competitive factors that influence the attitudes and bargaining power of customers, competitors and partners in this environment. Porter provides another tool for considering these factors, Five Forces analysis, which we describe later in this chapter.

Why?

The point of the following exercise is to figure out where you stand and how powerful (or not) you are in the value chain, and then to use this information to shape your business. Let's say that a number of these value-adding functions will be performed internally by your venture, and some by other external groups. The first question is: which ones? What are you currently capable of doing, and what is better done by others? The answer is unlikely to be clear cut. Depending on the circumstances, you'll probably have to weigh up the pros and cons of each possibility; for instance, building your own factory or outsourcing production to an existing manufacturer, assuming it will want your business. This leads to the second question: who are the other players in the chain? You'll need to identify them before you can work with them. And this leads to the third question regarding the competitive pressures your business faces: are you going to encounter any problems or resistance in the value chain?

Problems arise when a function you won't or can't perform yourself is controlled by a group of players who don't want to do business with you. This may be because your novel business is a threat to their established business, or the limited benefit they would gain or headaches they would encounter as a result of working with you make the situation not worth their while. In the first case, you may encounter no co-operation at all and your path to market will be obstructed; you may as well not have a business at all. In the second instance, a player may only be willing to work with you for a high price, in which case you could end up giving away a large chunk of business value to someone else, instead of pocketing it yourself. In either case, you must ask yourself whether it is more worthwhile to overcome that player's resistance – at a cost – or to build further capabilities yourself, also at a cost. All of these considerations will affect the balance between the pros and cons of performing a function yourself, working with partners or outsourcers, or – if you are *really* smart and the case requires it – changing your business model, product and/or target market to create a different value chain that links together more easily.

Let's look at an example of a new venture that used a value chain analysis to assess and adapt their business model.

Artica: sidestepping the incumbents

London-based start-up Artica, 2009 winner of HSBC's Start-Up Stars graduate award, designed and made ventilation and cooling systems that use only 10 per cent of the energy normally consumed by conventional air-conditioning systems. Installation costs are similar to those of conventional systems, but maintenance costs thereafter are far lower – practically negligible. Add the fact that Artica's patented units don't use the toxic coolant gases present in air-conditioners, and you have what appears to be a rarity these days: a low-carbon product that costs less money than a carbon-intensive one. The Artica unit works in temperate climates, such as those in Northern Europe, where its 'thermal battery' exploits the difference between night- and day-time temperatures. During the night, the system draws cool outdoor air over a highly sensitive (and non-toxic) phase-change material, which essentially freezes to store the cold. During the day, the unit runs warm air from the room over the same material, which now absorbs the warmth and re-emits the cooled air. As a result, a room can be kept at a comfortable temperature of 20° – 25° C on a really hot day. In addition, the product is easy to retro-fit, so the market can include both new construction and existing buildings.

Artica's founding team, led by industrial designer Mathew Holloway and comprising alumni from the Royal College of Art and Imperial College Business School, first applied to enter a start-up incubator in 2008, where they were asked to present a value chain analysis as part of their pitch to the investment panel. The typical value chain for their industry looked pretty simple at first, as did the functional areas they could occupy. In the upstream end of the value chain they spotted no serious problems with players. The technical solution at the core of the product – a phase-change material – was freely available to buy off-the-shelf, while the rest of the product design know-how belonged to Artica. Sourcing of other components and materials needed also wasn't difficult. Artica assumed, for the time being, that it would assemble the product, and also be responsible for marketing. See Figure 19.

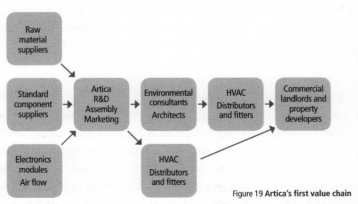

Figure 19 **Artica's first value chain**

In the downstream area of the value chain, the players standing between Artica and the end customer were more problematic, and the team spotted a bottleneck. Normally, products like Artica's are assessed by architects and environmental consultants, who then recommend them to their clients in the property industry. Artica did not foresee any problem raising the interest of these players. However, the physical sale and delivery of air conditioning products to property companies and developers is carried out by specialist installers, known as HVAC distributors and fitters. These players customarily enter into high-volume distribution agreements with existing manufacturers of commercial air-conditioning systems, such as Mitsubishi, Fujitsu, Carrier and Daikin. These large incumbent producers were unlikely to accept any of their distributors disloyally selling a radical new product offered by a start-up, and because an HVAC distributor would be dependent on a multi-million dollar agreement with a large company, it would be unlikely to do business with the new entrant. Such exposure could also present a danger for Artica: at the time of the analysis, they were not yet sure whether their product design was patentable, so there was also a risk that other companies could reverse engineer and copy the product.

Having understood and accepted this barrier, Artica would have to devise a way to reach some early-stage end customers without going through HVAC distributors. The team thought about their target market and asked themselves whether there were any potential customers who would never use an HVAC distributor anyway. There were: the owners and managers of listed and period properties. Installing modern air conditioning systems in such properties is often not technically feasible or not allowed because doing so requires installing a large box on the outside of the building. Artica's product does not require external units. Some buildings in heavily built-up areas have a similar problem with conventional air conditioning units because outside space is at a premium.

Further investigation revealed that, in Artica's home city of London alone, enough square footage of period commercial property existed to create a £50–100 million market for cooling units. In particular, the owners of serviced office space would be likely to see Artica as offering added competitive value for their business: their tenants could occupy an elegant period office with ventilation and cooling on warm summer days. If Artica could establish sustainable customer relationships with several landlords and prove the product's appeal and effectiveness, the company could penetrate this market further, while also pursuing potential opportunities in the conventional air-conditioning market, but doing the latter on an already solid footing. Building regulations today also often include sustainability criteria; Artica's product could potentially also appeal to the new-build or renovation market segment. Many public sector buildings fit this category.

The company directly approached a few landlords running serviced offices to gauge whether any interest existed. One such landlord asked them to install some units at two test sites. The trials were successful, leading to the company's first sales order for a wider roll-out across several properties. By this time, the product had also featured and won first prize on the CNBC series The Good Entrepreneur. The television programme and €250,000 prize brought further public exposure, customer interest and a bit of capital for additional marketing.

In summary, an analysis of the value chain and competitive environment led Artica's founders to think early on about a problem that they otherwise might not have considered. Had they assumed they could take the same route to market as an ordinary air conditioning manufacturer, they might have wasted precious time and risked competitive exposure by approaching the wrong group of distributors and customers.

Artica isn't alone. When a product is so innovative that it solves an old problem in a completely new way, it is common to expect resistance from industry members, and possibly in the market too, because companies and customers have already invested resources in doing things the traditional way. The challenge for these ventures lies in creating a new market with an easy route to the customer.

However, Artica's example so far only tells part of the story. If you decide to step around players in the value chain and go straight to your market, you'll have to develop a number of additional capabilities and relationships ('complementary assets') yourself, from scratch. The Artica team initially thought they'd design and make their product, but not sell it to the end user. As a result of their analysis, if they chose to go directly to their niche market of users, they'd have to develop their own marketing and sales operations and after-sales and maintenance services. These are functions that would otherwise have been performed by the more experienced HVAC fitters. Artica would thus have to spend time and money on developing these capabilities in-house.

Developing marketing and sales channels can be a very expensive activity, often more expensive than developing the product itself. For example, take Red Bull, the energy drink that is popular with university students and clubbers. The drink gained international popularity over the course of the 1990s, and became famous for sponsoring extreme sports events. However, it was founded in Austria as early as 1987. Red Bull's distinguishing feature as a company was its innovative approach to marketing. Since the company was launching an entirely new type of drink – not quite a soft drink (like Coke or Fanta), not quite a nutritional or sports drink (like Gatorade) – it would not be easy to position the product in mainstream retail outlets. The company would have to work hard to get shelf space in the supermarkets alongside established brands. Instead, in the early days the company marketed and distributed the product directly to trendy bars and nightclubs as a drink that would help customers to party through the night, and went directly onto university campuses to give away free samples of the drink, even paying for parties thrown by students. The company persuaded students to popularise Red Bull by word of mouth, and students then found the drink in their favourite nightspots. It was an astute approach, and cheaper than much conventional advertising (not that a start-up can ever afford television advertising), but still not cheap: in its first year alone, the company spent $870,000 on marketing, rising to $1.4m in 1991 – and that was when the company was only selling its product in Austria.[8] In this case, the founders were able to invest their own funds in the business at start-up. Entrepreneurs with less cash may have to undertake marketing activities more slowly, or may have to spend a fair amount of time proving the product concept before raising external investment which could go toward product launch and marketing.

For its part, Artica intended to follow its two trial site installations in 2009 with a wider product roll-out in the autumn of 2010. The plan changed, however: the start-up was approached and acquired in December of 2010 by Monodraught, a UK maker of natural ventilation systems and low-energy building concepts. Monodraught is a subsidiary of Denmark's VKR Holding, which in turn controls a portfolio of companies in the environmentally friendly building trade. Monodraught, already active in the market for environmentally friendly products, was clearly interested in Artica's innovation and the possibility of addressing a valuable new market segment while also diversifying its offer to existing clients. Although the acquiring firm may be selling different products to those of the acquired firm, it will already have developed complementary assets, such as an established sales department, credibility with customers and experience of providing installation and after-sales services, all of which should make the introduction of a new product easier.

Problems upstream

A final note on bottlenecks in value chains: in addition to distribution and other problems occurring downstream in the value chain, other types of problem may occasionally exist upstream. These could range from a university or inventor refusing to license the right to employ a proprietary technology in your product to difficulty securing a component supplier. However, for start-up ventures, problems are most often encountered downstream in the chain, where the product gets closer to the market and competition with other offerings consequently intensifies.

For all these reasons, use the value chain exercise as a tool to form a picture of your industry environment, and plot your venture's path of least resistance to a ready market.

How?

The following sections outline a stepwise approach to mapping your value chain environment. In time, you'll be able to follow this process more intuitively.

Step 1: Plot your value chain

To start you can begin to plot a value chain diagram based on your initial knowledge or assumptions about the players in the chain. Obviously, though, value chain analysis has to be based on factual information to be effective. To verify or correct your assumptions and fill in any gaps in your knowledge, you need to interview experts and preferred witnesses, as covered in Chapter 4. So, treat this exercise as an analysis that will develop and change over time, not one that you'll perform once and set in stone as the basis for all your future decisions!

Every venture's value chain is a little different, but a generic starting template can usually be divided into five segments, as previously shown in Figure 18.

Large companies are capable of 'owning' the entire value chain in order to control how their products are made and marketed and to extract the most profit from them. Start-ups generally cannot afford to operate across the whole value chain, so must choose in which segments they'll work and how they'll engage with other parties (partnerships or vendor–customer relationships) to provide the operations they won't carry out themselves.

The first step is to define what specific activities in your business case belong in those generic segments. Next, you need to decide which activities your venture will perform and which should be done by other players. When making this decision, consider both sources of value and complementary assets.

SOURCES OF VALUE

Ask yourself: what value will a customer be paying for, and which players provide it?

For instance, if your venture is going to create and sell a new beer, customers will base their purchase decision on a number of factors, not just on the drink itself. You can summarise these qualities in a grid, as shown in Figure 20.

Value elements for new beer	Players and holders of complementary assets
Visual appeal of packaging (first purchase)	Packaging designer Bottling/labelling plant
Taste appeal – quality (repeat purchases)	Developer of formula (brewing academy) Manufacturer (brewery)
Brand name and image (ongoing purchases and growth)	In-house marketing team or outside agency
Availability – easy to find and buy (ongoing purchases and growth)	Bars and restaurants Retailers (supermarkets and shops)
Drinking experience, ambience (repeat purchases and growth)	Specific quality bars and restaurants, or chains

Figure 20 **Sources of value for a beer product**

Which types of value will your venture have the capability of delivering? Which activities bring the most financial value? Which ones should you develop in-house and which should be delivered by partners?

COMPLEMENTARY ASSETS

The term 'complementary assets' was coined in 1986[9] by Professor David Teece of MIT. Teece investigated why inventors didn't always profit financially from their technological discoveries, and defined complementary assets as the additional resources and capabilities needed to bring a technology to market.

More specifically, complementary assets include:
- *Resources* such as a recognised brand name, a distribution channel or customer relationships
- *Capabilities* such as manufacturing know-how and facilities, sales and service expertise, and sector-specific marketing expertise

If you don't have the resources or capabilities needed to bring your venture to market, you will either have to work with other companies that do, or develop these assets internally. Developing your own assets will be expensive, and some resources, such as a brand name or customer relationships, can take years to develop. On the other hand, working with a resource-rich company means that you'll have to share some of the income generated by your invention. All ventures need to assess the most suitable trade-off in their particular case.

To return to the beer example, suppose you're a designer and your co-founder is a brewer who's come up with a new beer flavour. Between you, you'll be responsible for the packaging and the taste – but what about the rest? Will you recruit another team member with experience of marketing drinks and then set up your own marketing operation? Do you intend to set up your own brewery or open your own chain of pubs? Or are you going to co-produce the beer with an existing brewer, commission a marketing agency and sell through bars and restaurants?

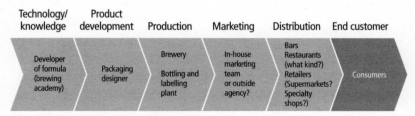

Figure 21 **Typical basic value chain for a beer product**

Figure 21 shows a first draft value chain for the new beer. If you were going to develop this business, you'd have to decide where in the chain to activate your company. Consider Artica, the air cooling company. Its expected business customers would be seeking and paying for 'value' in several areas:
- The benefits of the ventilation system itself (the product)
- Availability of distributors
- After-sales and maintenance services

Technology/ knowledge	Product development	Production	Marketing	Distribution	End customer
R&D by Artica designers and engineers / Phase change materials (from suppliers)	Artica's designers work out the specifications and test product	Component manufacturerers supply parts / Artica assembles product	Artica markets to architects, environmental consultants, HVAC distributors and fitters	HVAC distributors sell and install product at customer sites, provides after-sales service	Commercial landlords and property developers

Figure 22 **Artica's initial value chain assumptions (other players' work in darker shading; Artica's work in lighter shading)**

Their initial value chain would have resembled Figure 22.

When the company realised that this route to market wouldn't work because incumbent manufacturers influenced the decisions of HVAC distributors, they identified a different route to reach a specific customer segment. This meant that Artica would have to cover more of the value chain by providing distribution and after-sales services itself. The new value chain resembled Figure 23.

Technology/ knowledge	Product development	Production	Marketing	Distribution	End customer
R&D by Artica designers and engineers / Phase change materials (from suppliers)	Artica's designers work out the specifications and test product	Component manufacturerers supply parts / Artica assembles product	Artica markets to **niche segment** of period property landlords	Artica installs product at customer sites, provides after-sales service	Niche market of commercial landlords of period properties

Figure 23 **Artica's revised value chain (other players' work in darker shading; Artica's work in lighter shading)**

Step 2: Analyse your value chain

LOCATE POWER IN THE VALUE CHAIN – PORTER'S FIVE FORCES

Sometimes you can spot potential bottlenecks in your value chain fairly easily. Porter's Five Forces exercise can also help you to determine factors that influence the players in the chain.

Michael Porter identified five forces that affect a company's competitiveness, as shown in Figure 24. Each force may be powerful, making it difficult for a new venture to enter the market, or weak, reducing the difficulty.

Suppliers. Suppliers can increase their power when:
• The number of suppliers is limited, so they dictate the terms of business and the quality of their product.

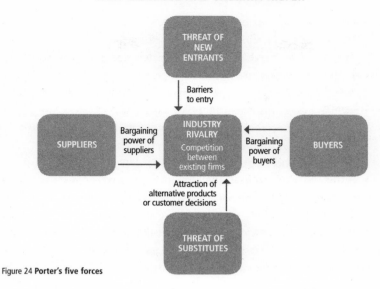

Figure 24 **Porter's five forces**

- They make a specialised, high-tech or bespoke product for you, or hold intellectual property rights for a technology you need.
- They have many other customers, and you're one of the smallest or least important.
- They want to expand into your line of business and become a competitor.

Buyers. Buyers wield power when:
- They purchase in large volumes so can dictate the terms.
- They have a wide choice of alternative suppliers to buy from, especially if your product is relatively generic.
- They're sensitive to price when choosing or switching suppliers
- They don't see much added value in your product.
- They are interested in 'integrating backward' (upstream the value chain) to produce or supply your product themselves.

Threat of new entrants. How easy is it for new competitors to enter your business? If barriers to entry already exist in your market or industry, you may initially struggle to gain a foothold. On the plus side, however, these barriers will also discourage many other ventures from competing with you.

Barriers to entry may be created by:
- Product differentiation or a unique selling point (USP)
- Intellectual property rights, such as patents and trademarks
- A reputable brand and customer loyalty
- Partnerships and established relationships with suppliers
- Exclusive deals with customers (or suppliers)
- Collusion between competitors, from partnerships to cartels
- Knowledge requirements, complexity of technology and shortage of qualified employees
- Size of the investment needed to enter the market, and time required to realise returns

The above suggest not only barriers that you may have to address when entering an industry, but also barriers that you may be able to create when planning your commercial strategy.

Threat of Substitutes. Customers may choose alternatives to your offering. Note that 'substitutes' aren't limited to your direct competitors but can also refer to an alternative purchasing choice or no purchase at all. A customer may test drive a Lamborghini to decide whether she prefers it to a Ferrari, but she may also be considering spending her money on a boat, swimming pool or art collection. Business customers also consider alternative ways to allocate money.

Substitute products may be more or less competitive in relation to your offering, depending on:
- Differences in price, functionality, performance, quality or perceived value to the customer. Does the customer need your product or is it an optional luxury purchase?
- High switching costs, for example if buying and using a new product requires the customer to acquire additional new equipment, redesign systems and processes, re-train staff and so on.
- New trends in the market attracting customers to certain products more than others.

Industry rivalry. Entry into an industry where existing firms are already competing intensely will obviously be more difficult. Factors that create rivalry include:

- Many competitors and low product differentiation, leading to competition on price.
- Powerful or few customers and the risk that they may switch to competitors.
- Slow industry growth, leading to fierce competition for market share.
- The need to shift high volumes of product as a result of high fixed costs (overheads) or because production capacity can only be increased in large amounts, causing sudden jumps in the ratio between product supply and customer demand.
- High barriers to exit resulting from companies being highly specialised and identified with a product, and thus unlikely to change or leave the market.
- Lack of an established or widespread technical standard in a new industry, prompting companies to lock-in loyal customers with a proprietary technology or format that's incompatible with competitors' products.

You may already possess a fair amount of knowledge regarding your value chain if you already work in the industry. But if you don't, or you need to fill some gaps in your existing knowledge, consult preferred witnesses who work in the sector (Chapter 4 has more on these).

Step 3: Deal with resistance and risk in your value chain

Once you have some idea of your abilities, strengths and weaknesses with respect to other players in your value chain, what do you propose to do about it? You can address problems in your value chain in three ways:

1. Find a way around a bottleneck, for example by following Artica's solution and locating an attractive niche market. This may require 'integrating vertically', in other words developing in-house skills and operations that would normally be performed by other players downstream in the value chain.

2. Find a way through a bottleneck. Can you negotiate more favourable terms with a player? Sometimes a partnership or exclusive agreement may offer a solution. In these instances, think carefully about what you are giving away as the agreement might prevent you from accessing other opportunities.

3. Change your product, service or business strategy to create a more favourable value chain. Consider the approach adopted by Emma Stanton in Chapter 1, in which she switched from a service for high-end consumers to a B2B offering for the corporate market.

If none of the above three solutions is possible, it may be better to let go of this idea and think of another venture to pursue.

In summary...

As with other tools in this book, constructing your value chain isn't a one-off exercise or an exact science; rather, the process provides a framework for taking a critical look at your venture's possible routes to market. You'll make new discoveries about your value chain as you interview preferred witnesses – industry experts and potential customers – and even when you go on to test your venture in the market. Assessing your value chain will help you determine the sort of business strategy you can adopt to reach your addressable market (discussed in Chapter 4), and whether and how you circumvent, negotiate or partner with other players.

6. PROTECTING YOUR BUSINESS IDEAS FROM IMITATION

What?

An important aspect of your venture's overall value proposition is the extent to which the value you create is *sustainable* over time. One element that can diminish or destroy your venture's sustainable value is competition from other businesses entering or already participating in your market or industry. Competitors may notice your new offer and skim off a part of your potential market share by offering the same products and services to your potential customers. Your venture may be at a less-than-fair disadvantage if others can take the ideas you've laboured over and then produce and sell your product or service more quickly and widely than you can – especially when those 'others' are larger companies with established complementary assets such as existing customer relationships, brand reputations, manufacturing processes and financial resources. Furthermore, it may be very damaging, not to say frustrating, to discover at a late stage that another party already owns exclusive rights to an invention or a part of an idea you've arrived at yourself.

Your venture's sustainable value is thus determined to a large extent by two factors:

- *Protectability:* the degree to which you can protect your business from competitors, through the use of legal property rights and other business mechanisms.

- *Freedom to operate:* the degree to which you can operate your business without infringing on the property rights of other businesses or individuals or without having to pay to utilise ideas, creations or technologies for which other parties own rights.

These are two sides of the same coin – referred to by academics as the 'appropriability regime' – and basically refer to the degree to which you or others can appropriate value from your potential venture.

This chapter covers how to protect your intellectual property (IP) and how to deal with infringements.

Legal mechanisms at your disposal include:
- *Copyright* – which is acquired automatically
- *Registered monopoly rights* – which must be applied for and refer specifically to patents, trademarks and registered designs
- *Trade secrets* – which are established by contracts between interested parties and safeguarded through operational measures

What we want to make clear in this chapter is that, depending on the type of business or product offering, there's rarely a sure-fire way to protect a venture, and protection may be very expensive for a start-up. Consequently, you need to consider the possibilities available to you, weigh up the pros and cons and determine an appropriate and selective protection strategy for your venture or idea – a strategy that not only determines the actions you need to take but also provides a timeframe.

Your protection strategy will also affect and be affected by decisions you take regarding your product offering, value chain position, and commercial strategy. Some business ideas cannot be protected by IP rights. This is the case with many service businesses, although the materials they create to distinguish themselves from other businesses, such as brochures, logos and brands, are protectable. We also describe ways of preventing imitation without IP in this chapter's section on trade secrets, and we touch on other ways of erecting 'barriers to entry' in Chapter 5 (in the section on 'Threat of new entrants') and of creating a strong market position when discussing commercial strategy in Chapter 7.

Intellectual property is a vast subject, and legal frameworks vary from country to country and case to case. Here, we focus on conventional practices in the UK, Europe and the US. When it comes to the specifics of your business, you need to consult both your national intellectual property agencies and a legal expert on the subject. The latter may be a solicitor who specialises in IP, who can provide advice, draw up contracts and conduct negotiations or litigation; or a patent and trademark attorney, who can likewise provide advice but is also specifically qualified to analyse, write and register applications for industrial rights such as patents and trademarks.

Why?

Our question in this part of the chapter is not why should you register your IP rights, but why should you devise an overall appropriability strategy, full stop.

As new technologies develop at exponential rates, making possible more and newer ways of creating and delivering products and services, IP and ownership issues are becoming increasingly complicated. If you ask an expert, such as a patent attorney, for generic information about an IP matter, their likely answer will be 'it depends'. Although the IP framework was developed to encourage invention and innovation by offering legal and economic incentives to creators and innovators, sometimes it results in ambiguity, controversy, opportunism, costly litigation and reputational and economic damage to companies. In fact, sometimes it stifles the innovation it was meant to foster.

Movements and business models have also arisen that eschew the use of stringent IP rights. This shift began with the software industry in the 1980s, since when a growing movement of developers has worked collectively to create open-source software, making source code openly available to use or modify for free, under liberal public licensing regimes wittily dubbed 'copyleft'. Under such licences, developers creating programs or code derived from open-source software must in turn make their own code available as open source. By removing constraints on the use and further adaptation of software, and reducing instances of incompatibility between different software formats, large open-source projects, such as the Linux operating system, have gradually gained mainstream acceptance with companies such as Novell and IBM, in parallel with the business computing industry's move toward a consulting business model based on software projects customised to client needs. The use of open-source software as a starting point reduces the development time and cost involved in creating customised or derived products and services, and makes it possible for anyone to do so.

In another collaborative initiative – without rejecting proprietary IP rights – the technology industry has begun to adopt 'open innovation'[10] practices, whereby companies enter IP cross-licensing agreements with partners in adjacent or complementary industries, not to collect revenue but as a way to pool knowledge, speed up research and co-develop new technologies and products.

Today IP is still central to many business strategies but opinions vary regarding its benefits or even necessity. However, if you do possess a solid piece of intellectual property, such as a patent, you're more likely to attract investors for your venture, because a solid IP right is an asset granting your business protection from imitation at an early date and the exclusive right to generate income from an invention. If you don't have sure-fire patentability, a well-considered protection strategy is still important to persuade a potential investor that your venture is worth a risk.

TomTom: the ups and downs of IP

Amsterdam-based TomTom is the European market leader in portable navigation devices using GPS. Its products range from route planners that sit on top of your car dashboard or are built directly into it, to route-planning software for your smartphone. In the world of technology products, TomTom has seen its share of IP-related lawsuits and controversies, culminating in its battle with Microsoft in 2009. The various disputes touch on hardware, software, open-source issues and an encounter with a so-called 'patent troll', illustrating that IP strategies must be selective to be economical, and thus cannot protect a company from all possible risks. Plenty of other companies have faced similar challenges; we chose TomTom for this case study because it's a well-known European technology company and we assume readers' familiarity with the products will help them to follow a story based around legal technicalities.

From its founding in 1991, TomTom's mission was to create software tailored to the needs and performance potential of portable digital devices. It chose to focus specifically on car navigation in 2001, released its first navigation software to run on other companies' PDA devices in 2002, and its first combined hardware and software device for cars, the TomTom GO, the following year.

While TomTom rapidly became the leading European company in this market, its biggest global rival was Garmin, which holds the largest US market share for in-car navigation devices. In 2006, Garmin sued TomTom in the US state of Wisconsin, alleging that the Dutch company was infringing claims contained in five patents registered by Garmin in the US for certain navigation features and methods in its own devices. TomTom held no patents in the US for technology it had developed itself, so it bought three patents from a US company, Horizon Navigation, and countersued Garmin, alleging that over 60 Garmin products infringed the patents it had purchased.

In April 2007, the Wisconsin court threw out both company's suits.[11] The judge ruled that Garmin had not infringed any of the claims in TomTom's patents. Similarly, she denied Garmin's eight infringement allegations against TomTom. On four of TomTom's allegations, she ruled that there had been no infringement because of differences in the two companies' products, and in the other four instances she ruled that Garmin's patent claims were invalid to begin with as they had been *anticipated by the prior art*. This term means that the combination of features covered by the patent was already publicly known in some form before that patent was filed, and consequently was not novel, prompting the court to invalidate the patent. In Garmin's case, some of the novel features claimed in its patents had already appeared in two pre-existing products – its own and another company's – while another set of features had already been anticipated in an academic textbook about the design of vehicle navigation systems.

Garmin and TomTom had lawsuits pending in Texas and the Netherlands, which dragged on for another seven months until they opted to settle out of court. Although the companies denied any connection, the timing of the settlements coincided with their competing bids to acquire TeleAtlas, a Dutch digital mapmaker.

While the case focused on the core technology of Garmin's and TomTom's products was thrown out, in 2006 TomTom lost a lawsuit filed by National Products Inc., a US maker of fastening devices, for a much simpler invention: the design of a mount used to attach a device to a car windscreen or dashboard, using a suction cup. The mount on TomTom's devices was ruled to be similar enough to the patented design to constitute infringement; the Dutch company was required to pay damages to National Products for past infringement and arrange to pay licensing fees for future exploitation of the features claimed in the US company's patent. TomTom stated, however, that the sums paid and owed weren't substantial.

'The bigger you get as a company, the more you get involved in these kinds of issues,'[12] a TomTom company spokesperson was quoted as saying at the time. The company may not have anticipated, however, that it would later come up against the world's biggest software company, and that financial expediency might ultimately prevail over legal argument.

In February 2009, Microsoft sued TomTom, alleging infringement of eight of its US patents. Five of the patents in question were related to vehicle navigation devices and other computing functions, while the other three were related to Microsoft's File Allocation Table (FAT), a method for storing and managing long filenames. Microsoft, which had tried to persuade TomTom to license the technologies for over a year before suing, also filed a complaint with the International Trade Commission in an effort to block the US import of TomTom's devices.

Microsoft stated that it had already licensed the navigation technologies in question to other companies making GPS devices, including Pioneer, Kenwood, Alpine and even Garmin, claiming this precedent alone proved its patents were valid, but TomTom was not swayed.

Three weeks later, TomTom countersued Microsoft, saying that Microsoft's Streets and Trips software – a suite of route-planning products for PCs, violated four TomTom patents for route generation in a navigation system.

Commentators and bloggers began to weigh in on the merits of Microsoft's suit, the debated legitimacy of its patents and of software patents in general,[13] but matters were stirred up further when the open-source community jumped into the fray. The TomTom software that Microsoft had singled out as infringing its FAT patents was based on the so-called Linux kernel, an open-source code. Although Microsoft had recently taken steps to befriend open-source organisations, previously the giant had made bold public allegations that Linux violated 235 of its patents. The open-source community now saw the suit against TomTom as a throwback to previous hostilities and a veiled threat to go after Linux at a later stage, in spite of Microsoft's assurances that it was only attacking specific, proprietary 'implementations' of Linux developed by TomTom.

A week after countersuing, TomTom joined the Open Invention Network (OIN), an organisation of Linux users that acquires software patents and licenses them freely to members, who in turn pledge to cross-license freely any new Linux-based software they create themselves. Commentators speculated that TomTom might use the coverage of OIN's patents to defend itself from Microsoft, but what seemed to matter more was the uproar and publicity generated by this alliance. OIN posted the text of the Microsoft FAT patents on its website, inviting the public to submit examples of 'prior art' (pre-existing and publicly known similar inventions) that might invalidate them.

Finally, just over a month after Microsoft filed the suit, the two parties agreed to an out of court settlement and to cross-license their technologies for five years. TomTom agreed to pay licensing fees on US sales related to all eight of the Microsoft patents. The Dutch company also agreed to remove certain file management functions that were comparable to Microsoft's from its products within two years – this was not seen as a major setback since the company could easily 'invent around' this technology.

For its part, Microsoft had to write the licensing agreement in such a way that it would not infringe the General Public License applicable to Linux and the OIN's patent portfolio, but the agreement also stipulated that Microsoft would not have to pay any licensing fees to TomTom for the patents in TomTom's countersuit.

Editorialists and IP experts conjectured[14] that TomTom must have chosen to avoid expensive and time-consuming litigation that could disrupt its sales; a patent suit can cost $10 – $15 million and drag on for several years, with the risk of an injunction on sales until it's sorted out; paying licence fees can often be cheaper. TomTom had just reported a €989 million loss in its quarterly accounts, after writing down the value of its investment in TeleAtlas, so protracted litigation would have meant unwanted expense and a risk to its reputation in the eyes of its investors. But, on the other side of the fence, observers also noted that Microsoft may have preferred to avoid testing its own patents in court. Indeed, this case marked only the third time that Microsoft had filed a suit for patent infringement in its history, although it had frequently persuaded other companies to pay for licences without resorting to litigation.

Along the way, TomTom and Microsoft were both sued by Acacia Research, one of a recent breed of company whose purpose is to acquire an interest in fairly obscure patents that aren't being exploited or defended by their owners (usually resulting from lack of money), then sue other companies for infringement. These so-called 'non-practising entities' – or, more derogatively, patent trolls – are seen as the ambulance chasers of the IP world. Acacia has achieved notoriety as one of the most aggressive and profitable patent trolls, with the highest number of such suits to its name, to the delight of both its shareholders and inventors who can't afford to sue by themselves, and the irritation of the large companies it's sued or forced to settle out of court – the likes of IBM, Yahoo, General Electric and Boston Scientific in the US and BMW, Philips, IKEA and SAP in Europe. Acacia sued TomTom in 2007 and Microsoft in 2010, and both companies chose to settle out of court.

What this story highlights is the fact that IP is frequently an unavoidable aspect of innovative ventures, and must be planned for carefully – taking into consideration whether and when to protect, the relative solidity of your protection and how to avoid infringing on other companies' rights. However, guaranteeing complete freedom from risk is almost impossible. It appears that TomTom did not file patents on all of its technologies and designs, nor in all countries where it operated, but this kind of selective patenting isn't uncommon. Once a company has a large portfolio of technologies, patenting everything in every jurisdiction may not be worth the enormous costs involved. A strong brand and a large market share can also be barriers to competitors, who will have to incur huge marketing expenses to introduce a competing product into the market successfully. However, if your company plans to export its product some day, one region for which patenting should be considered from an early date is the US. Not only is it a large and appetising market to sell into, but most patent litigation also occurs in the US, because it's the largest market with a single legal system for litigation, making a lawsuit potentially worth its cost.

How?

The sections below outline different elements of each type of IP right to consider when formulating your protection strategy:
- The nature of the IP right
- Eligibility and how to obtain the right
- Costs, duration and geographic coverage
- Freedom to operate, or how not to infringe other parties' rights

Copyright

Copyright is the oldest and in many ways the simplest form of IP, because it arises automatically upon the making of an original creative work (usually of literature or art, but it can stretch as far as software code). It gives the author a right to prevent the copying of the work or to demand compensation (by pre-agreed contract or litigation in case of infringement) for any copies made, such as royalties on the sales of a published book or a CD.

In commerce, copyright is most applicable to businesses or new ventures that produce and distribute multiple copies of some type of written, visual or musical content, whether printed, recorded, digital or a combination thereof. However, if your venture doesn't fall within this category, it's still useful to keep in mind that any documents you produce, any original content on your website, any technical drawings or photographs of your products, and similar creations may not be reproduced and used by others without your permission.

The most important caveat to remember, however, is that copyright does not protect the imitation of an *idea*, only its particular expression in a tangible form – an original collection of words, characters or symbols (such as a code), images and/or sounds. If you paint a portrait of, say, your favourite entrepreneurial role model, that doesn't prevent others from painting or drawing their own portraits of the same person in their own style; however, if someone takes a photograph of your original painting, you can control her right to distribute or sell that image, which is considered a tangible derived work. Similarly, if two people independently write two different books about the same subject, neither one is infringing the other's copyright.

If we apply this rule specifically to new ventures, you need to be aware that when you write a business plan for your venture, the document itself is copyrighted as a unique and tangible combination of words and pictures, but this does not legally prevent anyone from copying the business *ideas* within the business plan, which are *not* tangible. Keep this in mind if you ever show your business plan to other parties. Obviously, there are plenty of reasons why certain parties would not want or be able to steal your ideas if they were to learn about them, and such people would probably prefer to work with you than against you. All the same, choose carefully who you confide in and assess whether you need them to sign a non-disclosure agreement.

NATURE OF RIGHT

In short, copyright means the right to exclude others from making or distributing copies of your work, or any direct adaptations (such as a screenplay based on an original novel).

Material and moral rights. An author holds a material right, which is the right to economic compensation for copies of the work. Material rights may be sold to other parties or licensed for a royalty, as when a publisher undertakes to produce and print copies of a book and pays a portion of the income to the author.

An author also holds moral rights over his work, which cannot be sold or transferred. Moral rights include the right to always be identified and credited as the author of the work, and the right to prevent the work from being displayed or used in a way which the author deems distorting or damaging to his reputation.

Related rights. In cases where works are performed before an audience or broadcast to the public, performers and producers hold material rights to royalties for the specific recording of a work, such as CD sales or income from a broadcast.

OBTAINING COPYRIGHT

Unlike industrial IP rights, copyright arises automatically upon the creation of a work and does not require registration; however, you must be able to prove authorship and the date of creation in the event of a dispute over infringement, so it's important to keep records. Although your right arises automatically and does not need to be registered, it is prudent to mark a document or other work with a copyright symbol © or other relevant phrase, such as 'all rights reserved', followed by your name and the date. Doing so sends a signal to any viewers that you intend to defend your right. Digital registrations can now be made in many countries, such as the i-DEPOT from the Benelux Intellectual Property Office. These do not definitively prove authorship, but provide a confidential record that the work already existed and was in your possession on a given date, a fact which may help to support an infringement claim if the other party cannot demonstrate prior possession.

TERRITORY, DURATION AND COST

Unlike registered industrial rights (discussed further down), copyright is free. There's no such thing as an 'international copyright'. Each country has its own legislation and legal procedures, but most countries in the world have signed up to a number of international copyright treaties that establish minimum standards and require members to recognise rights protecting creations made in other contracting countries.

Duration of copyright is usually the author's life plus a set number of years following death, at which point the work enters the 'public domain'. In European Union countries and the US, copyright expires 70 years after the author's death.

COPYRIGHT AND FREEDOM TO OPERATE

If your business involves the copying or distribution of creative works in any way, then legally you need permission from the copyright holder, who may require you to pay royalties. The digital age has allowed for rapid and hard-to-trace copying and distribution of digitally stored content and prompted controversy over the right to copy; however, the laws haven't changed and infringers are increasingly being tracked down and prosecuted. However, you don't have to be running an illegal music download site to infringe copyright. Displaying someone else's text or photographs on your website is an infringement, although quoting an excerpt of a larger text – up to a limit defined in a specific country – is generally acceptable from the point of view of material rights, as long as you credit the author. It is still prudent to check that the author does not object under her moral rights.

You should also be aware that most countries uphold the rule, usually stated in an employment contract, that copyright for work created as part of an employee's job belongs to the employer. Copyright for works created during a freelance assignment or contract, in contrast, belongs instead to the individual author. If you're employed but create a work (preferably outside of office hours) that is not related to your job, you will usually be recognised as the holder of the copyright. Always check your contract and the legislation in force.

Industrial IP rights

Registered industrial rights differ from copyright in that they don't arise automatically and freely but require an application to a government agency, formal registration and payment of application and maintenance fees. (The only form of industrial rights that arise automatically are *unregistered* design rights, which are similar to copyright but arise with respect to the individual appearance – such as the shape or configuration – of a commercial product if the design is original and new.) In this chapter we limit our discussion to patents and trademarks. For those interested in the workings of unregistered or registered design rights, information can be obtained from the sources listed on page 118.

Protecting an invention: patents

Patents are the most widely discussed aspect of IP, as well as the most technical, complex and expensive. They're also typically the most alluring IP tool in the eyes of novice entrepreneurs because, unlike copyright, a patent protects an *idea* itself from unauthorised exploitation by other parties. It's even possible to register a patent for an invention or device you haven't physically built yet, as long as the idea is deemed technically feasible. This is a seductive proposition.

While patents can often create legitimacy for your product by reassuring investors and sending a signal to potential competitors, they're not foolproof commercial shields in all business sectors or situations, as the TomTom case demonstrates and this section aims to explain. Since patent law was initially designed to foster innovation for society's benefit – by encouraging inventors to publicly disclose their discoveries – not simply to make inventors rich, the law must accommodate a variety of interests that aren't always harmonious, including the legitimate interests of competing inventors. Thus it is not always easy to prove definitively that an invention meets all criteria for patentability, and such verdicts can be overturned at a later date. However, studying how best to use the patent system to your advantage can be advantageous, depending on your particular circumstances.

Many businesses cannot or do not make use of patents – such as service businesses. If yours is one of these, you may want to skip this section to pay more attention to those on trade secrets and trademarks, or focus more of your attention on commercial strategy, as discussed in Chapter 7.

NATURE OF RIGHT

A patent is essentially a deal between an inventor and the state; the inventor discloses details of an invention for anyone to see – thus furthering the social progress of science, technology and design – and in exchange receives a limited-time (20 years in most countries) monopoly right to exclude others from using that invention for commercial benefit, and in some jurisdictions even for non-commercial use, or to grant permission under agreed conditions, such as a license in exchange for royalties. (The wording of the law establishes the right to exclude others, rather than the right to 'practise the invention' (meaning take it to market), because some inventions incorporate other patented technology and thus require permission from the previous inventor – see the 'Patents and freedom to operate' section later in this chapter). A patent may also be sold or assigned outright to a new owner.

Conditions for patentability. It is not uncommon for multiple people in the world to think of the same or a very similar invention, at around the same time and to publicise their idea in various ways. Therefore, to be patentable, an idea or invention must meet three basic conditions, which vary slightly between Europe and the US:

1. It must be *novel* at the time the application is filed. Novelty means that whatever is claimed as an invention has never been publicly disclosed either in any existing products or processes, or described in any existing technical or academic literature, including anything written by the inventor himself (except in countries which allow grace periods for inventor publications). Any previously known instances or public disclosures may be considered prior art and invalidate the application. Note too that, although a patent is only applicable to the specific countries in which it's granted, prior art can originate from anywhere in the world, as long as it is public knowledge.

2. It must be *non-obvious* at the time the application is filed. Non-obviousness means that a person who is technically skilled in the subject matter (in legal jargon, 'skilled in the art') would not find the idea obvious. An idea might be obvious, for instance, because a very similar invention is already in the public domain, or existing technical literature already hints at or suggests such a solution (as in some of Garmin's failed claims against TomTom). The EU goes one step beyond the US by requiring that the invention be 'an inventive step', which means that it solves a clear technical problem

that has been identified in current practice. This is a legal rather than a technical test and is worth getting advice on if you think your invention is commercially valuable.

3. It must be capable of *industrial application* (EU) or *useful* (US). In other words, an invention is not patentable simply because it has never been done before. Industrial applications include agricultural or other technical, productive activities. In practice, few inventions fail this test.

Being rather broad, these conditions can be satisfied by a range of cases, such as:

- A radically new technology or invention based on scientific advances, as when semi-conductor circuits were developed for a function previously performed by metal wiring.
- A novel *combination of two* or more pre-existing technologies or products, to create a new contrivance, such as Unilever's patent for the Viennetta dessert. The patent describes the inter-layering of ice cream and wafer-thin chocolate (not new inventions in themselves), and the production method to obtain this delicate combination.
- A new or specific application for a pre-existing technology, as when the already existing internal combustion engine was first incorporated into the patented design of an automobile.

Exclusions from patentability. Some classes of subject matter are excluded from patentability in certain jurisdictions. These include:

- Scientific discoveries, theories, mathematical formulas and algorithms *per se* and aesthetic creations (but an invention that *incorporates* a mathematical formula as part of a device to obtain a useful technical outcome will be patentable).
- Animal and plant varieties *per se* (although *processes* for modifying genes to obtain specific biological effects have been patented).
- Methods or instructions for performing mental acts, teaching, playing games, administering medical treatment or doing business (although the US Patent Office has been more liberal in some such cases).

- Presentations of information (see the 'Copyright' section earlier in this chapter).
- Inventions deemed likely to encourage offensive, immoral or anti-social behaviour.

If you think your invention may fall into one of these categories, seek expert advice on where and how it could be patented.

Borderliners: software and business methods. As an intangible set of instructions, typically based on algorithms or mathematical formulas, a software program should technically fall under the patent exclusion criteria, while its expression in code may be covered by copyright. However, patent office policies on software have evolved considerably over the past decade, as IT has become increasingly embedded in all forms of industry. The European Patent Convention (EPC) formally excludes software 'as such', but allows patenting for technical inventions incorporating software to solve a technical problem. What qualifies as a technical problem is open to question; the use of a software program to run an industrial machine that performs a technical task is clearly an eligible 'software-related invention', but the use of software to run a piece of hardware on an everyday computer is more ambiguous. The US Patent Office has decided that software is eligible because it is useful and produces a tangible result, provided it meets the other patentability criteria.

Software is still a sticky area of IP, as the (far from singular) TomTom case illustrates. Much of the documentation for software inventions and practice exists in textbooks or in software programs themselves, making it difficult for patent offices to search for prior art. This leads to many cases where patents are challenged and even invalidated after being granted, with opponents arguing that the claimed invention was obvious or not novel. It is also easy to avoid copyright infringement of a software program by writing a different code to achieve a similar result; this situation creates a grey area between the protection that can be obtained from copyright (specific expression of an idea) and patents (a more broadly defined method for solving a technical problem).

Business method patents are another area of controversy. These patents cover practices such as Amazon's one-click internet checkout system, or the US State Street Bank's patented method of managing a stock portfolio, which was defended in a landmark court case in 1998. Since then the US Patent Office has considered business methods eligible for patents. In Europe, such methods are still considered too intangible and abstract to be patentable. The EPC excludes them, and the European Patent Office restricts patent eligibility to technological inventions, not commercial or financial inventions.

OBTAINING A PATENT

Patent application. You need to obtain patent protection in each country in which you intend to operate, although there are methods for grouping together applications in the early stages (described below). Patent applications are made up of a number of sections, including a title, an abstract, a technical description and possibly illustrations, but the most important section is the *list of claims*, which describes exactly which aspects of the invention the applicant wants to protect. This is where the skill of a patent attorney is crucial: the claims may have to be carefully 'written around' any potential prior art, to describe the specific innovative step to be protected, while at the same time making the claims broad enough to pre-empt or exclude potential competitors.

The claims. Claims broadly fall into three types (these are not legal terms, but broader conceptual categories we employ to aid your understanding), which are often combined in a patent application:
- *Process claim* – describing a method of making something, such as a new printing method
- *Application claim* – describing an industrial use for the invention, such as a new printing method's use in packaging
- *Product claim* – describing a specific object, such as a type of package that incorporates the invention

In legal terms, claims are divided into two types: independent and dependent.

An *independent claim* stands on its own, and usually defines the invention in the broadest terms that seem permissible by prior art, in order to cover as many bases as possible. If a claim is too specific, a competitor could design a minor variation on the invention, by changing one component or detail, and thus exempt it from any obligation relating to your patent.

A *dependent claim* defines a more detailed embodiment of an independent claim. Dependent claims can serve as fallback options if a broader independent claim is deemed to be invalid because of prior art or obviousness.

If the inventor is aware of any technical information that could be construed as prior art, he is also expected to clarify in the application how the invention claims constitute a genuine innovation with respect to the precedent.

Patent prosecution. Once the application is filed, the 'patent prosecution' phase begins.

1. *Search and publication.* An examiner at the patent office first performs a search for prior art in any products and publications that were already available before the application was filed, and sends these to the applicant for consideration. Once the search is completed, the patent office makes the entire contents of the application public, along with a search report detailing the patent examiner's findings. This allows the applicant to assess whether the office has discovered prior art of which he was unaware, while also informing the public about the invention. In the EU and US, publication happens 18 months after the filing date.

2. *Examination.* At this point, the applicant can choose whether to proceed with the application. If so, the patent office begins the examination phase, in which it analyses the evidence further with respect to patenting criteria, and finally determines whether the invention can receive a patent. The examiner informs the applicant of any objections, and the applicant may respond with justifying arguments or by making amendments to the application. Depending on the degree and length of this dialogue, the examination phase can take a year or more.

A patent application may be withdrawn at any point in the prosecution phase, either before or after publication.

Patent grant and duration. If the examination has a positive outcome, a patent is granted, usually lasting 20 years (in most countries) starting from the application date (*not* the grant date). This means that in fact you will have less than 20 years ahead of you during which to benefit from commercial use of the patent. However, most jurisdictions allow you to claim damages in respect of infringements occurring after the publication of the application.

Most jurisdictions require a patent holder to pay periodic maintenance fees during the life of the patent. If these fees aren't paid, the patent lapses before the 20-year point.

Territories and treaties. Contrary to a frequent misunderstanding, there's no such thing as an 'international patent'. Each country may grant a patent in its own jurisdiction, under its specific legal terms. An applicant thus needs to file in all the countries in which he's seeking protection.

However, while patent *grants* are national, there are two major international *application processes*, the Patent Cooperation Treaty (or PCT, involving over 140 contracting states) and the European Patent Convention (or EPC, presently involving 38 states), which help to streamline procedures and save time by allowing people to apply in several different countries at once through an umbrella body (the World Intellectual Property Organization or the European Patent Office). What you get at the end, however, is not an international patent but a bundle of national patents, reflecting national differences, for instance with respect to enforcement procedures and maintenance costs.

If you choose not to file internationally at first, you can also make use of the *priority date* rule, which is applied by all countries that have signed the Paris Convention for the Protection of Industrial Property (173 states at last count). This convention establishes that, if you file additional applications in other individual contracting countries or through the PCT within 12 months of your first country application, the date of your first application will count as the valid starting date in the other countries too, taking priority over any other applicants.

Cost. Patent costs vary, depending on patent attorney fees and national patent office charges. Attorney fees usually depend on the invention's complexity and the work required to draft a suitable patent, while national differences may depend on the number of claims contained in the patent, the duration of the application process and the post-grant maintenance fees required to keep the patent valid.

To get a patent in one country will typically cost several thousand pounds. To extend that protection internationally will require a budget of tens of thousands of pounds. Over the 20-year life of the patent you can expect to spend in excess of £100,000 per invention for reasonable geographic coverage.

However, the above is only a partial view in many cases, because new ventures often require more than one patent, and end up having to maintain *patent families* for years, in which case you have to multiply the above figure by the number of patents. This tends to happen especially when a new technology or product design evolves over a number of years, and inventors want to protect even the early versions or components of their invention that embody their fundamental developments. They file additional patents as the invention process generates further innovations or improvements.

PATENTING RATIONALE

Given the costs and timescales mentioned above, you need to think carefully about what and whether to patent.

Reasons to patent. Reasons to patent roughly fall into two categories: staking out your turf and generating revenue. More specifically, patents:
- Prevent competitors from imitating your business before you can build a substantial customer base.
- Protect the fruits of your R&D investments; they also give you the security to discuss your technology openly with other parties such as potential partners.
- Create bargaining chips for cross-licensing negotiations with owners of other technologies.
- Attract investors and lenders, who see patents as a form of security.
- Generate cash through licence royalties (although this practice is not as lucrative as is often believed).

Caveats and contra-indications. Some patents are more difficult to enforce than others. In biotechnology, for instance, patent claims for a new molecule and its medical application are unambiguous, and variations or alternatives are unlikely. It is difficult to 'invent around' an existing patent of this type to create a non-infringing imitation, so this industry treats patents as effective and essential. Software-related patents, on the other hand, create more controversy, as the TomTom case demonstrates.

A patent or patent family must be maintained, monitored for infringement and, if necessary, enforced in court by the patent holder, at her own expense. This can be prohibitively expensive and drain financial resources from other business activities (although the potential to sue may be enough to ward off a competitor).

As we have seen above, a court can invalidate a patent as well as award damages. Patents require public disclosure of an invention, which may not always be desirable. In some cases, secrecy may be preferred.

While patent licensing is an available option, the majority of patents don't earn substantial revenue through this passive method. Obtaining a patent for this reason alone, without starting a venture to commercialise products yourself, may not be a worthwhile pursuit (except in cases of high-priced, high-volume products, such as blockbuster drugs).[15]

Investors often won't take an interest until you have a patent or an application pending. This means that you may have to provide or obtain the money initially needed for patent applications yourself.

PATENTS AND FREEDOM TO OPERATE
Regardless of whether you intend to file a patent, you need to check for any possible infringement to other parties. In other words, you do not just want to consider whether you can obtain a patent, but more broadly whether you can realise your venture idea without infringing someone else's monopoly rights.

Existing and practised patents. First, do any other products similar to yours exist, and are they patented? You could start by conducting a simple internet search for similar products on the market, but you also need to perform a patent search for any inventions that may have been patented but not turned into commercially available products in the countries where you intend to operate. You'll need to determine if these patents are still in force or if any have lapsed or expired.

Pending patents. It is important to check also for pending patent applications because, if a patent is ultimately granted, the starting date of its validity will be the initial application date, rather than the date on which it was approved.

Consequently, if you put an identical or significantly similar product on the market during the period when the application was undergoing examination, it could later be considered as infringing on the patent.

As explained earlier, patent offices don't make applications public until some time after the application date, so a one-time search does not provide a complete guarantee that you're free to operate – you need to repeat your search periodically to check for any new developments.

Blocking patents. You also need to pay attention to so-called *blocking patents*, in cases where your invention is an add-on or improvement to earlier technology patented by someone else, or your product uses other people's patented technologies as essential components. In these cases, if you cannot find a way around using those technologies, you'll have to request a licence and usually pay royalties to the holders of such patents in order to make and use your own product offering or invention.

Discovering a related patent or application. Freedom to operate may become an intricate issue if you do find patented inventions very similar to your own invention, product or business ideas. In theory, you should either seek a licence from and pay royalties to the holder of the patent if you intend to practise the invention, or not use the invention at all. However, there are several possibilities to consider, described in the following sections, which are relevant both to your likelihood of obtaining a patent of your own and to your ability to realise your business without infringing another party's rights.

Circumvention. In consultation with an expert, you can consider how specific the claims are and whether you can 'invent around' the other patent. For example, if the patent specifies certain details of, say, a component of a mechanical device which could be configured differently but still fulfil the required function, is it possible for you to make a similar device that replaces those components with your own solutions, and therefore does not infringe the patent? TomTom might have considered this possibility when designing the fastener that secures its devices to the dashboard or windshield, but they probably didn't see this element as a core technology in their product; and ultimately the licence fees they ended up paying were modest.

Dubious validity. You might also analyse how defensible a competing patent is. As seen in the TomTom case, the company didn't file patents on all of its technology everywhere in the world, particularly not in the US. While this initially opened the company to a lawsuit from Garmin, the story also shows that it is possible for a court to overturn a patent if evidence is found to invalidate it. Companies or individuals may wish to avoid litigation if their patents are not very solid or they simply can't afford the process, as the settlement between Microsoft and TomTom suggests. On the other hand, patent trolls such as Acacia make a business out of litigating over patent rights acquired from small inventors, and research indicates that they specifically target obscure or simplistic patents that are easy for manufacturers to inadvertently infringe when developing new products.[16]

Defensive publishing. Finally, one of the simplest ways to secure your freedom to operate, if you have it to begin with, is to publish information about your own inventions. You can do so through a patent application, but if this is unaffordable, you may resort to a technical or academic publication. While this last option doesn't secure your monopoly over the idea, it does at least secure your right to use it freely, by creating prior art that will prevent anyone else from claiming it as their exclusive invention. Bear in mind that you will only have freedom to operate for *exactly* what you published. Also be aware that the US Patent Office allows inventors a 'grace period' of one year after such a publication to file a patent; Japan's patent office allows a publication grace period of six months.

A vast number of registered patents exist, so many that even patent offices find it increasingly difficult to conduct exhaustive searches for prior art. Some patent claims can be quite broad on the one hand and of uncertain validity on the other, so your search and analysis is unlikely to cover or pre-empt every far-flung eventuality. At the very least, you need to investigate the most obvious patent claims to avoid predictable setbacks.

PATENTING STRATEGY FOR A NEW VENTURE
There is no single strategy to fit every venture, but there are a number of decision factors to consider.

To begin with, for many ventures the choice isn't simply whether or not to patent, but whether you have or can obtain the budget to make such a decision and cover the costs over the long term. Many inventors run out and file a patent without giving this detail a thought, then realise that they cannot muster the funds to maintain the patent, file subsequent patents, monitor or litigate infringement or even practise the invention. So it makes sense to sketch the beginnings of a business case – an idea of the size and value of potential market segments (Chapter 4) and the commercial route you could take to market (depending on the value chain, as discussed in Chapter 5) before committing yourself to patent costs.

First, check whether you have freedom to operate, because if you intend to commercialise something, it is important to establish whether others can stop you from doing so or can demand that you pay licensing fees. Subsequently, you must decide whether it is worthwhile for you to establish the monopoly right to stop others from imitating you by obtaining a patent.

It is also important to identify specific parts of your invention which should be patented to obtain that commercial exclusivity, beyond protecting your freedom to operate. The cost of protecting freedom to operate by patenting *every* aspect of an invention could amount to more than the cost of setting up a business, and furthermore, freedom to operate can be established by other, cheaper means of public disclosure, such as publishing an article describing your invention. So, aim to identify the parts of your invention that are so-called 'showstoppers'; essential features of the invention, without which the product or business would either not work or not have competitive advantage over other solutions. Assess both freedom to operate and patentability in respect of those crucial features. Alongside this assessment, identify the less crucial or more flexible features for which, if you should not have freedom to operate, you can avoid infringing other parties' rights by making 'design-arounds'; in other words, by altering those features so that they still perform the necessary function but do not infringe. Finally, you might also identify details of the invention for which filing patent claims could be a superfluous exercise, because it would be too easy for *others* to design around them. You can discuss these issues in detail with a patent attorney.

If your competitive advantage lies in some essential features that are patentable and for which it would be desirable to prevent imitation, then it may be expedient to patent those aspects of the invention, particularly if you foresee that it will take considerable time to get your invention to market – time during which others might develop and patent an analogous invention. You don't want to later find yourself having to pay other parties for the right to use an invention you developed independently, simply because they patented and you didn't. However, in some industries and for some companies, the ability to enter the market speedily with a ready product and access customers through existing marketing and sales channels may be more central to business success than holding a patent.

Some interesting evidence suggests that a number of firms file for a patent defensively, in order to establish potential freedom to operate, and subsequently allow the application to lapse or withdraw it before the patent office makes a decision.[17] A patent application has the potential to turn into a granted patent as soon as it's filed, so the 18-month delay before the application is made public may buy a firm time to do market research on the commercial value of the invention to enable it to decide whether to proceed to the examination phase. Subsequently, once the application is published, the publication may establish prior art and thus give the applicant freedom to operate (provided that the invention was not found to be covered by another party's patent in the same territory). However, there are a few caveats to keep in mind about such a strategy. If you file with this defensive aim, and another party files for a patent application for a similar invention during the 18 months before your application is made public, that party will still have the possibility of obtaining a patent if you allow your application to lapse without being published, because the prior art status of the application is only established once it is published. In this case, the other party could limit *your* scope to practise your invention. And, as mentioned above, there are cheaper ways of establishing prior art.

You may instead opt to carry out an extensive commercial analysis before filing a patent application, to determine whether the patent (or likely patent *family*) will be worth its cost. The choice is a matter of how much IP risk you foresee and are prepared to accept as a result of postponing the decision.

Some inventions are so complex that they are by nature difficult to imitate or would take a long time for others to develop independently – for instance, if they contain a combination of complex inventions. This complexity could buy you some time, particularly if you know that the expertise behind the invention is fairly rare.

If patenting your invention seems difficult or problematic, or public disclosure of your invention isn't desirable, there are other options to consider. One frequently used legal device is the trade secret, described later in this chapter.

Protecting your identity: trademarks

Whereas a patent provides exclusive rights over an idea or invention, registered trademarks give your venture exclusive rights to a distinct identity, and consequently to the benefits you can derive from that identity, such as brand recognition and loyalty.

The building of a brand can become a powerful asset – although in a world of copious marketing noise, developing a new brand from scratch is neither easy nor cheap. However, assuming that you can build a distinctive brand and be seen as the provider of choice for a novel product or service before other parties take notice and attempt to imitate or overrun you, you need to protect your ownership of the brand.

A trademark allows you to prevent another party from imitating your name, slogans or the look and feel of your brand in ways that could cause customers to confuse that other entity with yours, or mistakenly buy the other entity's product when they intended to buy yours.

NATURE OF RIGHT

Trademarks typically combine words, phrases, visual symbols, colours or packaging shapes (such as the distinctive Coca-Cola bottle) that identify a certain organisation as the source of a product or service, as distinct from other organisations offering a similar product in the same country.

A registered trademark gives its holder an exclusive right to prevent others, through legal action, from imitating the mark. The aim of a registered trademark is to prevent not only the blatant counterfeiting of goods – such as a fake pair of designer sunglasses – but also unfair competition through an identity that is just similar enough to a well-known company brand to mislead a customer. Because it usually takes a long time and hefty resources for a company to build a solid brand reputation and relationships with clients, the trademark right prevents these assets from being usurped by other companies, or from being damaged if an imitator were to sell goods of inferior quality.

In addition to straight trademarks that distinguish goods and services, it is also possible to register collective marks and certification marks. Collective marks are registered by an association or trade body. Members of such a body are generally allowed to use the collective mark in their communications to indicate that they are part of such a group. Certification marks relate to a standard such as the CE mark in Europe, and can be displayed by any company whose products and services comply with that standard.

Trademarks may also be sold or licensed. For example, when Sir Richard Branson's Virgin Group sold its mobile phone operations to the UK cable telecoms company NTLTelewest in 2006, the new combined communications group adopted the Virgin Media brand under licence.

OBTAINING A REGISTERED TRADEMARK

Eligibility and application. To obtain trademark protection, an application is filed with a national trademarks register. The registration document includes a description and reproduction of the mark that is being protected, along with a list of the goods or services for which protection of this trademark is sought.

Depending on the country in which you apply, the registration may be examined and evaluated by the trademark office, including a search procedure to identify similar pre-existing marks. The application may also be published after a certain period of time to allow third parties to file objections to the trademark's eligibility within a certain time period.

To qualify for trademark protection, the mark must be not only distinct from marks used by other entities, but also distinctive in its own right from normal descriptive language and symbols. The trademark is a combination of words and the goods or services with which it is associated. The word 'apple', for instance, is a common word which cannot be trademarked by itself, but is acceptable as a trademark in respect of electronic products or software. However, no one can trademark the word 'apple' to sell fruit, as that is the common descriptive usage of the word. On the other hand, a fanciful or made-up name not found in the dictionary, such as 'skype', can qualify as a trademark for a wide range of goods and services.

It is also possible to register a distinctive sound as a trademark. However, original sounds can frequently also be protected by copyright. Once a trademark is obtained, it is usually up to the trademark holder to monitor the activity of other parties to identify infringement, and then take legal action in the courts.

Territories, duration and cost. Like patents, trademark protection is national. If your company intends to do business in several countries, you'll have to register your trademark in all of the national jurisdictions where you want protection. As with patents, however, there are a number of international agreements that can ease the international application process, including the right to claim a priority date.

Trademarks are maintained by active use, and the rights will lapse if they're not used for a certain period, set at five years in most jurisdictions.

There is also one exception to the rule of national trademarks: the Community Trademark of the European Union. Under this procedure, it is possible to register and receive a single trademark valid for all countries in the EU.

Costs vary in different jurisdictions. Average costs for an EU trademark, including the cost for a basic search and registration by a qualified expert, amount to around €1,500 in the first year for each mark filed. Monitoring for infringement costs around €500 per year. The trademark registration must be renewed every ten years, currently at a cost of €1,500 per individual mark.

TRADEMARKS AND FREEDOM TO OPERATE

Using another party's trademarks or confusingly similar marks to sell your own goods is infringement. Technically, it should be possible for two companies which belong to different industries, make different products or operate in different countries to have similar names or some similar brand elements, without infringing each other's trademarks. However, in today's business environment brands are increasingly valuable in their own right, and single companies are branching out into a variety of business lines under one brand, rather than branding each business line differently like an old-fashioned conglomerate. Examples of this phenomenon include the Virgin Group and the easyGroup in the UK. Even a century-old US brand like Marlboro has been licensed by its owner, tobacco group Philip Morris, to a line of casual clothing made by the Valentino Fashion Group in Italy. Consequently, the possibility for brand or trademark differentiation by industry is shrinking. If established brands are known to frequently launch new businesses, it becomes easy to mistake a product's brand origin. Since customer confusion is the determining factor in an infringement case, lawsuits for trademark infringement have expanded in scope. Naturally, these lawsuits are most often filed by large companies that can afford the legal fees.

Another reason why large companies protect their trademarks fiercely, even where product confusion doesn't seem a realistic threat, is that overuse of a verbal term or name may lead it to become a commonly used term, such as 'Kleenex' to describe tissues. This phenomenon can cause a brand to become less distinct, or 'diluted' in the eyes of potential customers, but can also potentially lead to trademark protection being invalidated. It is on this basis that US chipmaker Intel, which trademarked its 'Intel inside' tagline as well as its name, has filed an exceptional number of trademark infringement lawsuits in the last ten years, often against small businesses with no connection to the computer industry, alleging brand dilution – sometimes even referring to the use of the word 'inside'! Observers have criticised Intel for its exceptional zeal, adding that 'intel' is a common parlance abbreviation for 'intelligence' anyway. However, Intel is only an extreme example among large companies that file such suits. The company has lost similar lawsuits in European courts, where the brand dilution argument carries less weight than in the US. However, even if you think you can argue against a far-fetched infringement case, can your new venture afford expensive legal fees, loss of time and other possible setbacks? Many small businesses, when faced with a similar challenge, end up settling out of court and changing their name – a setback that can be avoided by the preventive measure of choosing your trademark carefully.

Even small companies will aggressively protect their trademark if they think the case warrants it. So it pays to do a trademark search before choosing your venture's name and brand, to avoid infringement risks in relation to any other company.

TRADEMARK STRATEGY FOR A NEW VENTURE

In a new venture, the first and most important aspect you need to consider with respect to trademark law is the choice of a name, and how quickly you need to act to register ownership of that name. Choosing a unique name is often a lengthier and more difficult process than entrepreneurs at first assume.

Once again, the issue comes down to your budget and your freedom to operate. You may choose to give the venture a confidential working title, assuming that this name hasn't been trademarked or used by another party, and delay your trademark costs until you're sure of your choice and have the budget to register and maintain it. You may also have reason to keep the name and prospective launch of your business a secret. The risk, of course, is that someone else may trademark the name in the meantime.

All of the other branding activity that applies to trademarks – logo graphics, slogans and the like – will usually follow the naming of the company or product.

Domain names. Domain names have raised interesting implications for trademarks and company identities; whereas trademarks are national, a URL is automatically international and there can only be one holder in the world for a particular domain name.

It is cheaper to register and maintain a domain name than a trademark or a slew of national trademarks, so if you've chosen an original name, registering it as a domain name before someone else does is a prudent step to take early on.

However, if your chosen domain name happens to incorporate another party's registered trademark anywhere in the world, that party can act to claim the domain from you. This claim is made through an international arbitration mechanism – the Uniform Dispute Resolution Policy – which is adhered to by ICANN, the international organisation that regulates the assignment of internet addresses and accredits domain name providers. Most such cases reportedly end with a resolution in favour of the trademark holder. So, freedom to operate is equally important with respect to domain names.

Protection without patents: trade secrets

Trade secrets may be used to protect knowledge that is not patentable, or even as an alternative choice to patents if these are not desirable. Put simply, if competitors never find out what's in your product, they cannot imitate it or steal the idea.

Most businesses will hold some information or knowledge which contributes to their success and competitive advantage, and should not be revealed to competitors. Depending on the degree of security needed, ways to maintain a trade secret include:

- Legal mechanisms such as non-disclosure agreements (NDAs) or confidentiality and non-compete clauses in contracts with employees, partners, manufacturers, investors and anyone else you need to work with.
- Complexity and tacit knowledge, as in cases when different, highly specialised experts are required to implement a technology or process, particularly if such skills are scarce.
- Built-in technical and design safeguards, such as parts of a product that cannot be disassembled, software files that cannot be opened or that self-destruct when tampered with, raw materials and ingredients labelled with code names and so on.
- Security arrangements in company offices, such as locked filing cabinets and password-protected computer files, access to knowledge restricted to a handful of company members, visitor escorts, limiting who can answer questions from the press or other external parties and so on.
- Incentives *not* to divulge trade secrets, such as giving employees a direct stake in the company's long-term survival and success, through equity shares or options (which may be lost if an employee leaves prematurely), bonuses, ensuring job satisfaction and so on; and granting partners and outsourcers exclusivity and royalty agreements.

Trade secrets don't need to be registered. The basic rule for managing a trade secret is to indicate clearly when information being disclosed within the company is classified, so that disclosure would be a breach of any relevant clause in an employment or third-party contract. In all countries, tort law on misappropriation of trade secrets requires a company to have taken reasonable measures to maintain the secret, and qualifies a legitimate trade secret as a piece of confidential knowledge providing a company with a competitive economic advantage, which would be lost if the knowledge were made public. (Other legal protection aspects vary among countries.)

Secrecy is cheaper in the short term than patenting, and if stringently enforced could last forever, whereas a patent only lasts 20 years. On the negative side, secrecy carries a high risk: once lost, it's lost forever! The damages awarded in a lawsuit for breach of secrecy may be poor compensation for the loss of a business opportunity. And your invention or technology may be vulnerable to reverse engineering or independent discovery by competitors.

One of the most successful and long-lived trade secrets (over 120 years old) is the Coca-Cola recipe. Only a few individuals in the company know the secret formula, which is stored in a bank vault.

TRADE SECRETS AND FREEDOM TO OPERATE

It should come as no surprise that, if you *independently* make an invention or acquire knowledge that an unrelated party has been holding as secret, you're not liable for misappropriation because you wouldn't have known there was a secret in the first place. It may also be possible for you to reverse engineer another company's unpatented product – namely, to take it apart as far as possible and figure out how it was made. In this case, you're also not liable because you didn't actually steal hidden information from the company, unless you are violating a clause in a customer license agreement, such as those that come with the purchase of software products.

However, if you aim to start a new venture that will draw on knowledge you gained during a period of employment or consultancy, and that knowledge has been classified by your employer or client as a trade secret, you face a strong possibility of prosecution. You need to check carefully your contract terms, the duration of any non-compete agreements and the status of the knowledge in question.

A final word on disclosure

If you aim to file a patent but have not yet done so, or you have a pending application that hasn't been published, you need to make clear to a potential investor or any other party that a disclosure is made in confidence, otherwise your conversation or correspondence may be deemed a public disclosure that will count as prior art. The simplest way to establish confidentiality is to ask people to sign a non-disclosure agreement (NDA), but in practice not everyone will agree to do so. Many investors refuse to sign them because all too frequently similar ideas are pitched to them by different entrepreneurs, leading to potential confusion regarding infringement. Experienced, reputable investors rely on their good reputations, and should normally respect confidentiality, but they will also recommend that you 'talk around' your invention, describing its competitive benefits or performance – which is what really interests them

– without revealing the secret ingredients within it. In other words: 'I don't need to know how you made it; just tell me what it does and why it's better than current alternatives.'

Searching for pre-existing IP

Patent and trademark offices in most countries, such as the UK Intellectual Property Office (UKIPO), offer searchable online databases that are accessible through their websites. The two international clearing houses of information, from whose sites you can perform worldwide searches and also find links to the respective sites of member countries, are the World Intellectual Property Office (WIPO) and the European Patent Office (EPO). You can search for European trademarks on the website of the Office for Harmonization in the Internal Market (OHIM).

In summary...

As we've seen, different types of intellectual property involve different technical, legal and financial implications. Protection is often not iron-clad, and the ability to generate licensing income from intellectual property without making products isn't always lucrative. It therefore makes sense to spend money on IP rights if you have something of enough commercial value to create a return and a strong risk of imitation exists.

When planning your new start-up venture, bear this advice in mind:

- Always check your freedom to operate (avoid infringement risk).
- Avoid having to pay others for something you created yourself –
  this may mean registering a patent if your invention seems
  vulnerable to imitation (for instance, if the resulting product can
  be easily examined and reverse-engineered, or if you anticipate a
  long lead time to bring your invention to market).
- Consider how to integrate your protection strategy and its timing
  with your foreseeable budget and other aspects of your
  commercial strategy (see Chapter 7 on entrepreneurial strategies).

7. CHOOSING ENTREPRENEURIAL STRATEGIES FOR ENTERING NEW MARKETS

What?

Chapters 1, 2 and 3 discuss how to evaluate whether a product idea, technology or solution is advantageous, compared to competing products and solutions, and how to compare the possible applications for a new technology. Chapters 4, 5 and 6 show you how to identify and evaluate market segments, business environments and intellectual property regimes that will be relevant to your business case. These fact-gathering and analysing missions should give you considerable information about the possibilities and limitations of your venture, and show how much more there is to starting and successfully growing a business than simply having a product to sell.

The combination of these considerations should inform your choice of 'business model'. Essentially, a business model defines the way in which you organise interconnecting aspects of your business to create and extract value from it (usually monetary, but sometimes other types of value, such as those associated with social enterprises or non-profit organisations). Since we assume our readers to be in the very early stages of creating a concept or case for a new business, we prefer to refer more concretely to *commercial strategy* – the route to market you will take to turn your idea into a commercial operation – and *revenue model* – the manner by which you'll collect income from your business.

Commercial strategy can be defined in either broad or specific terms. Based on our research into the routes taken by start-ups that not only survived but achieved significant growth in revenues and/or employees in their first five years,[18] we choose to start with the type of market that's likely to be most suitable for a particular venture idea: the 'market for products' or the 'market for technology' (or knowledge, more broadly). Each of these two market categories calls for a different type of strategy if you are to enter that market; the resources, capabilities and assets you'll need will also differ. However, we also identify a hybrid market entry strategy that addresses both markets, as well as what we call 'transitional' start-ups and consulting models.

Why?

New ventures are subject to huge uncertainty. Many unpredictable or uncontrollable external events can impact the success of a start-up, not the least of which may be unforeseen competition from other groups who've been developing a similar offering behind closed doors. While no one can be truly clairvoyant about a start-up's future, and a certain amount of trial and error will be likely in the early phases, a considered choice about the most realistic route to market and revenue model when you're developing your business case will hopefully avoid wasted effort, wasted money and frustration later on. Even if your venture should need to change its strategy when it is already knee-deep into the start-up phase, it's useful to have a structured framework for making these changes – even one from which you might consciously choose to depart if circumstances demand an exception to the rule.

Several of the case studies in earlier chapters of this book demonstrate the importance of using collected insights and foresight regarding environmental factors when selecting a commercial strategy. In a fair number of these stories, the strategy finally adopted turns out to be different from the one first envisioned by the entrepreneur, due to an environmental limitation, an opportunity or both. Many of these cases positively illustrate some of the issues we discuss later in this chapter, even though they weren't part of the original research that gave rise to our strategy framework.

Jean-Marc de Fety (Chapter 2) initially intended to build a price comparison platform aimed at local customers, to provide information about local shops and their inventory to nearby residents and shoppers. However, when he realised that persuading high street retail chains to provide the inventory data needed to make his idea work would be a complex endeavour, he decided that he couldn't afford to spend two years getting the necessary relationships and agreements in place. So he modified his strategy to enter a more accessible, simple *market for products* (or, in this case, for standardised services). He still focused on a local market segment, but avoided the retail chains, building a supportive and exclusive social network for a niche segment of affluent London mothers, mummysworld.co.uk. His reasoning was that, if he could build up an influential and attractive base of users of his service, this base could later attract partnerships or commercial agreements with businesses eager to understand and tap into this market segment's needs. By so doing, de Fety was able to fund the launch of the company from his own savings, and earn some early revenues from subscribers and advertisers.

In the case of Artica (Chapter 5), the founding team recognised early on that the typical downstream value chain in the mainstream market for business air conditioning systems was unlikely to be receptive. Air conditioning distributors and installers who normally sell to business clients were unlikely to sell Artica's innovative cooling system because they had lucrative contracts with major incumbent producers of conventional systems, such as Mitsubishi, which they would not want to antagonise. Fortunately, the team was able to identify a sizable and valuable niche market that could not be served by conventional suppliers, thanks to building regulations for period properties. They thus decided to create an offering tailored to serving this particular segment in the *market for products* by developing a close understanding of these niche customers' needs. This decision also meant that the company would have to create its own sales and installation operations, and would need to determine whether these resources could be built up gradually and funded by customer revenues, or put in place at start-up by raising external investment.

CropDesign (Chapter 3) is an example of a technology-based company that changed its strategy several years into its operation. Initially, the company thought it would not only develop its platform technology for application to a specific crop, but also sell directly into a market for products: it would produce and distribute genetically modified (GM) rice seed to farmers, therefore integrating its operations from technology at the upstream end all the way into distribution at the downstream end of the value chain. This choice was based on the observation that there was no significant competition from powerful incumbent suppliers in this market. Unfortunately, this initially attractive lack of competition was subsequently explained by the fact that there was also no significant demand for GM rice seed, prompting those incumbents to direct their efforts and marketing power into the more attractive market for GM corn. However, if CropDesign had tried to enter the corn market as a product supplier, going head to head with the likes of Monsanto and its peers, it would face barriers in its downstream value chain similar to those faced by Artica, because the distribution channel in this industry was dominated by the incumbents. Nonetheless, the performance potential of CropDesign's technology could offer a true step change in improved crop yield, meaning more crops per acre, a desirable and competitive selling point. So the company changed course and entered the *market for technology*, by selling *itself* – the whole start-up, complete with patents, equipment and highly specialised employees – to an incumbent. The start-up's investment in technology development, particularly applied to corn seed, needed to reach the point where the method was proven or 'de-risked' enough to attract an incumbent such as BASF, which already possessed the commercial structures and relationships needed to deliver a product to an end market.

Finally, TomTom (Chapter 6) provides an interesting example of a company that moved from one type of market to another, well into its operational life, and was ultimately successful. In its first years in the early 1990s, the company (initially named Palmtop) operated on what was essentially a consulting business model, receiving commissions from business customers to create tailored software. Their first customer was 'an entrepreneur who was importing wooden ducks from India and needed a bar code reading system'.[19] The company's technical speciality was creating special software that would operate efficiently on handheld devices, which presented technical challenges resulting from limited memory, storage capacity and processing power. Beginning thus with order entry and bar code reading systems, the company later struck up a partnership with Psion (through one founder's contact with a former university classmate), and moved into making and selling standardised consumer applications for the increasingly popular Psion, Palm and Hewlett Packard personal digital assistants (PDAs), such as dictionaries, personal finance tools, games and route planners.

The partnership and new direction introduced the company to relationships with distributors and retailers and helped build repeatable revenues for standardised products. Finally, as satellite navigation technology and infrastructure became more reliable and accessible to the civilian market, the company saw that demand for navigation software was growing faster than for other PDA features, and decided to move into making proprietary hardware devices on which to run its navigation software alone under the new brand, TomTom. Along the way, the company nearly lost its shirt in an unsuccessful technology partnership with Ericsson to develop navigation software. TomTom is therefore an example of a 'transitional' start-up, which began in a consulting services role in the market for technology, explored several options in the technology and hybrid markets and eventually specialised in a single market for products (a process that spanned over ten years, with some hiccups along the way).

How?

While the cases above offer some insight, other businesses cannot entirely resemble your own venture, especially if you're aiming to start an innovative venture for which there are few or no direct comparisons. How, then, can you choose a strategy and decide what resources and capabilities you will need to implement it?

You may be asking yourself:

- Will I sell products or technology, and which market segment should I focus on?
- Which activities in the value chain can my venture perform, and which will be performed by other parties?
- How important will registered intellectual property rights be for my business?
- What sort of capabilities and relationships will my venture need, and how will it be funded?

The model we describe in the following sections ties together the insights gained from our research and will help you to to choose a venture strategy.

Our approach, shown in Figure 25, matches up the two principal types

Figure 25 **Choosing a strategy**

of *market* a new venture may enter with the *resources* and capabilities needed to build a growth business in that market. These choices depend on *environmental factors* pertaining to each case, indicating the most appropriate *commercial strategy*.

Markets

MARKET FOR PRODUCTS

This is the most commonly known way to do business: create a usable product or standardised service,[20] which suits the needs or desires of an identified set of customers, then market and sell it. Selling is either done directly to retail customers or via commercial partners downstream in the value chain, such as distributors and existing retailers. Demand–pull business cases usually operate in this market category, offering a product designed specifically to solve a problem experienced by an attractive market segment, and generally employing a combination of established technologies and technical methods (albeit perhaps using them in a new application). Companies operating in this market usually focus on creating value through generating revenues and building profitability from an early stage.

MARKET FOR TECHNOLOGY OR KNOWLEDGE

The main distinguishing feature of a market for technology is that a company operating in it doesn't invest in or deal with the production or manufacturing of end products; rather, it focuses its efforts on building and selling its intellectual property or intellectual capital.

Markets for technology have existed in some form since the nineteenth century, but have experienced resurgence and growth over the last three decades, as innovation and intellectual property rights (IPR) have gained economic value and visibility. Defined very broadly, 'technology' may include a specific patentable invention, such as a new molecule, mechanical part or computer chip; an intangible creation, such as a software program based on an algorithm, or a method for drug delivery; or more simply an organised body of scientific or technical know-how that may be used in a variety of projects. Consequently, the market for technology may include licensing patents for a variety of different applications, the outright sale of a patent, the selling of an entire company that possesses a technology or the provision of services based on specialist know-how.

To realise a high financial return from a technology business, entrepreneurs and investors generally try to sell the entire technology start-up company to an acquirer operating in the market for products. As Chapter 6 on intellectual property makes clear, this equity approach has been found to create more value than licensing out patents. Start-ups choosing to operate in the high-growth market for technology, therefore, don't aim to serve end customers directly, but rather try to build a portfolio of intellectual property that will attract an acquirer. In a few cases, such companies might opt to remain independent, as application developers for larger companies. This is often the case with biotech start-ups that enter into contracts with a number of large pharmaceutical companies.

HYBRID, CONSULTING AND TRANSITIONAL MARKET STRATEGIES

As we will see later on, some types of technology or product do not lend themselves to a single market approach, so start-ups pursue hybrid strategies enabling them to operate in both markets.

When neither a standard product nor a sellable technology approach are possible (as a result of factors explained further on), an entrepreneur may opt to provide knowledge-based, customised consulting to clients on a project basis. However, consulting in this way is not generally considered a fast- or high-growth business.

Finally, some companies may be termed transitional start-ups; they initially operate as consultants with a view to moving into a more scalable market at a later stage. This approach involves its own challenges and a successful transition is not guaranteed.

Resources

In order to operate and implement a commercial strategy, a company has to build or acquire an appropriate combination of resources or assets:

- *Human resources*. The managerial, commercial, technical and operational know-how of the founders, top managers and other key employees.
- *Social resources*. These are relationships and partnerships with other firms, which provide a start-up with additional capabilities, expertise and/or learning opportunities.
- *Technological resources*. Put simply, these involve the technologies or specialist knowledge that a company has at its disposal, either

through direct ownership or other relationships. Some companies choose to use proven or established technologies within a novel product design or application, while others set out to commercialise a nascent and as yet unadopted technology. A new technology may have a variety of possible product applications, and consequently many potential streams of revenue.

- *Financial resources.* A new venture will need money to both start and continue its operations. The amount of money it will need, the timeframe in which it will need it and the way in which it will raise the money will all depend on the type of business offering and the appropriate strategy. Money may be raised, for example, from the savings or personal assets of the founders, from customer revenues, from angel investors or from venture capitalists (more about this in Chapter 10).

Environmental factors

As described at length in Chapters 4, 5 and 6, environmental factors play an enormous role in the success or failure of a business, blocking some routes to market while making other routes possible. For this reason a company's commercial strategy – the market area it will enter and the resources it will use to do so – needs to depend on an insightful evaluation of the following factors.

CUSTOMER ENVIRONMENT: IDENTIFIABLE AND READY TARGET MARKET SEGMENTS

A new business will need customers at some point (but not always immediately, as we'll see), so a determining factor for commercial strategy is the existence and nature of attractive, interested market segments, either large or well-heeled enough to make your business profitable. Chapter 4 covers market segmentation.

However, some product or business ideas may not yet have a clearly identified or ready target market, although a prospective market may exist in the future. This is often the case with a very new technology or idea, which may offer solutions to problems not yet considered urgent by prospective customers. For example, although environmental damage in various forms has long been a subject of public discussion, governments, industries and consumers have only gradually adopted solutions as the impacts – high energy bills, expensive landfill costs and hotter temperatures, for example – have become more evident. In addition, a new technology may not yet be technically developed or perform well enough, compared to older solutions, to satisfy potential target customers. Start-ups in this situation usually need money to invest in further development and improvement of the technology (as did CropDesign), and will not expect to see revenue for some time. In both of these cases, we'd say that the business is 'not close to market'.

In your own case: you need to clarify and demonstrate whether you have a product or solution to a clear problem, for which there are customer segments prepared to adopt and pay for your product offering today. Or, on the other hand, is your business dealing with a cutting-edge idea or technology, not yet fully proven, or for which there is not yet a clear or ready customer?

INTELLECTUAL PROPERTY ENVIRONMENT: IMITABILITY OR PROTECTABILITY

On the other side of the market issue, you need to determine how protectable your business is from imitation. We discuss the ins and outs of intellectual property rights, especially patents, in Chapter 6. Patents are particularly important when your business is *not* close to market, because the exclusivity afforded by a solid patent can buy you some time by preventing competitors from encroaching on your idea while you develop applications. However, patent portfolios are expensive and so only worthwhile if you can expect a high return on the investment made in them. In addition, not all inventions are equally protectable, not all patents are equally solid, and patent litigation may be an expensive risk. Certain patents may be easy to 'invent around' or to challenge in court. Software is especially risky in this respect, as software patents may be difficult to defend (in Europe especially), and even the copyright on software code may be invented around, by writing a program that performs the same functions but is coded differently. 'Application patents' claiming protection for a new use of a pre-existing technology may also be difficult to defend, depending on the degree of inventiveness or obviousness. And some types of knowledge or skills, as listed in Chapter 6, are simply not protectable through intellectual property rights.

In your own case: how imitable is your business idea or invention? Are there solid grounds for protection through intellectual property rights? If not, in what other ways might you protect your business from imitation?

BUSINESS ENVIRONMENT: THE VALUE CHAIN AND PLAYERS' GRIP ON COMPLEMENTARY ASSETS

Chapter 5 describes the structure of a business environment as a chain of players who carry out different value-adding functions in a product's journey to the end market, from creating the basic technology to the development of a specific product design, to production, marketing and distribution activities. Large, incumbent businesses typically aim to own or control operations across most of this value chain so as to maximise profit through control over intellectual property, market share, commercial relationships and other competitive factors. Small start-ups tend to avoid performing many of these functions at the beginning of their lives, if they can, for the simple reason that doing so is too expensive, time consuming and risky. Building an entire proprietary value chain would delay market entry, increase the funding needed from investors, and mean that there's more to lose in the event of failure. So start-ups must choose where in the value chain to focus their operations.

'Complementary assets' in the value chain refer to the commercial capabilities or relationships that need to be in place for a new product to reach the market. In some cases such complementary assets are not only crucial to reach the market but are also tightly controlled by incumbents, which erect barriers to entry such as exclusive contracts with distributors, retailers or specialist marketing firms, or outright ownership of major marketing and distribution channels. In these cases, which we call 'complex value chains', it may be difficult for a new business to reach the market, and some form of co-operation with incumbents or other players will be required – which means that these players will exact a cut of the value or revenue of your business, assuming they're willing to work with you in the first place.[21] This was the case for Artica, when the team observed the nature of the relationship between distributors and major producers in the air-conditioning sector. Similar examples can be found in the pharmaceutical and medical device industries; for example, doctors, who commission treatments and also influence the National Health Service's choice of products, are accustomed to receiving information from reputable marketing departments that are highly specialised in the sector.

In contrast, in some other businesses, complementary assets are fairly simple, unimportant or unencumbered. In such cases, a start-up can access the distribution stream and make itself known to players relatively easily, or may be able to market and sell directly to customers.

In your own case: take a look at your value chain. Are you able to access all the links in the chain that you need, especially downstream of your core position, so that your offering can reach the end market without obstruction? Or are certain valuable assets tightly controlled by other companies, potentially requiring you to share or give up some revenue value, intellectual property, exclusivity or other assets?

SALES PROCESS: SIMPLE OR COMPLEX

If the value chain in your business sector is uncomplicated and a start-up can approach prospective customers directly, you may nonetheless come up against a complex sales process.[22] As we discuss in Chapter 4 in relation to market segments, a complex sales process is one whereby prospective customers are large organisations with lengthy, multi-stage decision-making processes. In other words, procurement decisions require the consent and co-operation of multiple managers or departments with different priorities and interests. Selling to those clients involves engaging the interest and gaining the consent of all these players; obtaining each new client will thus take considerable time and effort.

Extreme examples of complex sales processes can be found in public sector procurement, such as government departments and public-sector agencies, or international non-governmental organisations (NGOs). In these cases, new suppliers may only have a chance of entry every few years, when there is a call for tenders. In general, large organisations or companies often won't accept a small start-up as a supplier of important goods or services, since the risks of a small supplier going out of business or being suddenly unable to meet demand for high volumes of product are seen as significant liabilities. At the other end of the spectrum, a simple sales process is one whereby prospective customers may be single individuals or even small businesses, in which the decision will be taken by a small group of people who work closely with one another or by the business owner alone.

In your own case: what kind of customers is your business aiming to serve, and what level of complexity will the sales process require? As Chapter 4 explains, it is especially important that you research the answers to these questions for B2B offerings because these factors will affect the speed at which you can make and grow sales. In sectors involving a complex sales process, start-ups can operate successfully when the team of founders includes people with past experience and relationships in that industry.

Environment complexity

(e.g. importance and accessibility of complementary assets; complexity of sales process)

	LOW	HIGH
LOW	**1 Value proposition based on product offer (or standardised service)** • Specific product / market niche • Control over the value chain • Diverse founding team with experience in industry • Funding from founder's own capital, debt, or possibly an Angel, followed by early revenues *Revenue growth by selling standardised products to customer segments*	**2 Value proposition based on technology offer** • Focus on developing one application • Build a technology team • Establish technology partnerships • Source specialised VC for startup and development capital *Employment growth to build up intellectual capital with view to a trade sale*
HIGH	**4 Value proposition for customised services or consulting (possibly a 'transitional' startup)** • Specialist knowledge or technology used in bespoke projects for single customers • Build team with technical, consulting and customer-relations skills. Keep tacit knowledge confidential • Direct access to customers (usually small businesses) • Low capital requirements: 'bootstrapping' *Organic growth through customer relationships, but not really scalable: 'Lifestyle' business*	**3 Hybrid value proposition based on technology offer and market approach** • Acquire technology • Establish commercial partnerships • Acquire partners in downstream value chain • Source specialised VC in different funding rounds, for startup, development and acquisition capital *Revenue + employment growth*

Left axis: **Environment uncertainty** (e.g. strength of IPR; target market clarity)

Figure 26 **The entrepreneurial strategy matrix**

Putting it all together: the entrepreneurial strategy matrix

They say it's not a business analysis if it doesn't come in a two-by-two matrix. Well, here's ours. Use the model provided in Figure 26 to decide which market to enter and which strategy to pursue.

The value chain and sales process are indicators of *environment complexity*, while the clear presence or absence of target markets and/or solidly protectable IP are indicators of *environment uncertainty*.

Assess whether these indicators score low or high in your business case, and then decide which quadrant of the matrix pertains to you.

QUADRANT 1: LOW UNCERTAINTY + LOW COMPLEXITY ➤ GO TO THE MARKET FOR PRODUCTS

The ideal situation in this quadrant is one in which you have a very clear and attractive target market (market certainty) that you can access fairly easily (low complexity), either directly or via downstream players who are receptive to your offering.

Growth path. Successful companies in this quadrant become profitable quickly and grow in monetary value by increasing sales and profits. They usually aim to keep staffing and fixed costs as low as possible to enhance profit. These are the 'garage' enterprises that start in cheap offices with a small team of multi-talented, multi-tasking staff. If your offering is in this category, aim to develop and deploy your resources as described in the following sections.

Technology resources. Companies in this quadrant usually rely on already proven technologies, but employ them in the design of novel products. They aim to develop a specific quality product for a valuable niche market. Once they've established a name by offering a prized product to that niche, they may expand to develop a related product tailored to another niche and so on. Although they are offering something novel, these companies try not to sink too much money into filing costly patent portfolios – which delay and dent profits – if they can acquire market acceptance quickly and quietly, establishing a strong niche brand instead.

Social resources. Successful companies in this quadrant operate independently without need for partnerships (unless these present significant opportunities), focusing rather on building direct and trusted relationships with customers. By doing so, they control their value chain and get to keep more of their revenues and profits for themselves.

Human resources. Companies in this quadrant benefit from having a small team of founders with diverse skills (technical, marketing, financial), in which at least part of the team have past working experience in the market segment the firm is targeting, and thus have prior relationships with and insight about customers.

Financial resources. These companies are generally started with some of the founders' own savings. Since they are able to develop and sell products relatively quickly, they can often access bank loans once they get their first customer orders, and gradually self-fund their operations through cash flow from sales. While they might occasionally attract an early angel investor, they're not suitable for venture capital (VC) or large external investors; the funding they need to get up and running is too small for VCs, and the return they would have to provide such investors is unappealingly high.

Critical success factors: customer insight and speed to market. A company in this segment succeeds by forming a rapport with clients as a supplier who solves a problem and meets their needs, and by building market share fast. But don't confuse 'speed to market' with 'first to market'. Who cares about being first if you cannot establish a reputation and ramp up sales quickly, leaving space for the next entrant to overtake you? First to market is achieved initially by going 'under the radar' of big incumbent firms and addressing a market segment that they're ignoring. But *speed* is achieved by creating an offering that's *easy* for your customers to adopt.

When setting up the specifications of your offering, you need to think about anything that might be an obstacle or an attractor; this can include user-friendliness, the client's cost of switching from another product (including the time and expense of new learning or staff re-training that might be required), compatibility with the other equipment or systems that the client uses, maintenance, follow-up services and the cost of replacement parts, your price and the time it will take for the client's purchase to produce benefits (payback), preferred revenue models such as selling versus renting, leasing or special sector models like 'software as a service', and any other insight that's relevant to your customer segment.

QUADRANT 2: LOW UNCERTAINTY + HIGH COMPLEXITY ➤ GO TO THE MARKET FOR TECHNOLOGY

If you're in this quadrant, you may have a very novel offering and one or several target markets in mind, but cannot access them quickly or easily. Ideally, you'll have protectable intellectual property.

Growth path. Companies in this quadrant aim to grow their intellectual capital and the value of their technology, rather than revenues, to attract a technology buyer. So they tend to use investors' cash to hire teams of expert technical staff to improve the starting technology – its performance, reliability and applicability. They also hire highly regarded top managers. If your offering is in this category, try to develop and deploy your resources as follows.

Technology resources. Because it will take time for your offering to reach the market and because you're going to have to bargain with incumbents in order to access it in the first place, intellectual property rights are important in this quadrant, as both a time-buyer and a bargaining chip. Intellectual property rights define very clearly what you own and have a right to be paid for. If you have a platform technology that can potentially be used in diverse applications, you should focus your company's efforts on further developing one application that appears the most promising in terms of technical feasibility *and* early market demand. Once you can show that the technology works reliably in that application, prospective users in other sectors are likely to become receptive, and potential acquirers can see market possibilities.

Social resources. Successful companies in this quadrant develop fruitful technology partnerships or research alliances, either with established companies recognised for their research and development (R&D) or with scientific institutes. These partnerships not only speed up the development process through trading (protected) complementary know-how and offering a virtually expanded pool of employees, they also bolster the start-up's reputation, giving it much needed credibility in the eyes of investors, future customers and acquirers. If such organisations are willing to work with the start-up, the logic goes, there must be something of value in it. CropDesign (Chapter 3) used this tactic, establishing partnerships with established organisations known for their R&D activities, such as the Pioneer Hi-Bred, and Stine Seed in the US. Start-ups in this area also engage in significant PR activity to get press coverage for their inventions and activities as a way of signalling legitimacy.

Human resources. The most important human capital in such a start-up is a skilled technology development team, large enough to deliver the needed application in a reasonable time, with an impressive chief technologist to signal capability to potential partners. This group should be flanked by a small but authoritative business leadership team. The top business managers of such start-ups need to be specialised in the industry (and have relevant contacts), usually experienced in the management of a previous start-up, and capable of negotiating successfully with partners, investors and potential acquirers.

Financial resources. Because of the hefty amount of capital needed for technology development and the long lead times to reach a payback, these companies need to raise venture capital. They should seek investors who are specialised and well-connected in the start-up's industry to facilitate the creation of partnerships and the approach of suitable acquirers.

Critical success factor: legitimacy. Chances are, if any kind of market demand exists for the functions provided by your new technology, there'll be similar or competing technologies aiming to solve the same problems and enter the same market. A new industry in this situation is described as being 'in ferment'.[23] As famous examples in business history have shown (such as Betamax versus VHS in the 1980s), the best quality technical solution doesn't always win in the race to become the industry standard. Beyond the technology itself, every action your company takes should signal legitimacy – from the expertly qualified managers you hire, to the reputable technology partners you sign agreements with, the quantity of PR communications that get picked up by the technical or general press, the influential industry members you persuade to endorse or talk about you, and the well-appointed offices you occupy.

QUADRANT 3: HIGH UNCERTAINTY + HIGH COMPLEXITY → PURSUE A HYBRID MARKET ENTRY STRATEGY

Some entrepreneurs or inventors find themselves in a difficult position: they may have a technology for which no clear market application exists as yet, or they've devised a concept to solve a problem that prospective customers don't yet think of as a priority, meaning that demand isn't urgent. So the environment is 'uncertain'. These entrepreneurs also face a difficult value chain, in which incumbents are powerful and perhaps not interested in the start-up's offering, or gaining access to potential end markets involves a complex sales process. They may also have a product offering that's difficult to protect from imitation, such as software, making it risky to enter partnerships with large incumbents. These entrepreneurs know they have an original idea or offering of value, which could provide a fine solution to a problem, if only they can gain the market access needed to prove it.

Growth path. These companies aim to increase the value and legitimacy of their technical solutions, the size of their company, and their market share and revenues. But they do so by gaining a commercial foothold in the market, rather than a technological one.

Ventures in this quadrant require the most resource-intensive strategy to succeed. If your offering is in this category, your resources need to be developed and deployed as follows.

Technology resources. While the start-up might begin with some proprietary technology or ideas, it may also be necessary to acquire some complementary technologies to create an integrated product offering that fits potential customers' needs (for instance, by embedding the new technology as an improvement to an existing technology product). When speed to market is needed, buying such technology ready-made from other companies (or buying those companies) is faster than developing from scratch. If this option isn't feasible, the start-up may hire technical staff to develop integrated, market-ready products in-house.

Social resources. Rather than technology partnerships, this type of start-up needs commercial partnerships with other businesses that have sizable, established distributor or customer relationships, in order to worm its way into the value chain and gain access to those 'complex' customers. Even better, if the start-up can acquire some specialist distributors or small businesses with loyal and attractive client lists, it can leverage those established relationships of trust and habit to introduce its novel offering to customers and/or embed its innovations into the existing product lines, creating competitive advantage.

Human resources. With this strategy, you need managers to oversee the development of technology, products and sales. However, while some of these people will be hired as part of the management team of the initial start-up, others will come on board through acquisitions. You therefore need to make decisions about whether and how the acquired subsidiaries and their managers are absorbed into the parent company – whether in a full company merger or by retaining different operating companies. Our research suggests that it is preferable to retain the managers of the acquired companies in order to benefit from their customer knowledge and keep tabs on cash flow of these new units.

Financial resources. Naturally, the product development and acquisitions will require a lot of money. Companies operating in this quadrant need to raise substantial venture capital in multiple rounds of funding, but they'll also require investors with multiple specialities. At each phase of the strategy, investors should be brought in with expertise in that area: start-up phase, technology/product development phase and the aggressive acquisition phase.

Critical success factor: acquiring and retaining credibility with customers. The challenge for these companies is to get end customers to buy very novel products, which often may imply a change in customers' behaviour or business processes. That is why such ventures aim to reach the market by acquiring profitable small companies that have established names and customer relationships in the target sector, or by building commercial partnerships with other companies. Pre-existing customer relationships will lend initial credibility to new product launches because customers already trust a company they know. Obviously, the manner in which new products are introduced will also affect customer retention, so skill must be applied to retaining rather than destroying that credibility in the process of acquiring new customers. For this reason, an attempt should be made to retain managers from acquired companies to create smooth transitions to new business lines.

QUADRANT 4: HIGH UNCERTAINTY + LOW COMPLEXITY → ENTER THE MARKET FOR KNOWLEDGE

This is the least attractive quadrant in terms of growth prospects, but in some cases it may be the only plausible one, at least in the early days of a new venture. Your business may be following either a *consulting model*, offering a customised service, or a *transitional start-up model*, waiting for the right moment to enter the product market. Both are described below.

In this quadrant, you may have a skill or technology of value to offer, but you have not identified a sizable market segment that would currently adopt your offering as a standardised product or service. In other words, you could not sell many identical copies of the same product. You may also not be able to patent your know-how or protect it from imitation, making it difficult to safely enter the market for technology. Incumbents may also be uninterested in partnering with you or buying your technology, precisely because they can't see a high-volume market for a standardised application. However, your offering could be a valuable ingredient in bespoke projects for clients who need a particular skill or product at a particular time, on a contract basis, and who may even pay well for it. An additional reason for providing your offering as a bespoke specialist service is that you can structure your service in a way that keeps unpatentable know-how from being leaked to customers.

Many types of traditional business fall naturally into the bespoke consulting model, such as legal services, design services (architecture, graphics and product design consulting) and IT consulting. In some cases, however, innovative start-ups also operate in this quadrant because of the environmental factors outlined above. This is frequently the case for new information technology, such as an algorithm that allows a software to perform a new smart function, but which for now is only sought after in very specialised or rare projects or situations.

Sometimes, in contrast, a start-up is destined to stay in the fourth quadrant, and may be labelled a 'lifestyle' business, capable of paying a decent living for the founders, but growing only very slowly as a company, if at all. In other cases, however, a venture may start in this bespoke mode to build experience and some reputation until it can switch to one of the other, more scalable, strategies later, if and when an attractive prospective market emerges. TomTom falls into this 'transitional start-up'[24] category.

In *Crossing the Chasm*,[25] Geoffrey Moore proposes that all new technology start-ups (particularly in the IT sector) should begin doing business in consulting mode, in order to test, improve and legitimise a technology by working closely with a few visionary clients. They should subsequently make a transition to the product market, for instance by developing an off-the-shelf software product for a wider market. However, our experience shows that the challenges involved in making such a transition shouldn't be taken lightly. To change your company's business model, you may need to change the type of skilled staff you employ – from consultants to product developers, from client relationship managers to e-marketers, and the like. Doing so can create organisational turmoil, and if both models – consulting and transitional start-up – are being pursued at the same time, care must be taken to clearly define roles to avoid situations in which product developers, for example, are pulled into emergency consulting work and other such muddles.

Not transitioning may also be risky, such as when competing ventures move to 'productise' a bespoke service like yours. For instance, in the early days of the world wide web, many small businesses and organisations required the services of expert web developers in order to get their first websites up and running. Today, however, content management systems (CMS), some of which are increasingly user-friendly and refined, and frequently offered as open source or 'freemium' software, are making it possible for relatively inexpert people to build websites of sufficiently good quality by themselves. This makes bespoke web developers not quite the hot property they once were, at least not for small clients. This kind of competitive risk, however, will depend on how exclusive and specialised your consulting venture's technical know-how is.

Growth path. Some companies in this quadrant do become large over time but, as a rule, you should not expect steep or fast growth. These companies grow gradually through repeat business and referrals, but because of the customised nature of each service, they need to add more staff in order to serve more customers, and staff pay is one of the highest costs in any company. The business can only become rapidly scalable if it can eventually develop a profitable standardised offering.

Technology resources. A start-up like this usually begins with a kernel of specialist knowledge. The intellectual capital that it needs to build to be competitive is the so-called 'tacit' knowledge of its employees: the ability to adapt this specialist know-how to a variety of different projects, built up through experience. If the start-up's special ingredient isn't patentable, the company needs to keep it confidential as a trade secret (with the exception of products and services based on open-source software licences; see Chapter 4).

Social resources. The start-up's most important social resources may be the founder's affiliation with a prestigious institute and/or previous employer, such as a university or reputable company in a relevant business sector. Beyond that, satisfied customers are an important source of referrals and publicity. Collaboration with other companies may be needed, but this may often occur on a case-by-case or outsourcing basis related to bespoke projects, rather than through a formal partnership agreement.

Human resources. A company like this may simply begin with one or two founders, selling their services directly to customers. In certain areas of highly specialised consulting, prospective clients will demand to speak directly to and question the consultant or technology inventor, rather than deal with a sales representative. If the business grows and establishes a reputation, other professional managers may be added, such as a business development director, as well as other consultants.

Financial resources. Usually a start-up like this finances itself by 'bootstrapping' – entrepreneurship jargon for self-financing. Because the company works on a contract basis, it may be able to sub-contract or outsource equipment and other services as needed so that it doesn't have high fixed costs (such as full-time salaries). This means it can usually begin with a small office and a bit of the founder's savings, and cover costs by billing them to clients or receiving partial payment for services in advance or partway through a project. The slow growth trajectory of such companies means they are not suitable for angel investors or venture capitalists, who would demand a high return on investment within three to six years.

Critical success factors: gradually built-up reputation and customer references. Companies in this quadrant generally succeed by adding one satisfied customer at a time, and relying on referrals or references. As the reference customer list grows, so do the company's reputation and capabilities.

In summary...

As with many other parts of this book, the model above is not fool-proof, nor will every reader's venture fit precisely into one quadrant. However, this model should at least present some guidelines for considering how your initial business idea is likely to develop best as a venture, and most importantly how environmental conditions will impact your market opportunities and resource requirements. It will also give you an idea of the extent to which your company can be self-sufficient or will otherwise need external partners and/or investors, and the specific kinds of relationship that will help the venture succeed.

SECTION III
PROOF OF CONCEPT

8. USING PROTOTYPING

What?

Earlier chapters in this book talk about analysing and evaluating business ideas on paper and through discussion with industry and market experts.

At some point, however, anyone who aims to become involved with your venture – from partners to investors to customers – will require a more tangible demonstration that your concept is realistic and that the qualities that would make it an attractive business proposition are achievable. In fact, you need proof of these qualities yourself before you sink your money, energy and time into the launch of a new venture.

'Proof of concept' can be sought and tested in a number of ways, and prototyping plays an important role. The word prototype derives from Greek and means 'first impression'. This meaning is important, because it highlights the fact that a prototype need not be a perfect replica of a final product, especially not at an early stage of your product concept or business case. Rather, it's an approximate replica that demonstrates or tests some important aspect of your idea in a concrete way. In a very early stage, your prototyping activity should also be crude and experimental enough to keep some creative options open for decision making at a later stage. As your venture's journey moves through the stages and hoops necessary to become a business reality, you can make increasingly sophisticated and refined prototypes to match your evolving decisions and needs.

Beyond this book, there are other, longer and more detailed sources of information on prototyping. Our purpose here is to give you a short overview to help you consider how prototyping and design will be useful to you.

Why?

Prototyping has three main purposes: to aid design development, to gather customer feedback and to be used for communication and persuasion (especially with investors).

Prototyping as a design aid

The practice of prototyping was initially developed in the design and manufacturing industries as a way of trying out or testing design ideas and decisions at various stages in the product development process. Prototypes can demonstrate either functionality or the look and feel of a product, and late-stage prototypes demonstrate both. Anything from folded paper models to taped-together mechanical parts can serve as a very early prototype!

However, prototyping also plays a further role in the design process; it aids inquiry and stimulates discussion and further idea generation within a product design team, especially if the team members have different technical backgrounds and expertise.

At later stages, successive prototyping allows for increasing refinement of a design, to the point of obtaining complete production specifications.

Prototyping as a market-testing aid

By providing a concrete impression of a proposed product or service, a prototype helps potential customers to understand the idea, possibly try out the experience of using the product or service, comment on their likelihood of adopting and buying it or suggest how to improve it.

Potential users are likely to give you much more valuable and tangible comments if they have a prototype than if they're given only a verbal description of a product or service.

Prototyping for communication and persuasion

Finally – and very important at the earliest stages of your venture – when trying to attract investment, partnerships or other types of support, a prototype can offer potential stakeholders a tangible demonstration of the product's expected qualities, and some proof that the concept is feasible.

Investors are more likely to take a business proposition into consideration if they're shown even a simple or relatively crude prototype. A prototype demonstrates not only a product's technical feasibility but also something of the sincerity, invested time and commitment of a venture's founders. Early-stage, visual prototypes also help stakeholders (including your company staff and marketing or PR people) to envision the product's future merits.

Ceres Power: demonstrating the market benefits of a new fuel cell

Ceres Power, an alternative energy company spun out of Imperial College in 2001 on a patented and globally unique technical approach, was never going to be a 'three years to market' company, but much more a ten-year serious investment and business building enterprise. From its start as a public limited company (plc), behind all the classic team building, technology development, IP protection and product/market definition activities, the senior team realised early on that it could benefit from the power of design in its widest sense. One of the issues they faced is that, whilst the science and technology was interesting, it was complex at the operational level, and thus explaining in simple, succinct terms to investors, potential partners and the new company staff how this great technology benefited the end user, and where it offered advantages in the massive energy market, was difficult.

The background to the core technology, which had been developed by academic researchers in secrecy during the early 1990s, consisted of a metal-supported, wafer-thin fuel cell with unusual new properties. However, the management knew that developing this science into a fully proven commercial product was going to take considerable time and financial investment. To raise both interest and investment, the company needed to find a way to demonstrate the potential and future benefits of their proposition at an early stage.

Fuel cells create electrical power and heat directly from an electrochemical reaction and are thus highly efficient at turning the energy in fuels to usable forms of energy for, say, combined heat and power (CHP) devices, powering cars or providing electricity to the national grid. The Ceres fuel cell's design, however, meant that it could be used in ways that competing fuel cell technologies could not. Ceres sits in the category of so-called Solid Oxide Fuel Cells (SOFC), which are fuelled with conventional and easy-to-get hydrocarbon fuels, such as natural gas, eliminating the need to source and feed in pure hydrogen gas, which is harder to come by. However, such cells typically operate at very high temperatures (800–1000° C), and can only be used in large, industrial-scale systems. Not so with the Ceres cell: thanks to the use of a new application of ceramic material as an electrolyte, it is able to operate at lower temperatures (500–600° C) than its direct competitors. Lower operating temperature also allows for the ceramic to be mounted on a base layer of stainless steel, as opposed to more expensive materials needed at higher temperatures. Most importantly, the resulting compact, lower-cost design means the Ceres fuel cell can be used inside domestic-sized appliances, so conventional wall-mounted boilers can be replaced with micro-combined heat and electrical power devices. The technology could therefore be made affordable and accessible for consumers without affecting the layout of their homes or their habitual way of using power, but allowing them to save on energy bills and reduce carbon emissions by several tonnes per household per year.

The problem was: how does a new company with a new technology and a new market proposition communicate the magnitude of this potential convincingly to business investors and possible industrial partners?

Showing a fuel cell by itself, which looked like a small sheet of coated metal to the untrained observer, would not do much to stimulate investors' imaginations or show how the risk of getting the technology to the market in a worthwhile portfolio of products could be managed. In addition, in the first couple of years, there was no working prototype demonstrating the end-user experience. Instead, the purely functional prototypes looked like bulky, ugly and mysterious pieces of kit you would find in an engineering lab – a long way from finished products that would fit seamlessly into a home. The company's commercial management realised it would have to do better if it was to raise the additional capital needed to develop its product line and commercialise its technology.

Within a few months of starting, in 2002, Ceres won a competition to take part in a business support programme funded by the UK Design Council. Ceres Power worked with Chris Thompson, founder of innovation consultants Viadynamics. Thompson applied a range of tools and techniques to help develop a clearer strategy for bridging the gap between what the company had at that time and the potential product and market proposition for a range of stakeholders; from an end-user to an investor to a potential new member of staff. He also worked with the management team to refine and communicate Ceres Power's value proposition, product portfolio and brand vision. This work not only resulted in an added sense of cohesiveness for the growing Ceres team, but also enabled the company's commercialisation roadmap to be stress-tested. One very tangible outcome of this process was a simple communication tool to help explain the Ceres business proposition. An animated video was produced using computer-aided design tools, showing how a stack of wafer-thin Ceres fuel cells would be enclosed, alongside other components, in a wall-mounted unit the same size as a household boiler (another step up on the competition, which made larger, floor-mounted units) to produce a combination of heat, hot water and electrical power for the home. The unit was shown connecting to the normal gas supply, plumbing and electrical systems of a conventional home, as well as connecting to the thermostat, and in turn supplying the household's power and heating requirements.

Through this video, which lasted under three minutes, the unique, complex technology could be communicated in images and a flowing story that showed its ultimate effect on the end consumer's everyday experience in a number of significant energy market segments. These visualisation techniques, and the ability to spread risk across several potential product lines, helped Ceres to raise £10 million in early equity capital, prior to the company's flotation on London's alternative investment market (AIM) in 2004.

Ceres takes raw materials, manufactures its unique metal-supported fuel cell and uses these cells to create a powerful, compact heat and power device – the fuel cell module. This module then becomes the platform for a variety of energy applications, including the domestic micro-combined heat and power device – the micro-CHP unit. Figure 27, which is an example of the company's communication through visual prototyping and design, shows this journey.

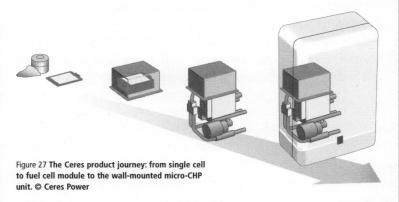

Figure 27 **The Ceres product journey: from single cell to fuel cell module to the wall-mounted micro-CHP unit. © Ceres Power**

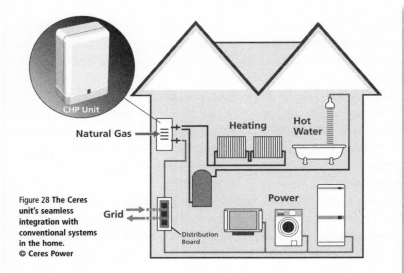

Figure 28 **The Ceres unit's seamless integration with conventional systems in the home.** © Ceres Power

Figure 28 also illustrates for the layman how the Ceres wall-mounted micro-CHP unit efficiently produces heat and hot water for the home and electricity for use by the home owner or for exporting back to the national grid, all using the same natural gas and home infrastructure used by a conventional gas boiler.

Naturally, Ceres also engaged in typical industrial and manufacturing prototyping to develop the finished product. Design played an important role in enabling British Gas and Ceres to enter a £5 million product development programme in 2008 with significant forward orders for micro-CHP units. At the same time, British Gas invested £20 million in the company. Other significant product development and supply programmes exist with Calor and Bord Gais, Ireland's incumbent gas utility company.

Design is now used widely throughout Ceres, not just in the engineering functions. It offers a powerful set of tools to aid areas as diverse as specification, IP protection and communication.

How?

Words of warning

Before we discuss how to go about prototyping, we'd like to express a few caveats.

Large companies often have ample financial and human resources to dedicate to design and prototyping activities from an early stage of product development, whereas new entrepreneurial ventures often do not. Time is also a limiting factor. Therefore, you should aim to make the *simplest* kind of prototype that will suit your particular purpose (and your resources) at a given stage in your product or business development. Before rushing out to lavish money on a pre-production, full-feature prototype, think about what you actually need a prototype to demonstrate *now*, and what medium and level of sophistication will be good enough for that purpose.

You should also understand that prototypes can never fully simulate a finished product. Some compromise is always involved in the prototyping process. Users' expectations of a prototype's performance may also be higher than its actual performance. For this reason, when testing a prototype (especially an early one) with potential product users, you need to specify exactly what you're asking users to assess, such as a particular function or design feature, while asking them to overlook or place less emphasis on other aspects of the prototype.

Consequently and finally, keep in mind that prototypes cannot eliminate *all* product risk.

Prototyping stages and types

Prototyping takes place in stages, moving from very crude or 'lo-fi' (low fidelity) prototypes to refined beta and pre-production prototypes. While prototypes were once used exclusively in the domain of product manufacturing, a newer class of 'services prototyping' has also evolved.

EARLY-STAGE AND LO-FI PROTOTYPING

While the term lo-fi may be mistakenly equated with 'low-quality', this 'poor man's' prototyping is frequently essential to early-stage entrepreneurship, yet sadly overlooked. It can be an important tool for collecting early data from potential users and testing your design and market assumptions, with a view to making a more persuasive proposal to early-stage investors. We strongly recommend that you read and consider this section especially carefully as you build your early business case and strategy.

'Paper' prototyping – for market testing. So-called 'paper' prototypes are essentially simulations of a product experience in the same way that a game

of Monopoly simulates the experience of acquiring (or losing) property and wealth. While they're not necessarily made of paper, the term is used to denote simplicity and low cost.

In her book *Paper Prototyping*, Carolyn Snyder[26] illustrates a test for a mobile phone interface in which the potential user and the tester pass drawings of a mobile phone back and forth. The tester asks the user to pay a phone bill using the mobile phone. The user acts out functions such as pressing keys on the keypad, and the tester responds by colouring or writing on the drawing to show how the phone would behave in response. Although users may at first find this process strange, they eventually settle into it and actively participate. A third observer notes the user's choices and reactions to determine how user-friendly or intuitive the phone's planned interface is.

One of our own students needed to test his concept for a new online consumer financial service by illustrating it to several focus groups. Because he had neither the time nor money to create a beta website – and doing so would've made little sense at that early stage – he brought specially designed imitation banknotes and playing cards to the focus group sessions to simulate the experiences of investing money, receiving financial returns and obtaining relevant information from the proposed online service. By doing so, he was able to gain useful insights on how consumers felt about the financial service itself, which was specifically what he wanted to test, apart from how they might react to, say, the colours or graphic design of any website that would deliver it. He was also able – at an early, penniless stage – to tell some potential investors that a sample of consumers in his demographic target had so far reacted positively to his idea.

Experience prototyping – for early design development and user testing.
This approach has been described by the international design firm IDEO[27] as an early-stage method for designers to understand a user experience and identify the features required of a new product or service. Experience prototyping is lo-fi, allowing the designers to test a very specific need.

Among several examples, the authors from IDEO described a project to design a computer–user interface for a remotely operated underwater exploration robot. They placed one designer, A, in a room scattered with chairs, operating a video camera. Another designer, B, in a separate room, watched the video images on a screen, and issued verbal instructions to A, directing her to move about the room among the chairs, and to move the camera in different ways, while searching for an object. The difficulties encountered in giving and executing directions – while A and the chairs got increasingly tangled in the video cable – gave the designers and their client valuable insight into the challenges faced by a pilot remotely operating an underwater robot, and suggested design specifications to overcome these problems.

Virtual prototyping in CAD simulations and animation videos – for presentation. Although these may seem too slick to be termed 'lo-fi', we categorise them as early-stage prototyping since they offer a way to present a product concept before actually building the finished product. The digital age has provided immense opportunities for visualising objects through computer-aided design tools, animation, and especially three-dimensional simulations, which allow the viewer to virtually move through a picture, see an illustrated object from different angles, look inside it and so on. While images and animations may not be useful for tangible user testing and feedback, they go a long way toward communicating what a final product is expected to do and how it will look, stimulating the viewer's imagination, and can often steer design decisions as well.

PHYSICAL/MANUFACTURING PROTOTYPES

This is the classic domain of prototyping, and highly technical! The information below is a simplified overview.

Concept models – the basic idea. Concept models apply to the early stage of manufacturing prototypes, in that they're simply meant to render an impression of the product. Depending on the context, this could be a two-dimensional illustration, a computer simulation or a small three-dimensional model constructed from a simple material such as cardboard or wood.

Industrial design prototypes – look and feel. So-called design models are meant to simulate what a product will look like, such as the shape and colour. A plastic cast of a new sports car that shows its sleek shape – but perhaps has no moving parts – would be an example of a design prototype.

These are most often used for collecting customer feedback or for presentations to investors.

Development prototypes – functionality. These are also called 'proof-of-principle' prototypes or 'breadboards'. Development prototypes generally overlook any aesthetic specifications, and are simply meant to demonstrate or test a specific functionality: will this technology or contraption in fact do the specific thing that engineers and designers thought it would? An early development prototype could be a clumsy-looking collection of tubes, wires or other parts that you wouldn't want to have in your sitting room, on your desk, or wherever the product is meant to be used. The point of this model is to check performance for a specific purpose; you refine the look and feel of the product later.

In large companies, development prototypes are generally for internal engineers' use only. However, an entrepreneur may opt to show them to early-stage investors or potential users if time and financial constraints mean developing a more refined model is currently not possible. A development prototype shown alongside a concept model or design prototype indicating the intended final design (even if this is just an attractive drawing) creates a more accurate impression than verbal description alone and is more likely to elicit a good response.

Alpha prototype. An alpha prototype models most of the full features and functions of the expected product, using the same materials and properties, although there may still be some differences in look and size. Alpha prototypes are generally used internally for testing, not released to external commentators. They tend to be made with a semi-manual or customised manufacturing process since they are not produced in large quantities.

Beta prototype. This is the version that's most often shown to potential customers and released widely and numerously for testing and comment. Beta prototypes include the full features and scale of the final product, and are also produced using the industrial mass-production process envisioned for the final product. In the case of software and websites, as opposed to physical products, beta versions are those products that internet users are accustomed to downloading and/or trialling for free.

Pre-production prototype – final pilot. These are mostly used internally to test and refine the final manufacturing process and tooling, but might also be released to a sample of preferred users.

Rapid prototyping. Digitalisation has made possible a range of techniques for creating accurate pre-alpha prototypes quickly and cheaply using a combination of computers and machinery. One of the most popular of these is three-dimensional printing, which lays down successive thin layers of a material, such as plastic, to build up the intended shape of the model. Without going into extensive and dry technical detail, other techniques in this category include stereolithography, selective laser sintering, fused deposition modelling and computer numerical control (CNC) prototyping.

NON-PHYSICAL AND SERVICES PROTOTYPES
This is a fairly new area of prototyping, but is becoming an increasingly popular practice as design firms move into the area of designing not just products but also standardised services. Once again, the information below is a simple overview.

Storyboarding. Borrowed from the film and advertising industries, storyboarding provides a visual illustration of a customer journey from first contact to the provision and conclusion of a service, such as the experience of booking a plane ticket online, booking a hotel during the same internet session, travelling to the airport, checking in luggage, walking through the airport, boarding the plane and completing the journey. Many events may happen along this continuum to influence the customer experience, and these can be included in the storyboard to explain the rationale for adding particular features to the service.

Storyboards may be presented as a series of drawings or photographs, or as a video or animation. They can be used for design development, user feedback or in a presentation to potential investors and partners. However, beware the temptation to present a slick storyboard or video animation to an investor without also collecting some commentary from real prospective customers (see Chapter 9), or at least from preferred witnesses (see Chapter 4).

Role playing – improvised or scripted. Role playing with live participants is another way to either demonstrate or test a service. An improvised role play allows for spontaneous and perhaps unforeseen responses from users, so is a useful tool for design development and testing. Scripted role play may be a live alternative to a storyboard.

Role play may be used in conjuction with paper prototyping.

Running a pilot test. A further step on from role playing is to run a short pilot programme offering the service to a larger sample of users in a real business setting, while recording the experiences and reactions of both the providers and users of the service. A pilot may even be compared to a control group using a different or older version of the service.

A pilot is essentially the beta version of a service prototype.

In summary...

Proof of concept and prototyping are important tools, both for developing and testing your business idea and for communicating it to others. Whether you're testing your idea or selling it, making use even of lo-fi or early-stage prototypes will be more effective than using words by themselves. Take care not to overstretch yourself too soon: create an appropriate type of prototype at an appropriate cost for the purpose required and the development stage of your venture.

9. TESTING
THE MARKET

What?
As you take your venture idea out into the world, you'll probably be asked questions along the lines of 'how do you know if people will want to buy this?' and 'are you sure this is the best solution for the problem?' Potential investors, as well as potential partners and distributors, will typically want to see some evidence of interest from a target market segment before making a risky commitment to a new business proposition.

The more specialised your customer segment – imagine, for instance, that you're developing a device for diabetes patients to self-inject insulin – the more you'll need to understand about those customers and users to make a product that addresses their difficulties, needs and desires. Market tests may thus help you to identify product design refinements or to make a choice between alternative technology applications or product features. Sounding out potential customers is also a tool for deciding on a viable price for a product or service.

Furthermore, entrepreneurs and inventors tend to fall in love with their ideas, and can consequently develop blind spots or misconceptions with regard to users' and customers' needs. This is an especially important consideration for technology-driven business ideas; translating a new technology into a usable product requires an understanding of the people who will use it and whether the product is compatible with their habits, with the other products and practices they adopt and with the way they live their lives (in the case of consumers) or carry out business (in the case of business customers).

Testing is not a panacea, and care needs to be taken to consult impartial testers (not, for instance, your doting parents or best friends) and to interpret the information collected in an impartial manner.

While market testing is no crystal ball, avoiding or ignoring it altogether can also be a deadly mistake for entrepreneurs, causing them to overlook fatal flaws in a product or business proposition that might have otherwise been spotted in a market trial and put right. Early-stage start-ups typically cannot afford the extensive, technical (albeit not always accurate) market testing performed by large companies, but some form of objective reality check with potential customers, matched with intelligent observation, is doable and advisable. This chapter outlines several different approaches that may fit different business propositions, stages of development and customer types.

Why?

Shortly before the iPad tablet went on sale last year, Steven P. Jobs showed off Apple's latest creation to a small group of journalists. One asked what consumer and market research Apple had done to guide the development of the new product. 'None,'' Mr Jobs replied. 'It isn't the consumers' job to know what they want.'

New York Times[28]

If I'd asked my customers what they wanted, they'd have said a faster horse.

Henry Ford[29]

It may seem strange to begin a chapter on the subject of market testing – that is, collecting reactions to your product or business idea from potential users and customers – with two celebrated entrepreneurs' claims that doing so is pointless. In the popular imagination, a capable entrepreneur is believed to be so insightful as to know exactly what customers want before they know it themselves. Often, this is the case, but not always.

Even popular fiction weighs in on this point. In an episode of the television series *Mad Men*,[30] advertising creative director Don Draper berates a marketing psychologist for her reliance on focus group discussions: 'A new idea is something they don't know yet,' he says of consumers, 'so it's not going to come up as an option. ... You can't tell how people are *going* to behave based on how they *have* behaved.'

In other words, people don't truly *know* whether they want a new product until it already exists, so you can't expect them to explain what they want beforehand. In real life, a similar view is held by marketing professor Gerald Zaltman[31] of Harvard Business School, who argues that the thoughts that motivate people to buy or reject products are mostly subconscious and more emotional than practical or intellectual, making it difficult for consumers to articulate their preferences in words. Unpicking these subconscious emotional drivers should be the marketer's real task. Zaltman, however, doesn't advocate forgetting market research and replacing it with entrepreneurial intuition; rather, he suggests doing research in a different way.

Psychology certainly applies to the relationship between innovative new ventures and market research: it is indeed difficult for potential customers to rate reliably a product that is so novel as to be beyond their habitual everyday experience. They may be intrigued by the ingenuity of a new idea, but won't have enough familiarity with the product and how it might affect their current habits or routines to predict whether they'll really adopt or buy it at the end of the day. (They usually fare better, however, when rating an already familiar product that has been upgraded with novel or 'new and improved' features.) So, to some extent, innovative entrepreneurs must try to interpret the market and guess its future direction in the absence of any useful test, as the fictional Don Draper frequently does for his clients, and as Steve Jobs and his colleagues at Apple have done *most* (not quite all) of the time.

In fact, aspiring entrepreneurs sometimes assume a bit too glibly that they're as insightful as Steve Jobs – and also forget that even he has launched a famously unsuccessful product, the Apple Newton (a failure from which he undoubtedly drew valuable lessons for developing products such as the iPod and iPhone). Furthermore, they might consider that customers won't be obliging if the entrepreneur should make a wrong guess about their needs.

In their enthusiasm for a new idea, entrepreneurs may also leave testing until too late – thus wasting time and money developing a product with the wrong features – or may test the wrong attributes, as the case study in this chapter illustrates.

boo.com's failure and the elusive nature of a new market

UK retail site boo.com was perhaps the most famous of Europe's dotcom failures. Founded in 1998 to sell high-end fashion and sports apparel over the internet, the company's three founders were contemplating a future of growing online commerce, and were keen to capture first-mover advantage as online fashion retailers. Their problem was not that they had a bad idea, but that it was, if anything, too forward-looking at the time. Technical details that may have appeared mundane to them proved a turn-off to customers.

The founders of boo.com ('boo' for short) created a technically advanced, highly attractive and engaging website: stunning 3D photographs of items of apparel could be spun around on screen to be viewed from various angles, and even 'tried' on a virtual mannequin – a visual experience as close as possible to sampling a product in real life. The site also featured a stylish and entertaining animated character of a female shopping assistant, Miss Boo, who could guide users through the searching and buying experience.

Had it been founded a few years later, boo might have been a success; however, in 1999, most home consumers were still using slow, dial-up internet connections. It could take several minutes for a single page of boo.com's exceptionally byte-heavy content to download onto a user's computer, making a conventional trip to the shops seem an acceptable or preferable alternative. Add to this the fact that internet retailing was still in its early years, and many consumers were still unaccustomed to shopping online, sceptical about online payment security and wary of purchasing products they couldn't see or touch. Consequently, only a tiny percentage of early visits to boo.com converted into sales – 0.25 per cent in the first week – regardless of the enormous (and expensive) media and marketing hype that had surrounded the launch. Customers in the US were especially peeved by the site's slowness, and sales in that country far undershot the company's projections, in spite of the US having a greater proportion of internet users than Europe at the time.

Today, you might ask yourself how the company could have overlooked something as simple as download speed. Did boo's founders not market-test the service before launch? Co-founder and CEO Ernst Malmsten's own account[32] of boo's story indicates that they did, but, in their enthusiasm for all the site's bells and whistles, they underestimated the importance of download speed until it was too late.

The problem that the founders wanted to address related to shopping, not technology. Malmsten and co-founder Kajsa Leander, two well-travelled Swedes who'd lived in New York but grown up in a small Swedish town, observed that many trendy fashion and sportswear brands could only be found in certain countries or in major cities. You could buy a copy of *Vogue* nearly anywhere, but not the fashions that were featured in it. The internet seemed an excellent medium for a virtual department store that could be visited from anywhere. It was being touted as the central pivot of a new economy and, as none of the three founders was a software developer or information and communication technology (ICT) specialist, their over-confidence in the technology may have been understandable. All the same, it was also untested and misguided.

The first prototype of the boo.com website, which the founders took to investor presentations, was a slick dummy site that ran on a laptop. It contained the intended 3D features and performed all the right operations when someone clicked its buttons, but was not actually connected to the internet. It wowed the likes of Bernard Arnault, the chief of French luxury goods empire LVMH, and Italy's Luciano Benetton, who were approached for investment.

Now, what's wrong with this approach, you might ask, seeing as Chapter 8 extols the virtues of Ceres Power for presenting a clever computer animation of its future product to potential investors and industrial partners? The difference is that Ceres had already built a purely functional prototype, knew that its technology could work in the manner envisioned and had adequate technical data to prove it.

In their ambitious goal to exploit the global reach of the internet from the start, boo's founders had set themselves an immense task, building not only a website but an enormous back-end system to serve 18 country markets at once, accommodating different languages, currencies and taxation regimes. The company became aware, while building the system, that speed at the back end could be a problem, so the management purchased an enormous server able to process the quantity of simultaneous operations that would be demanded of the system. This solution couldn't, however, tackle slowness on the consumer's end of a dial-up internet connection. Relatively few consumers at the time either had access to or were willing to pay for higher-bandwidth connections.

And finally, we come to the market test. Once construction of the website and back-end systems had been completed, the company did run a pre-launch pilot trial in which friends and family of staff were invited to try buying items from the site and even returning them, and to send feedback to the company. It may be argued that friends and family aren't the most impartial of product testers, but even despite this bias, they reported the site's slowness as their chief complaint, while rating highly other aspects, such as the site's attractiveness and the company's quick delivery execution.

By now the system had been built, at great expense and with much effort. After months devoted to their dream, it's somewhat understandable that the founders would hold onto their optimism, underline the positive feedback and play down any warnings about download speed. Beholden to their investors, months behind schedule, they'd invested too much, personally and financially, to delay the launch any further to tinker with the system and make it faster.

We raise this last point about personal investment to emphasise the importance of carrying out market research and testing early and gradually, even if it means starting with humble lo-fi prototypes (as described in Chapter 8) or talking to prospective users and customers about a product that you have not yet finished designing or building. In fact, you could even start indirectly, by finding out what customers think of alternative products and services before you make your own. If you don't ask questions early, you could find yourself in a position at a later stage whereby you won't be able to acknowledge problems dispassionately or have enough time to solve them.

Had the boo founders, after coming up with their idea, questioned a sample of people about the experience of surfing or shopping on the internet, what they thought of existing shopping sites and what might discourage them from making an internet purchase, they might have uncovered some useful insights. Better yet, if they'd performed an 'empathic design' exercise (described later in this chapter) and simply watched people surfing the internet on their home computers, they might have incidentally observed how consumers felt about download times.

Or, quite simply, they could've started with the question, 'if this is so great, why isn't someone else already doing it?' – a classic refrain voiced by start-up investors and coaches who mentor entrepreneurs. Perhaps, if they'd considered doing even some informal first-hand research, they'd have noticed people playing video games at home and wondered why 3D animations were used in video games but not yet online. Why were people using the internet for something relatively simple such as book purchases (on Amazon.com or its imitators in other countries) but not playing Tomb Raider over the internet? Surely the media and software developers who created Lara Croft were aware of the internet, probably knew web developers and might have considered the possibility? Boo's founders might have decided it would be preferable to identify a different unique selling point for their website, and perhaps scale up to 3D animation gradually, as broadband access dropped in cost and rose in uptake.

Instead, here's what happened: after the boo.com site launched officially in November 1999, ongoing customer feedback confirmed that low download speed was a major complaint. The site received a scathing review in *The Industry Standard* – the magazine then considered 'the Bible of the Internet Economy' – after its columnist, James Ledbetter, spent 81 minutes trying to make a purchase, discovering along the way that the site didn't work on Macintosh computers (a problem the founders knew about but chose to overlook). By the time the company had taken steps to reduce download times by 50 per cent and sales conversion rates had improved to nearly 3 per cent (after four months of trading), it was too late: the dotcom crash was underway. The company's investors had by now put a whopping $130 million into the venture, on heady initial expectations that the website would go live six months earlier than it did, and that the company would move swiftly to an IPO within six to nine months of launching. With New York's high-tech NASDAQ market now plummeting, the majority of boo's investors lost confidence as well as patience, and refused to inject the additional cash needed to keep the company afloat until it could achieve profits. Thus, boo.com went into receivership in May 2000, only six months after launch.

Of course, misconceptions about users' needs were not boo's only problem – unrealistic expectations about the internet's financial returns were the order of the day – and today a site like boo.com wouldn't encounter the same problems, thanks to the wide availability of broadband internet access. But underestimation of simple user requirements and timing played a part in a way that's often emblematic of new industries, new markets and novice entrepreneurs.

In spite of boo.com's complexity and the capital expense it entailed, the more conventional aspects of the business worked well. Warehousing, distribution, delivery, returns and call centre assistance, for which tried-and-tested business methods already existed, ran smoothly. The problem was in the execution of the most innovative (and consequently riskiest) aspect of the business: the front-end experience of browsing and ordering over a website – the point at which customers ultimately lost patience.

In a new market space, it can be easy – for potential customers and entrepreneurs alike – to overlook problems that fall outside habitual perceptions, and Malmsten's memoir frequently demonstrates that, in spite of their enthusiasm for technology, boo's founders were thinking along the familiar lines of the fashion retail industry rather than those of the new internet industry. Enthralled at the idea of presenting boo as a futuristic lifestyle and fashion experience, they overlooked more pragmatic criteria for consumers: convenience and ease of use.

Market testing an innovative business concept in a new market or industry requires careful and watchful consideration not only of *what* needs to be investigated or tested and *which* feedback is most important, but also *when* and *how* to do the testing. The most important problems facing an innovative business may elude even an entrepreneur with some prior start-up experience.

How?

Below is a brief outline of traditional market testing methods and some more novel approaches, along with suggestions for further reading.

Customer comment: focus groups and surveys

Focus groups and customer surveys are the most traditional tools of market research, used by small and large companies alike.

A focus group is a small gathering of people (usually six to ten) selected from a target market or demographic category. In an informal and interactive setting, a moderator facilitates a discussion between the participants about their opinions or emotional responses to a topic, problem or product.

Because a focus group is more flexible and open-ended than a customer survey, allowing the conversation to follow the direction taken by participants, it is possible to collect a good deal of qualitative information about potential or existing customers. The conversation may also uncover new issues that weren't foreseen or expected. It is also less costly than conducting large-scale quantitative research, although its validity may depend on how astutely you select your sample of participants, compared with how novel, niche or mass market your business proposition is. A niche market may be more willing to adopt a new product that calls for a change in behaviour, and its members are more likely to have a set of strong needs and opinions in common than a broader sample of mass-market customers. Sometimes it may be useful to conduct several focus groups for specific sub-categories of your target market (for example, by age, gender or other relevant criteria), as a group that is fairly homogeneous tends to interact more openly, thus providing more information.

Ideally, to be effective a focus group should be conducted by a trained moderator. If you don't have one to hand or can't afford to hire one, here are some simple guidelines for conducting a focus group:

- Ask participants to introduce themselves at the start so that everyone feels more at ease.
- Introduce the topic clearly, ask some open-ended questions to stimulate discussion between group members and then let the conversation evolve. Use visual aids and props (prototypes, photographs, brochures) as prompts.
- If new ideas are produced by group members, improvise and ask more specific questions in response to participants' comments. However, as with lawyers questioning a witness in court, avoid asking leading questions that might elicit an expected or conditioned response from participants. Do, however, make sure that all the topics that need to be examined have been addressed by the end of the session.
- Aim to prevent one or two people from dominating the discussion, as can sometimes happen, and encourage participants to express individual opinions if needed, rather than falling into a 'groupthink' situation.

- Allow the session to run for one or two hours, and end it on a positive note, including a wrap-up stage in which participants review and evaluate the concepts raised, and their relative strengths and weaknesses.
- Close by thanking all participants.
- Consider audio- or video-recording the session for future reference.

SOURCING PARTICIPANTS

We now live in a world full of networks, societies and interest groups, so there are many ways to source participants for focus groups, particularly if your business proposition has one or several niche targets. Charities, hobby groups, trade associations and clubs may all provide access to certain types of consumer, business or professional. Many people appreciate being asked for their honest opinion and are willing to help when approached.

Digital focus groups. Increasingly, focus group exercises are also being conducted online rather than in physical meetings, or by video conferencing. Informally, participants can be found through existing social networking groups and forums and consulted through online chats or posts. Specific online business tools such as GutCheck can be used to organise formal online qualitative market research; they also provide access to pools of suitable target customers at a much lower cost than that of hiring a market research agency. Bear in mind, however, that such tools are currently in their early days as new ventures, and as yet little is known regarding their efficacy.

Surveys. Using information gleaned from focus groups, a market researcher may then draw up a survey questionnaire to use with a wider sample of people in an attempt to test or validate the opinions expressed in the groups on a larger, more quantitative scale. However, for a small new venture with limited resources, it may be difficult to survey a sufficiently representative and objective sample of people. A survey of 100 of your friends and colleagues will not be seen as reliable information if you report that a large majority of respondents liked your product. Quality will depend on your contacts, but when presenting survey results you must be clear about how the sample was sourced and any demographic, professional, personal or other affiliations that survey respondents share. In fact, even if you survey anonymous people on the street, you must be clear about the location at which the survey was conducted.

User observation: empathic design

As Don Draper notes, many people do not know what they want, or do not perceive problems with their everyday products or lifestyle that could be solved or bettered. Habit can make us impervious to dissatisfaction and prevent us from considering improvements.

This is the thesis held by proponents of *empathic design*, who say that carefully observing product users in action – especially in their everyday home or work environments – can be more illuminating and useful than questioning them directly and collecting verbal comment.

Whether you observe people using competing products or your own prototypes, an empathic design exercise may highlight problems as well as positive attributes of a product that users would not have thought to mention in the more artificial setting of a focus group discussion. You may also observe people using a product in novel ways, suggesting further business opportunities or product enhancements.

In their excellent and concise article on the topic, Dorothy Leonard and Jeffrey Rayport[33] of Harvard Business School cite five types of information that empathic design practices can provide more effectively than traditional market research:

- The specific circumstances that prompt people to use a product, which may be different from the circumstances imagined by the product designers.
- How a product fits into users' environments and habitual routines, suggesting alternative uses to those that the designers initially intended.
- How users add features to a product, modify it or combine it with other products, suggesting added attributes that could be designed into the product itself.
- Users' interest in some of the peripheral (non-core) features of a product, whose importance could be highlighted or enhanced in the future.
- Previously unexpressed user needs, or difficulties in using a product which users have taken for granted, not realising they

could be addressed or improved through redesign. Users would be unlikely to comment on these in a focus group.

Consider visually recording (photographs or video) users in a live setting; the recordings may reveal details that weren't noticed by observers on the spot. You may even give users video cameras to tape themselves using a product at home or work when you are not present. Leonard and Rayport also outline a method for performing an empathic design study and making use of the information gathered; you can purchase their article from the *Harvard Business Review* online service as an initial guide.

All the same, empathic design is not intended to replace traditional market research entirely. New solutions designed in response to empathic observation should also be tested more traditionally to gauge whether they appeal to potential customers.

B2B, radical innovation and customer collaboration: lead user groups

Because it is an aid for early product development, lead user research sits somewhere between market research and prototyping, helping a venture to align a novel application with the needs of its likely first customers.

Lead users, as described by MIT professor Eric Von Hippel,[34] are companies in a specific sector that are more likely to adopt a novel product or technology than their peers – and at an earlier date – because some aspect of their business causes them to experience certain technical or operational problems earlier than other companies do. If the problem is important, these groups will be more likely to adopt a novel solution, even if it requires some change to or reorganisation of their habitual way of working. A telltale sign identifying a lead user is that the company is already undertaking some internal R&D or product development to try to solve or mitigate the problem itself, even though doing so may temporarily rob some resources from its core activity. However, if as an inventor and entrepreneur you have already developed a platform technology or solution that could help, such companies will find it more convenient to adopt your application than to develop their own, provided that you can customise it to their needs.

Lead user exercises are typically structured as workshops lasting one to several days, in which representatives from identified lead user companies meet with the developers of a novel technology to analyse the needs of these potential first customers. The goal is to identify a common set of specifications that will be required of the intended applications or final products. These exercises aid the development of working prototypes, which can in turn be trialled by the lead user group.

The US corporation 3M, most commonly known for inventing the Post-it® note as well as producing many other cutting-edge products, was an early adopter of the lead user method. According to a 2002 study,[35] 3M obtained faster development times and generated new product lines more successfully in cases where it adopted the lead user approach than when it employed traditional product development methods.

While an entrepreneurial venture may not have the financial and human resources of 3M, this does not preclude it from performing lead user research on a smaller scale. Preferred witness research (Chapter 4) may identify some potential lead users. Since entrepreneurs often innovate in industries in which they have prior experience, a past employer or client may also have the characteristics of a lead user. We also recommend the methods described in Von Hippel's articles, books and tutorials, most of which are freely available on the internet.[36]

Although lead user methods were designed and commonly intended for business-to-business (B2B) propositions, there may also be situations in which individuals could be considered lead users – and consequently co-developers – of a new technology or design, such as people with special needs.

The real purchase decision: in-market testing

While the approaches above are designed to offer some guiding principles for developing a potentially successful product, the real proof of success only comes when customers are actually invited to *buy* the product.

Unfortunately, what people say in a focus group or other opinion forum doesn't always match what they *do* when the time comes to open their wallets. That's why you cannot be entirely certain of a venture's success until that time. This is especially the case with extremely novel products, where customers may not have enough experience to provide a reliable opinion about whether they would buy or use them. In their minds and conversation, people may be seduced by the idea of a futuristic new solution, but only a few of those people may be willing to change their everyday habits to adopt it. The gradual process by which a large number of people very gradually transferred many of their activities – such as banking, shopping and reading the newspaper – from the physical to the online realm is a case in point.

Consequently, for some entrepreneurs, going straight to market with an innovation may be the only test worth pursuing, although they might start with a simplified first version of their product or low volumes to avoid overstretching their resources. However, it may also be possible to run some simulated in-market tests or pilot trials before a full-scale launch.

A simulation or pilot may take a number of forms, on a small or large scale, depending on the nature and style of the product or business proposition. A venture may sell a limited amount of product for a limited time, perhaps in conjunction with a special event or at a time of year that fits the product. The founders of innocent ltd took this approach when they first came up with the idea of starting a business selling American-style fresh bottled smoothies in the UK. Before going through the expensive and time-consuming process of registering a company, designing a brand and packaging the product, they performed a simple market test by running a stall in a place where they expected to find members of their target market segment. The cheeky, purposely earnest nature of the test matched the later style of their product and brand image. In their own words:

> In the summer of 1998 when we had developed our first smoothie recipes but were still nervous about giving up our proper jobs, we bought £500 worth of fruit, turned it into smoothies and sold them from a stall at a little music festival in London. We put up a big sign saying 'Do you think we should give up our jobs to make these smoothies?' and put out a bin saying 'YES' and a bin saying 'NO' and asked people to put the empty bottle in the right bin. At the end of the weekend the 'YES' bin was full so we went in the next day and resigned.[37]

The internet is also a useful medium for market testing certain products or services, making it possible to collect statistics on how many visitors click an advertisement link, which pages are read the most, how many visitors 'convert' into buyers, at what speed and so on. It can also allow visitors to post comments and suggest improvements. A venture may even run a simulated sale on the internet, interrupting the purchase before the buyer enters payment details, although the founders should think of an appealing and suitable way to apologise and compensate any disappointed purchasers for their time.

Another option is to test-sell a limited amount of real product over the internet. As the founders of Cars Direct in the US showed, this can even be done with big-ticket items. The founders built a test website advertising cars at invoice prices, which could be bought through the site. They ran the site for one weekend, during which they sold four cars. After verifying the sales by telephone, they bought the four models themselves, at normal list prices and delivered them to the customers, paying the price difference – which amounted to less than $20,000 – themselves. For a relatively low cost and in a short time, they had demonstrated the existence of consumers who were willing to buy a car over the internet to save money. When the company launched for real, it sold $250 million's worth of cars in its first year.[38]

Pricing for your target market

Market testing is also an important check to optimally and realistically price a product or service. Pricing is discussed in depth in other books, and with particular reference to entrepreneurship in *Marketing That Works*,[39] so here we only offer a quick overview. Although we use the word 'price' here for brevity, it could refer to any number of ways of collecting revenue, such as rental fees.

COST-PLUS

Large companies with powerful marketing channels typically use *cost-plus* pricing methods – they calculate the cost of a product's manufacture and then 'mark up' the price to create the desired profit margin. This approach is fine when a company can expect to sell its product in large volumes, and its ample financial resources make a large up-front investment in manufacturing possible.

For new ventures, however, which often begin their operations selling small volumes to niche markets, this type of pricing is unsustainable and may even diminish the product's revenue potential.

VALUE PRICING

Since new ventures aim to distinguish themselves from competitors by offering something new and – by implication – better than current offerings, a new venture would do better to aim for *value pricing*, whereby price is set at a level expected to generate the highest profit possible. This price is often determined during market testing by asking a sample of people in the target market segment what price they'd be willing to pay for a product – preferably one that they can see and touch for themselves.

When asking potential customers what they'd pay for a product, beware of giving them a choice between prices: they'll understandably tend to pick the lowest price under consideration. It's better to ask them how much they'd be willing to pay for the product, or else suggest the highest price in your hypothetical range and gradually work your way down if respondents reject it, until you reach the price they'll accept. You may also ask them whether they might give up any product features for a lower price, or pay more for added features. (The most sophisticated way to test preferred features with preferred prices is called *conjoint analysis*, whereby you present a number of feature combinations in such a way that the consumer cannot understand what's being tested. This subject is too large for the pages of this book, however, and can easily be looked up in marketing textbooks.)

An important caveat for value pricing is that the highest price quoted by potential customers won't necessarily deliver the most revenue. Aim for a combination of price and likely sales volume that will deliver the most lucrative result, as shown in Figure 29.

Price/unit	Units sold @ price	Revenue	Cost (£50/unit)	Contribution (towards fixed costs and profit)
£100	5,000	£500,000	£250,000	£250,000
£150	4,000	£600,000	£200,000	£400,000
£200	2,500	£500,000	£250,000	£375,000

Figure 29 **Choose the most lucrative combination of price and likely sales volume**

You may also consider offering an *inducement* to customers, by setting a price discounted below customers' perceived value but higher than the price of an existing reference product.

Instead of looking directly at a comparable product, the *perceived value* could also be identified objectively by factors such as the amount of money customers would save by using your product or the improved performance they would achieve (see Figure 30).

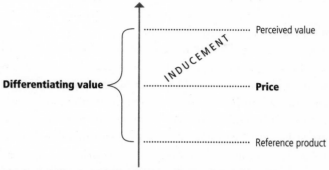

Figure 30 **Inducement: pricing slightly below customers' perceived value of a product**

Of course, if it looks as though you cannot make a profit at the price that customers are willing to pay, you may need to rethink the design of your business offering or find a way to reduce costs. A re-design may imply a different product or combination of products, but it may also mean a different way of delivering the product, such as renting or leasing, licensing, subscriptions or selling ancillary products and services such as advertising.

THE ATTRACTION OF FREE

New ways to entice users and customers are always popping up, including novel pricing models. The 'limited time offer' has been replaced by 'free' with a twist, or 'freemium' pricing, particularly for software and media products. The British pop band Arctic Monkeys shot rapidly to fame by (quite innocently) giving away copies of their first CD at concerts, just as Lily Allen's ascent resulted from uploading her first songs to MySpace, where they could be downloaded for free. Developments such as these, along with the free file-sharing movement whose model Apple borrowed and transformed into a mainstream commercial business with iTunes, demonstrate how free pricing over the internet can also work as an early market test. Many online businesses today offer a basic software or media product for free, to quickly build a base of users (who may also be beta testers), and later charge a fee for a premium version of the product with enhanced features. This freemium model is becoming increasingly mainstream for a variety of products and services, and also allows for early market testing of a product concept, which can help to shape the premium product version and other enhancements.

In summary...

Market testing is no magic bullet and only real sales can offer the final proof of business success, but never testing your entrepreneurial assumptions is also dangerous. As one of many tools at your disposal, market testing can lessen some of the uncertainty inherent in shaping a new venture, giving you a more thorough understanding of your customers. If you pay close attention, it may also uncover new insights about customers that you might otherwise have missed, helping you to either avoid mistakes or consider new opportunities. Based on your earlier preferred witness research (as discussed in Chapter 4), think carefully about which testing methods are most appropriate for your business proposition and which aspects of your business require testing.

SECTION IV
MARSHALLING RESOURCES

10. SETTING UP VENTURE TEAMS

What?

These days, technology has made it more possible than ever for people to start small one-person businesses – witness, for instance, the proliferation of iPhone apps created by single developers. However, it usually takes a combination of abilities and multiple human resource hours to start a venture with higher growth ambitions and a more complex product offering.

You may already have one or more co-founders with whom you plan to start your venture, but in addition to co-founders you'll eventually need other types of collaborator, from employees and managers to board members and investors. You may not be in a position to put a full team together yet, but since a good team will be one of the resources needed for a viable business, this chapter outlines some information and advice for future thought.

Opinions differ regarding what constitutes a good venture team and what an entrepreneur's priorities should be when assembling a team. Investors typically say that they want to invest in a team with the best technical and commercial expertise available, a board with contacts and a CEO with previous industry experience. Once upon a time, 'previous industry experience' might have meant appointing a director who hailed from a large incumbent company, but nowadays investors look more specifically for a CEO who has headed another start-up (or more than one) in the same industry. This may put you at a disadvantage if you happen to be trying to start your first company, and is why team members with a range of different expertise and experience are needed to complement whatever you can bring to the table and make up for anything you can't. If you're a novice entrepreneur, you might find that you have to give up some control of your first venture in order to see your idea come to fruition with the help of additional collaborators with a range of experience.

In addition to skill and experience, passion and drive are also seen as important attributes, and occasionally certain investors in certain circumstances will prioritise these qualities over industry experience, asserting that passionate, motivated and open-minded entrepreneurs will learn to do whatever it takes to go to market and remain unswervingly committed to the goal.

The optimum conditions may lie in a combination of these factors; however, as all start-ups and starting conditions are different, what's important is that the team should be composed and managed in a way that satisfies the internal needs and external demands of the business. Internal needs include requirements for smooth operations and good decision making. External demands include the ability to attract and retain target customers, investors and future acquirers of your business, and delivering the technology, products or services at the right time. In the case of a new venture, all of this usually must be done in a shifting environment of changing demands, as a young company learns about its market and business setting and hurries to adapt its products and practices in response. Venture teams therefore frequently need to be primed for speed and flexibility.

Attributes you must consider when trying to assemble a successful team will include not just technical skills and industry experience (possibly from diverse industries), but also networks and contacts, personality and thinking styles, and previous acquaintance or shared work experience.

The key ingredient, however, is attitude, because the kind of team you'll assemble and the company you'll build, at least in the early days, will be different from the type of team you would find in a large organisation. It takes a different animal to accept a position in a start-up company as opposed to a large organisation. The risk of failure, lack of job security, long hours, high commitment and adaptability required, and low starting pay are factors that will be tolerated only by the right kind of team member, in exchange for other incentives and rewards such as the thrill of innovation and independence, the chance to express one's talent, the opportunity to learn and develop new skills, and the prospect of long-term rewards (and kudos) if the venture succeeds. So the culture of the start-up is just as important as its product. While this difference is widely understood in the

US, it is sometimes less of a given in Europe, where the new venture community is smaller and working practices tend to be more conservative.

A team's success comes from its ability to coalesce around a set of clearly understood and shared values and goals, as well as its talent in implementing those goals. As coalescing is easier said than done, you need to devote as much thought to how you recruit, organise and retain the loyalty and commitment of your venture team as you do to your strategy and product offering.

Why?

Investors in start-ups typically state that the management team is more crucial to success than the business idea. A strong team can make something out of a second-rate idea – or modify it into a better idea – but a great idea will not succeed if the team that carries it out is not fit for purpose. If your venture will need outside investment, this alone should prompt you to pay close attention to the people aspect of your venture.

Your venture will also require different team attributes as it develops through stages – from evaluating and developing the idea (as you're presumably doing while reading this book), to raising capital, starting operations, and implementing and growing the business if you're successful in the previous stages. Managing these operational transitions effectively is another skill you'll need to develop if your venture succeeds in launching.

Bear in mind that how you effectively manage people, skills and roles in a start-up is likely to be different to the approach taken in larger organisations.

Handshake Solutions: order out of chaos

In 2003, Wouter Van Roost was appointed CEO of Handshake Solutions, a new venture within the Philips Technology Incubator in Eindhoven, The Netherlands. The incubator was set up after it was recognised that existing divisions in Philips weren't organised to exploit the company's R&D discoveries beyond its traditional markets and product lines. Believing that it would be necessary to enter new markets to remain competitive, Philips' chief technology officer, Ad Huijser, created the incubator to foster an entrepreneurial environment of small, versatile firms with a higher risk tolerance and longer-term commercial objectives than are typically found in a corporate product division.

However, when Van Roost was introduced to his new employees and colleagues, he immediately thought that the team did not seem right for an entrepreneurial venture. All 12 members were technology experts, and all were recruited from among Philips' employees; essentially, they were all alike.

Van Roost had spent the previous three years successfully preparing another activity developed inside Philips for spin-out, and was consequently invited to lead Handshake Solutions. As a philosophy graduate with an extensive career in marketing behind him, his strengths lay in understanding motivation and managing people. After being introduced to the Handshake Solutions team, he began to address them politely by saying 'Now, although I don't really understand your technology, I....'

Before he could continue, he was met by a chorus of smirks and laughter. The team members, accustomed to working in purely technical roles and departments, couldn't understand how Van Roost could be their boss. If anything, they believed, a boss should understand the technology even better than they did. At that moment, says Van Roost , in order to build and lead a business, 'I saw that I was going to have to do something new and different.'

The value proposition that Handshake Solutions was tasked with creating was certainly challenging. The R&D behind the new venture was a solution for making asynchronous or 'clockless' microprocessor chips. These consume less power and radiate less heat and electromagnetic energy than conventional chips, which contain an internal clock. This difference could potentially make clockless chips attractive for mobile devices, with their demand for longer battery life, or for applications where heat and electromagnetic interference could be an issue, such as medical devices. Although Philips was not the first company to create a clockless chip technology, previous attempts by competitors had been unsuccessful as a result of low performance, poor compatibility with the other electronics components and – most importantly – the fact that chip designers and electronic engineers would have to be extensively retrained to use clockless technology in their designs. Consequently, existing clockless technology was being used in simple, low-power applications such as smart cards, but the industry was sceptical about its suitability for more complex products. Although Philips was already using Handshake Solutions' technology in-house, the venture would ultimately work to overcome wider industry resistance, not only by offering better technical performance through its technology, but also by providing a set of design support tools and partnering with a mainstream industry partner, Britain's ARM. Nonetheless, the firm's proposition at start-up represented a radical departure from the industry norm. While technology was an enabler, thought Van Roost, the company's ultimate success in achieving its goals would depend on the attitudes, motivation, responsiveness and talent of its combined team.

Van Roost began by interviewing each of the 12 team members. He asked them if they really wanted to be engaged in a start-up. Would they be prepared to accept the degree of uncertainty and change that was inevitable in such a venture? Two of the original team members eventually preferred to leave the company.

From that point, Van Roost's approach to recruitment, hiring and management focused on fostering a way of thinking and behaviours that would drive the high technological and entrepreneurial performance needed, as the company grew from 10 to 25 employees over the following two years.

Recruitment and hiring

Handshake Solutions recruited new employees through the contacts and networks of existing staff, which already provided an initial filter. Interviews were geared toward assessing a candidate's mindset rather than skill set. Early attempts at using formal recruiting agencies, whose agents only paid attention to candidates' skills, had yielded unsatisfactory results.

The company sought people who were willing to learn, who wanted to develop, who were open to new and often shifting ways of doing things, and who weren't afraid to challenge accepted ideas when they thought another idea could work better.

It was agreed that ample time spent interviewing candidates thoroughly would be worth the investment. Each potential employee was interviewed by six or seven team members over a day. Each interviewer, while discussing the job and company, would be tasked with exploring a particular aspect, such as the candidate's personality, life experience, values or attitude. Van

Roost held the final interview with each candidate, during which he did not even discuss the job but only sought to get to know the person. In each case, he said, he was looking for some 'small element that might enable that person to initiate change'. The aim was to introduce enough variety to the team to prevent it from becoming blinkered and set in its ideas, because the technological and commercial environment around the company was expected to change frequently. At the same time, each person should be able to fit into the existing culture.

At the end of the interviews, the team met and reached a consensus decision about the candidate. Staff members who had not taken part in interviews were still informed about the candidate and the conversations.

'I never hired the obvious,' said Van Roost. Trying to please the boss would disqualify a candidate at interview. Discussing meaningful life experiences, showing emotion, asking challenging questions, possibly even showing a hint of disrespect – in other words, being a risk-taker – would score positively. For instance, the only member of the company (besides Van Roost) with a purely commercial, non-technical role had no previous experience of business development or sales. He was a procurement manager from Philips. When Van Roost asked him why he wanted to work in a start-up, he replied that he'd been reflecting on his life and wanted to move beyond the narrow way in which he'd been living. His motivation to do something new and challenging, not his past job experience or skill set, marked him out as a good candidate. Another person who was hired had shown little interest in discussing the job position itself, but instead talked at length about the bigger issues and problems she perceived the company facing, and which she expected to help solve. Although her skill set was in technology, her vision stretched further.

Management

While assembling these diverse people, Van Roost also created a flat, nimble and cohesive team structure. There were no organisational charts or official job titles. However, the company's procedures and operations were fully transparent, so everyone always knew who was doing what. The boss did not take all the decisions; requirements were discussed and solutions developed collectively by the team members directly involved in any issue. This allowed decisions to be taken as necessary, every day.

To keep the small company cohesive and prevent it from breaking down into isolated silos, no two people performing similar jobs were seated near each other. There were no 'technical' or 'marketing' departments with separate or competing interests; all functions were seen as complementary and intertwined.

Communication was a crucial factor in making this system work. All decisions and new developments were logged weekly on an online platform accessible to all employees. These decisions didn't just include those related to product development but also those on hiring, firing, rewards, customer support issues, strategic discussions and so on. The company held a live weekly meeting to communicate anything that hadn't yet been logged on the platform, and to handle any questions. 'Everyone was aware of what was happening and where we were going,' says Van Roost. The team members were aligned in working toward the company's goal, 'to become the company that will change the way semiconductor firms design their chips.'

Finally, Van Roost wanted the team to have a strong sense of identity and connection with the company, to feel that it was their company. The company logo was exhibited everywhere possible; specialists were even hired to carve it into the thick carpet in Handshake Solutions' office space (under cover of night, when the incubator management had gone home). To reinforce their solidarity, team members had discretion to buy a gift of up to €50, at the company's expense, for any colleague who had either done something well, dealt with a difficult problem or possibly even made a mistake but learned in the process. Company members began to socialise and share personal interests, hobbies, sporting activities and sometimes even holidays. The more they developed informal connections, Van Roost believed, the more productively they would work together.

Performance

If this set-up sounds too chaotic and informal to make a venture productive, think again. Handshake Solutions achieved its business milestones on time or ahead of the schedule set by the incubator. Its ratio of cash burn to revenue was also lower than that of other start-ups of a similar age within the incubator.

In annual employee engagement surveys conducted by Philips, Handshake Solutions consistently scored higher levels of employee engagement and motivation than the average scores for companies in the incubator, or for

Philips as a whole. Handshake Solutions' employees gave especially positive responses with respect to trusting their managers, understanding managers' expectations, belief that their talents and skills were being used well, and receiving the information needed to do their jobs effectively. Alongside this, the company tracked employee absentee rates over five years; Handshake Solutions scored an absentee ratio of 0.36 per cent, compared to the 4.5 per cent registered at the time for the entire Philips group.

In 2006, Handshake Solutions was audited by the Bell Mason Group, a leading innovation and corporate venturing advisory firm that methodically assesses venture performance with respect to typical stages in a start-up's development path. Handshake Solutions received a high overall rating from Bell Mason, scoring particularly well on business development and sales, management and financial criteria.

Finally, the team's flexibility was a key advantage for the company. It frequently happens that a start-up needs to alter its business strategy or product offering in response to new market insight. Such change often leads to staff turnover, which may temporarily disrupt and slow down operations or, alternatively, an increase in the headcount, because new skills and job roles are required to implement new initiatives. Handshake Solutions changed its business plan but was able to do so while keeping its original team in place, and without adding additional staff. The lean, well-connected and responsive team was able to redistribute work, skills and priorities, adapting quickly to the evolving requirements of prospective customers and partners. 'We could design and turn out a new product in six months, not two years,' says Wouter. 'More and better work could be delivered by a smaller, less costly team than you often find in companies tasked with transforming R&D into market-ready offerings.'

How?

The research

A plethora of differently named methods and theories about team formation, team analysis and team management exist, and new ones are regularly devised by consultants and academics. Van Roost, for instance, based his approach on ideas from chaos management theory as it relates to high-performing teams (particularly on work by Dr Marcial Losada from the University of Michigan), as well as adaptive leadership methods set out by Dr Ronald Heifetz of Harvard University. What seems more important to us is that Van Roost was able to apply these ideas in practice with success. It matters less what method you subscribe to in name than what you are capable of applying in practice, and whether it fits a need.

Broader research into characteristics that have an impact on the success of teams[40] indicates that the main ingredients are the following.

INTERNAL TEAM NEEDS

Recruitment and hiring: diversity and similarity between team members. The relative merits of diversity and similarity between start-up team members have been studied at length. Obviously, a new venture will require diversity of skills and roles: technical, operations, marketing and sales, finance and so on. In the early days, when a team is small, some members may have to cover more than one area, with at least a partial understanding of each domain (or an inclination to learn), backed up when needed by the services of outside professionals such as accountants and lawyers. So, professional skills are one form of diversity, but the division is not clear cut in a small team, and often not the most important measure of diversity.

Looking beyond skills, research indicates that diversity or similarity in personality and thinking styles (for instance: analytical, empathic, visionary, tactical, risk-taking, conservative) also influences a venture's development and performance. So does previous acquaintance of team members in another environment, especially if they've worked together before. People who have similar work experiences and thinking styles and/or have worked together tend to share a common language and approach, which makes such teams good at taking decisions and implementing them quickly. However, homogeneous teams can also become overly comfortable with a narrow view of the company, and get stuck in a rut, which can be a drawback in fast-changing business environments.

On the other hand, highly diverse teams are good at exploring and comparing new ideas and developments that could impact strategy because each member has some unique insight to contribute; but they're are also slower, initially, at making decisions and taking action. As team members become better acquainted with one another over time, however, they develop a common language too, making them better at implementation but, gradually, less exploratory.

For reasons similar to those that make diversity desirable, research has also found that some occasional disagreement between team members and even co-founders is productive, as long as it remains in the realm of healthy debate over ideas and doesn't become personal (or taken personally). In practice, this may be easier said than done, but depends largely on how carefully the company manages its culture.

Not surprisingly, new companies that grow successfully contain a combination of diversity and similarity between team members. Looking back to the Handshake Solutions story, Van Roost began with a homogeneous team of people who'd all worked at the same parent company and consequently shared a common way of doing things, but he gradually fed in new members who could contribute alternative viewpoints and approaches. During interviews, he consistently sought an element in a candidate's attitude or personality that distinguished her from the rest of the team.

Organisation and decision making. Small team size and the likelihood that the venture will frequently change its shape in response to new developments mean rigid job descriptions and corporate-style titles such as CEO, CFO and CTO are inappropriate in the earliest stages of a new venture. Some people in the company will clearly have more experience, and consequently more authority, than others. However, it is important to be clear about who is responsible for what roles or tasks at any given time, so that needs are covered and work is not duplicated unnecessarily.

Decision-making style is also crucial to a new venture's success because the environment of uncertainty surrounding a nascent business requires new decisions to be taken and tested frequently. Van Roost's story illustrates how relying on the combined intelligence and talent of all team members (particularly in a diverse team) pays off in both the quality of decisions and the commitment of the team to those decisions, provided that all members of the company are aligned behind an understood common goal.

Communication. A venture team that's required to be versatile and agile cannot perform well without regular communication about ongoing developments and decisions. Communication should be structured into the venture's modus operandi. While it may seem an obvious requirement, start-up companies sometimes fail in this respect because it's taken for granted that in small groups word gets round and team members naturally align. When the team ultimately grows larger, steps aren't taken to facilitate communication flows beyond word of mouth. Andy Abramson, founder of Comunicano, a strategic communications agency for US and European technology start-ups, has noted this problem: 'You would be surprised how often, when we visit a client company for our initial strategy session, more often than not different team members have a different idea of the company's purpose and direction, and explain it differently. They listen to each other's comments and say, "Oh, is that where we're going?"'

No matter how busy you are building a product or developing a customer base, the investment of effort in communicating about all aspects of the business, as is the case at Handshake Solutions, is worthwhile. Keeping people in the dark about important issues or changes, either because you're short of time or in an effort to retain control, will jeopardise trust and impede effective decision making.

Culture. Decision-making styles, organisation style and communication enable the creation of a culture within the company, the glue that holds it together. A clearly understood, shared sense of the company's purpose and goals is important, as demonstrated at Handshake Solutions. But it is also important for team members at all levels to feel that the company goals are aligned with their personal goals and interests, and that the work is based on a set of shared values. This is highly desirable in any work situation, but crucial in a new venture where the risks are high, changes in strategy and demands may be frequent and, consequently, commitment to something beyond each individual's domain of responsibility is needed. While material rewards, such as equity or share options, may provide a way to stimulate people's commitment towards a long-term goal, culture provides the day-to-day motivation.

Research supports the notion that a culture of openness and mutual support between team members will foster good working practices. A high degree of interaction between team members, possibly both on and off the job, also has a positive effect.

Good teams also need a strong leader, but, as Van Roost's example proves, a strong leader isn't necessarily one who decrees all the rules or single-handedly takes all the decisions. The leader's broader role is to foster and champion a company purpose and culture that allow for good decision making and will encourage members to work cohesively, perform well and create a winning product or service. The leader is also the individual who is tasked with representing and defending the company's goals and decisions to the board of directors and other external parties, so she must also be a person capable of fronting the company in these external relations.

EXTERNAL TEAM

Research on entrepreneurship also highlights the importance of the external or 'extended' team, including investors and a board of directors, an advisory board, other firms with which a venture forms partnerships or alliances, and the management team's network of industry contacts.

Ideally, your board of directors will include people with knowledge of your business sector, expertise to help steer your company in the right direction and a reputation that will lend credibility to your new venture. An advisory board doesn't have the governing power of a board of directors, but may also include experienced and reputable individuals who act as 'key influencers' in your industry or market. An alliance or partnership with a larger company (such as the product development partnership that Handshake Solutions formed with Britain's ARM, a leading chip designer, in 2004), also builds credibility and may provide the most viable route to market.

The people in these groups require as much care as the members of your internal team, so building and maintaining a trusting relationship through frequent communication and interaction is also essential to securing their commitment, ongoing support and help when it's required.

The everyday reality

In practice, you may not be able to line up all the success factors mentioned above to create the theoretically optimal start-up team described in the research, because you may not have control over all these factors. You may have to choose the best options available to you at a given time, in a given place, and find a way to make them work.

Let's start with the extended or external team: an entrepreneur (especially a novice one) rarely has the opportunity to choose investors, in the sense of having more than one offer on the table at the same time. While it is certainly a good idea to approach investors who have already invested in your industry, at the end of the day it's often the investor who will choose you, not the other way around. So, the extent to which an investor can offer valuable industry expertise, time or network contacts will vary with each circumstance. In addition, your investor(s) will have a deciding say over who sits on your board of directors.

Legally, a board of directors is mandated to take decisions in the interest of the company's survival and prosperity, and to serve the interests of all shareholders equally. Majority shareholders can rightly exert their influence in shareholder votes on decisions taken at shareholder meetings, but a shareholder who sits on the board should act impartially when weighing in on decisions that are the board's responsibility. In practice, however, conflicts of interest have been known to seep into the boardroom. The best antidote to this risk is to appoint an independent chairperson who is not otherwise employed by the company or by any of its shareholders, and who can effectively manage the board.

While you should obviously aim to build an optimal internal team, your ability to attract the most suitable set of people may depend on where your business is located, what kind of talent is available locally, economic and industry conditions that affect the competitiveness of the job market, cultural attitudes to risk and so on. You may not always find the optimal combination of technical ability, passion and open-mindedness in each person. Sometimes you may find people who have the right qualities or experience but are only available or willing to work on a part-time or consulting basis. Turnover is to be expected, especially when the venture must take a strategic change of direction and certain members are either not capable of or won't change jobs if necessary.

In the end, when juggling all these variables, the one area in which you can have a substantial influence is the culture that you foster within the venture: the trust, confidence and motivation that you are able to build among internal and external stakeholders; this is the glue that will hold the operation together, and hopefully will influence the other factors.

We like Wouter Van Roost's radical approach to building and managing a high-performing team, and the results he was able to achieve. However, we recognise that such a radical departure from typical practice may be outside the comfort zone of many people. Here are a few suggestions, based on situations encountered in more 'traditional' situations.

CO-FOUNDERS, VALUES AND THE MANAGEMENT TEAM

A start-up will often have two or three co-founders. These individuals will own a significant stake in the company at founding, alongside the initial investors. They may share an equal level of authority, although they're often specialised in and responsible for different business areas, such as technical product design and commercial strategy. A founding team of two is probably the ideal number; more than three usually makes shared decision making difficult.

Although founders may come together because they share an interest in a business sector or product and have complementary skills, the key to their being able to *stay* together is an understanding of and agreement on shared values and common goals. If the founders' objectives aren't aligned, the company won't function smoothly. Before entering a co-founding relationship, discuss and gauge agreement on these values and goals in detail. What kind of company does each of you want to build (not just what kind of product)? What do you see as the company's primary purpose, in addition to making money? What kind of personal reward is each of you seeking, and within what timeframe? Are you happy to face some lean years and then cash in when the company is solidly successful, or do you expect to drive a company car in six months' time? Do you want to run the company yourself for many years, as a lifestyle business in pursuit of a personal passion, or quickly build up its value and sell it in five or six years' time? If you're not sure about this point now, when and how do you expect to make a decision? If resources are scarce, how will you prioritise spending needs? How will you handle your relationship with external investors? What approach will you take when hiring employees or consultants? How do you want the company to be perceived by your employees, your customers and the public at large? What should the company do to foster those perceptions?

Values and goals such as these will drive future behaviour, so if you don't establish an understanding early on you face disappointment or conflict at a later date. Worse still, you may find yourself trying to manoeuvre around such differences – at the expense of a coherent business strategy – in order to *avoid* overt conflict with your co-founders.

Depending on the nature of the business and the amount of capital available, the company may include other individuals, at start-up or in the early stages, who perform significant or crucial roles. However, rather than extending the founder pool to an unmanageable number, it is preferable to take them on as employee managers (typically referred to as the top management team). Although these managers may hold specialised roles and have more experience and authority than more junior employees, avoid 'chief' job titles such as CTO, CFO and so on. It may be necessary to create the role of chief executive officer to represent and champion the company in its relations with the board of directors and outside world, and probably of a finance director to steer the company's financial strategy. Beyond this, chief titles tend to magically instil divergent ambitions and agendas. Each chief will come to see her domain as a separate department, with resource needs and priorities that must compete with those of the other 'teams'. In a small new company, it's important to keep everyone pulling in the same direction – the one that will lead the company to success. Create managerial roles if they're needed to organise the work effectively, but not to mete out false prestige or power through superfluous titles.

In summary...

Much of the advice in this chapter will come naturally to people who are more inclined to work in an entrepreneurial start-up than in a large company, and will be a selling point when recruiting this type of person.

However, you cannot always be certain of finding the right kind of people just when you need them. Always bear recruitment in mind, and keep a mental (even written) list of people you meet through your networking and other business activities who may fill a role your venture is likely to need. Remain visible to those people and keep them up to date on your activities and plans. In the case of people who appear to be a very good fit, it may even be worth bringing them on board, even in a light (perhaps temporary or advisory) capacity, a little time before you really need them, provided you can agree to terms that your venture can afford.

In time, the company may reach a point where it will be necessary to replace yourself and to appoint a chief executive with a range of experience that's better suited to the more evolved company. This, too, is something for which you should prepare in advance by keeping an eye out for possible successors. If you have a good board of directors and an experienced chairperson, they can provide significant assistance, both with search and recruitment from their pool of contacts, and in determining the profile of the candidate required.

11. SEEKING SOURCES OF CAPITAL

What?

The word 'entrepreneurship' is often uttered in the same breath as 'venture capital' or simply 'VC'.

Venture capital, however, is one of the hardest types of finance to raise, the most expensive to the entrepreneur and not suited to every type of venture or stage of the venture journey. Depending on the nature and condition of your business at a given time, it might be more advantageous to seek subsidies, debt or angel investment, among others. As Chapter 7 on entrepreneurial strategies and routes to market makes clear, some types of business manage to avoid raising expensive venture capital altogether, thanks to their ability to obtain customers and collect revenue early in the life of the company. Other ventures need so much capital to develop their offering that they won't be able to reach the market without raising VC investment first.

This chapter doesn't aim to show you how to raise capital step by step – many other books explain this in detail. Rather, we assume you're reading this book at an early stage in your business concept, so we introduce you to different sources of capital, the related pros and cons, and explain how different sources of capital are more or less suited to different ventures and commercial strategies. Our overview should allow you to consider what your fundraising path is likely to be as you develop your business case. At a later date, we recommend you do more research on the fundraising process itself before you raise money – taking advice, in person or on paper, from experienced investors[41] – as well as recruiting a good finance director and a suitably experienced lawyer.

Why?

It's often said that you need to spend money to make money. Some entrepreneurs are able to fund the start-up costs of their businesses themselves, through personal wealth perhaps accumulated from previous business activities. Stories abound of now-mature entrepreneurs who started with a small business and slowly developed an empire by ploughing their earnings back into it, using loans to grow it once it was stable and perhaps ultimately selling it to start another venture.

In today's world of high technology, innovation-based ventures and knowledge-economy markets, entrepreneurs frequently don't have the luxury of a long timeframe; certain new technologies need considerable capital and time to develop a product offering to launch on the market, and capital must often provide staying power until a new market catches on and becomes profitable. Many new entrepreneurs don't have enough funds to go the whole distance by themselves, so must resort to other people's money. Some sources of capital, however, require a founder to give up some control of the business, so it's important for you to consider whether this is something you can accept, and also if it is truly necessary.

One thing we can say for certain is that, in most cases, raising money from external sources is going to be a longer and more arduous process than you'll possibly envisage. You and your co-founders would likely rather spend your time building a first-class product or business, but you can't do so without funds, and persuading providers of finance to part with money for an unproven new business isn't easy. Thus fundraising becomes a necessary chore for many entrepreneurs.

You can't raise money without also taking into account the viewpoint of the other party providing the capital. On the one hand, your desire as a founder will be to raise capital at the lowest possible cost (specifically, at low interest rates or by ceding a low ownership stake), so that you can collect as much value from your business as possible. Lenders and investors, however, have their own requirements. They are businesses in their own right, aiming to make a solid return on their invested money. Furthermore (with the exception of individual angel investors), they must also answer to their own shareholders. Any financing agreement, therefore, spells out an acceptable common ground that, essentially, allows each side to place an acceptable bet on the venture's future.

One of the ways in which investors hedge their bets is by releasing funds in instalments or tranches, and agreeing on a set of milestones the company must achieve before it can access the next tranche of investment.

Milestones can be a double-edged sword. Metaphorically, a milestone signals a distance covered on a journey, and therefore an achievement. However, milestones are literally, well, stones planted into the ground. Driving a monolithic stake into the soil of a volatile new market – such as those targeted by innovation-based ventures – can be rather like trying to build a house during a spell of earthquakes.

It is crucial, therefore, for investor-backed entrepreneurs to keep communication lines open with funders, to retain their trust and manage their expectations effectively. Investors should know that the market landscape can change very quickly, but this doesn't preclude them from being taken by surprise if your company suddenly has to move in a different direction to the one described in the business plan in which they first invested. In fact, your business plan should preferably indicate that there are alternative routes to market, in the event that your preferred commercialisation strategy suddenly becomes out of place, as in the case below. An experienced investor should see value in an entrepreneur's consideration of possible fallback options.

Siruna: the paradox of mobile milestones

If you've ever found yourself becoming tetchy while trying to scroll horizontally through a website that doesn't fit the vertically orientated screen of your mobile phone, it will have occurred to you that websites must be redesigned for mobile browsing. In fact, large website owners such as the BBC and Google make adjusted versions of their content available for mobile phone browsing from a dedicated URL.

What you may not know is that the process of modifying websites for mobile use can be cumbersome and expensive. Different brands and models of mobile phone run on different software operating systems and, until recently, any website designer or owner wishing to release a user-friendly mobile version would have to manually code a variety of mobile websites compatible with different phone models. An early response to this problem, known in technical jargon as 'device diversity', was provided by a number of fully-automated tools to transcode websites into mobile software formats.

However, these were rather crude, could only transcode very simple websites and couldn't adjust graphic design and content features to optimise them for a phone screen.

In spite of these technical drawbacks, technology analysts were already predicting in 2007 that demand for mobile internet content would grow rapidly as more consumers switched to smartphones, creating a $1 billion global market for related technologies by 2010. There was clearly a gap in the market for better technical solutions.

Belgian start-up Siruna was founded in 2007 to commercialise a technology first developed at Belgium's Internet Broadband Research Institute that simplified the conversion of desktop websites into mobile websites. Siruna's technology platform addressed the problem of phone diversity with a semi-automated tool, which solved both software coding and design problems. Using the Siruna tools, a web designer could manually optimise the design and content of a desktop website for use in a mobile version, while the technology automatically dealt with the software complexities of different mobile phone systems.

In order to deliver the correct format to a mobile phone, Siruna would host mobile websites created with its technology on its own server platform, which functioned as an intermediary between the mobile phone user and the original website. When a phone user visited a Siruna website, the server detected the make of mobile phone and displayed the website in the appropriate format.[42]

Siruna's founders financed the first two years of the venture with a combination of their own savings, plus grant money and a convertible loan from a public venture fund, amounting to total seed funding of €500,000. They used this period to conduct lead user projects with several companies, including Dutch airline KLM and Belgian telecoms group Belgacom Mobile, to test and optimise the technology. Subsequently, they sought and obtained funding from a syndicate of venture capital firms, and closed a €4 million deal in the spring of 2009.

Siruna's original business strategy was to operate as a managed service provider (MSP), offering a turnkey mobile internet solution for big ticket business customers, such as:

- System integrators (SIs), which are ICT consulting companies that combine off-the-shelf software applications from different vendors into customised systems for their customers.

- Value added resellers (VARs), which would bundle the Siruna platform software into their own software packages.
- Independent software vendors (ISVs), which sell tailored solutions in niche sectors, such as banking, logistics and media, where internet and intranet content would need to be optimised for mobile handsets.
- Large web agencies, which could use the Siruna platform to create mobile website extensions for their customers.

Revenue would be collected through a combination of licensing and fees. This was the strategy spelled out in the company's business plan.

With the technological landscape of mobile telephony remaining fragmented among many models and operating systems, demand for Siruna's solution seemed a sure thing. Then a hiccup occurred in the market: the thundering success of the iPhone, and the consequent vogue for downloadable applications – 'apps'. Around the same time that Siruna raised the finance needed to roll out on a large scale, the service companies it had targeted as customers stopped looking for tools to create multi-device mobile websites because their clients were asking them to make iPhone apps to jump on the bandwagon (regardless of the fact that many consumers were still accessing the internet from other phone models).

At this point, the €7000 annual licence fee that Siruna aimed to charge target customers for a mobile website toolkit was no longer a viable proposition. The company had to reposition itself to serve the lower end of the market: the smaller businesses and organisations that built their own websites, often using open-source content management systems (CMS). However, at this end of the market Siruna realised it could only charge around €300 per toolkit. The founders reasoned that this market would require a do-it-yourself kit, which was easy to download. The product would have to be marketed worldwide at low cost to create economies of scale, so customers would be attracted through a freemium package, allowing them to try out a free basic version and then pay for a premium version with enhanced features. Thus was the OSMOBI platform born: a 'software as a service' (SAAS) product, derived from the Siruna technology, which allowed owners of websites created in popular open-source CMS, such as Joomla!, Drupal and WordPress, to adapt them for mobile phone browsers through the user-friendly OSMOBI editor.[43]

Siruna's analysis of registered OSMOBI users revealed that the service appealed to website publishers who remained primarily concerned with reaching a wide public on any make of mobile phone: these included local governments, tourist boards, religious organisations and charities. Siruna's management estimated that OSMOBI would have to accumulate a critical mass of around 10,000 free users of the basic package before significant revenue from fee-based upgrades would begin to flow in. The company drew on user feedback to make improvements and identify feature enhancements that would create the most demand, and began to draw up plans to add m-commerce (mobile commerce) and advertising solutions to its offering.

Unfortunately, Siruna then encountered a problem. The milestones that had been agreed with its venture capital investors were all based on the B2B managed service provider strategy, a model of which the investors had ample previous experience. When the second tranche of funding was needed, Siruna's VCs had difficulty justifying changes to the business plan, and the new milestones proposed by the company, to their own investment committees. Since the shareholder agreement with Siruna's new investors referred to milestones and stages of development described in the business plan, the business plan was essentially a legally binding document. At the second funding round in spring 2010, the investor syndicate collapsed and funding was denied on the basis, among other reasons, of the company's departure from its milestone agreements.

Siruna's back-end technology and servers were sold to a large web development agency, which intended using them to build mobile websites for its clients, and the start-up company was wound down.

Of course, there is seldom an attractive market without multiple competitors, and other start-ups always gain from the removal of a competitor. Today, the up and coming provider of a similar mobile web solution is Mobify,[44] a Canadian start-up also founded in 2007, whose two young founders, Igor Faletski and John Boxall avoided both angel and VC funding and opted to 'bootstrap' the company's growth gradually, thus retaining control over their business strategy. The founders first developed a mobile SMS messaging solution for the Vancouver public transit system during their final semester at university. Substantial media attention to the product, as well as the early licensing revenue it generated, prompted them to form a company upon graduating. Further revenue came from another client contract with a local television channel. The founders later switched their focus to the challenge of mobile web conversion. In order to develop their solution, they obtained an industrial research grant of C$150,000 from Canada's National Research Council and raised US$30,000 of investment from friends and family, a funding model that allowed them to remain majority shareholders. A short spell in Silicon Valley helped them to raise further licensing revenue from client projects. Finally, generous federal R&D tax credits helped them to get more out of those early revenues to plough back into their technology development. Eventually the company released Mobify Studio, a self-service platform for mobile web conversion with similar functionality to Siruna's OSMOBI. Thanks to the founders' early marketing efforts in Silicon Valley, Mobify Studio was adopted, among others, by *Wired*, the iconic and agenda-setting technology magazine. In 2010, in response to growing interest in mobile e-commerce, Mobify released a new-generation product that moves the website conversion process directly into a mobile device's browser, rather than routing it through an intermediate proxy server. This solution improves security, allows a retailer to set up a mobile site more quickly and keep the same URL (without that 'm' normally added to the beginning of mobile URLs), and is also optimised for tablet devices such as the iPad. So, the founders' choice to obtain the lion's share of their finance through subsidy and contract work, while growing their headcount very gradually, seems to be paying off.

The web development industry, too, has begun to reframe the problem of device diversity. With the release of the Android operating system and the emergence of Android apps, web developers now find themselves faced with the inefficiency of 'app diversity', and are reconsidering the appeal of mobile websites as opposed to mobile apps. Siruna's ultimate problem was perhaps not one of business strategy, but of timing.

How?

By this point, you may have made some considered decisions about what you're planning to sell, whether you want to enter a market for products or technology – or pursue a hybrid strategy – and where the value lies in your proposition. You're likely to have some idea of whether you can collect revenue fairly early or will need a lot of capital to sustain a long development process (as, for instance, in a typical biotechnology venture) before you can either sell to customers or sell the company itself, complete with its technology and human resource assets. This is not to say that your plans will materialise as you envision them, that you won't revisit them in the light of new events at a future date and possibly change your strategy, but you at least have a starting point for considering a possible funding scenario.

Figure 31 is a greatly simplified diagram of three types of funding path for a new venture. At an early stage, the kind of external capital to seek will depend on the amount the entrepreneurs already have at their disposal and their market entry route, in particular the point at which the company can generate revenue.

The information in the rest of this chapter further clarifies these pathways.

Cheapest sources of early capital

THREE FS: FOUNDERS, FRIENDS AND FAMILY

Early sources of capital may include the founder's own savings, possibly supplemented by loans or equity investments from sympathetic friends or family members, hence the term the 'three Fs': founders, friends and family (some people also add 'fools'). Some entrepreneurs not only spend their savings but also remortgage their homes or overload their credit cards. Think very carefully about whether those last two routes really are the best or cheapest options in the long run.

SUBSIDY

Beyond the three Fs, an external source of cheap or free capital is public sector subsidy. Subsidies may be granted by local, regional or national development agencies or government departments, or the European Union. They may be offered directly to start-up companies or funnelled through other channels such as universities (for inventors in academia) or research councils, and are usually aimed at supporting specific objectives, such as scientific or medical research, product or technology development, proof of concept or local job creation. Usually subsidies take the form of grants, although these must usually be matched by the

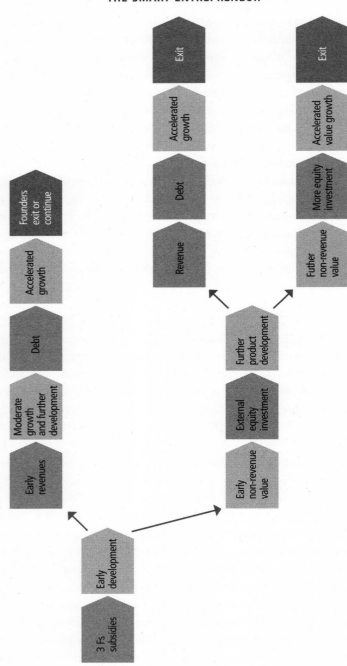

Figure 31 Three possible funding paths for a new venture; financial steps in darker shading

entrepreneur's own investment or some other source of capital. In practice, some ventures seek subsidies later in their lifecycle as a result of this requirement. Some private foundations also offer grants and incubation for entrepreneurial activities. Incubators may offer a combination of money, office and laboratory space, and services such as mentoring or legal and financial advice, though some actually charge fees or provide capital in the form of a loan.

Public sector subsidy programmes for business can change name and availability frequently, in line with changes in public policy. Currently, up-to-date information for the UK is available on the government's Business Link[45] website.

Prizes and awards are a useful source of free, no-strings-attached capital – from design or technology competitions, business plan competitions and so on. Beyond offering cash, awards often provide some publicity and visibility, which, in the case of the more prestigious competitions, may attract the attention of early-stage investors who use such events to scout for entrepreneurs worth keeping an eye on. Prizes may also include useful in-kind services for new companies. Some prizes or competitions are open to individuals or teams before they've registered a company, so provide a useful way to gather feedback on a business idea or product before taking the real plunge. However, avoid becoming so occupied with entering competitions that you put off starting or developing the real business.

BUSINESS CUSTOMERS

Prospective business customers may be a source of capital. If you're developing a product or service offering for businesses, you may find a company with a strong need or keen interest in your offering that would be willing to pay your venture to develop the product, possibly tailored to that specific customer's use. This method of financing a new venture is frequently used by software companies, and anecdotal evidence for its success includes the early beginnings of companies such as Microsoft and TomTom. However, this practice can only be considered a 'cheap' source of capital if you organise the development project in such a way that the single client doesn't absorb all your time and resources or lay claim to all of your intellectual property. You need to orient such projects and agreements to help rather than hinder your aim of developing a product for wide release in a large market. In other words, the client should pay you to make something you were going to develop anyway. You might add a few client-customised features or create a specific application that is a little different to your planned product but doing so shouldn't eat up too much of your resources. On the plus side, the project may help you trial your product's capabilities.

BOOTSTRAPPING

In any new venture, bootstrapping seems to be the most interesting path to commercialisation, as the case of Mobify illustrates. Financing yourself with your own capital, keeping your costs down to make that capital go as far as possible and reinvesting early revenues back into the company allows you to both hold onto control of the business and keep all of the future prize. Not all ventures or entrepreneurs have the scope to get to the prize on their own steam alone, and hence some must resort to external sources of capital.

Business sources of capital

After tapping into available sources of soft capital, you may need to turn to more formal and costly business capital if you need further funds to fuel growth. The two main forms of external capital are debt – in simple terms, taking out loans – and equity – selling ownership shares in your company to parties that typically invest in early-stage ventures. A third source of capital and other useful resources may result from entering into strategic partnerships with other firms. Partnerships can take a variety of forms, and are discussed further on in the chapter.

DEBT

Bank loans. The commonest form of debt is a bank loan, although other sources may include public development agencies or special programmes to help new businesses.

> *The lender's viewpoint.* Most people are familiar with personal bank loans attached to some form of collateral property, such as a mortgage on a house: if the borrower defaults, the bank forecloses on the loan and claims the property. Actually, banks prefer not to have to foreclose and would rather get repaid by the borrower. This preference is even more pronounced when banks lend to businesses:

they may secure a loan against collateral, but that is not their purpose in lending. A bank would rather avoid taking possession of a factory or office equipment because such assets are not its true line of business. A bank lends to a company on the expectation of receiving cash payments in the form of interest on the loan plus recovering the loan principal itself, in order to make a profit. Consequently, banks lend to businesses that are making sales and producing money that can go towards interest and repayments, or those that are seen as very likely to do so in the near future (for instance, if the business already has some customer orders).

The entrepreneur's viewpoint. Debt is far cheaper than equity, so theoretically preferable for the entrepreneur. Due to higher risk, interest rates charged for a loan to a young start-up are always several percentage points higher than the going rates charged to more established businesses, but still low compared to the return demanded by equity investors, who aim to receive around ten times their invested money by claiming a sizable ownership stake in the start-up. However, debt has two potential drawbacks. The first is repayments on most loans need to start soon after the loan is taken out, so interest and capital repayments will begin to siphon off some of the firm's cash. This is why debt makes the most sense if the company is already earning cash revenues and needs the extra finance to fund expansion, which will bring in even more revenue to both repay the debt and increase profit. The second drawback is that it is difficult, if not impossible, for the majority of new ventures to obtain debt at an early stage, as explained below.

Availability and suitability of loans. Some new businesses could be referred to as 'micro-technology ventures' with low start-up costs, such as a software developer selling an iPhone application over the internet. A micro-technology venture can be a good way for an entrepreneur to get started in business as they can sustain low overhead costs (writing the code on their own computer) and make sales fairly quickly. However, more ambitious early-stage start-ups in more capital intensive industries often need considerable funds to set up, pay rent for premises and salaries, buy materials and so on *before* they reach the point of trading with customers and earning revenue. Ventures offering innovative products and services may also take more time to develop and test a finished product, and longer to build up sales in a new market, compared with more conventional businesses.

If a venture manages to fund its pre-launch activities with the founder's funds and/or grants and awards, it may be able to start trading and make sales before running out of money, and will be able to apply for a loan once it can demonstrate some fairly reliable cash flow. In this case, debt is a better option than equity to fund the company's further growth plans.

However, if revenue is unlikely in the near future, loans will be difficult to obtain. Furthermore, raising money via a loan that must start to be paid back with interest the following month doesn't really make sense; a pre-revenue start-up needs to spend its capital on the activities that will lead to the launch of the business, not on repaying loans. A pre-revenue company is more likely to have to raise equity investment first, and then raise debt at a later stage when it's entered the market and begun earning revenue.

Government loan guarantee schemes for new businesses may provide help in obtaining bank loans. The UK government currently provides an Enterprise Finance Guarantee, which guarantees the repayment of 75 per cent of the amount of a loan made by a bank to a qualifying business. Such a facility may allow a start-up a bit more leeway in obtaining and managing debt finance; in the UK's scheme, for example, repayments may be postponed temporarily if the company experiences fluctuations in cash flow.

Suppliers. Suppliers of parts or raw materials may provide short-term (a few months at most) debt by agreeing to take payment a certain period after delivery of merchandise. However, start-ups tend to be offered far less generous terms by suppliers than established businesses as a result of risk: an unproven start-up could fold suddenly and be unable to pay arrears to its suppliers.

Leasing. A final way to obtain debt finance may be by leasing equipment and other fixed assets rather than buying them. As with a loan, leasing repayments and interest must be made monthly, so leasing does not eliminate a company's need for money, but slows down the rate at which it is spent on certain items. Equity investors frequently like their investee companies to lease equipment, so that more of the investors' cash can be dedicated to important value-adding activities, such as product development and marketing.

EQUITY
Because it is difficult for innovative new ventures to obtain debt finance at an early stage, equity remains the commonest source of funding for small businesses with high start-up costs.

The equity investor's viewpoint. Whereas lenders think in terms of monthly repayments, an early-stage equity investor takes a long view and is willing to wait several years before profiting from an investment, but exacts a high price for this wait and for the risk taken. This is not simple opportunism but a matter of hedging one's bets: an investor has money engaged in several ventures at a time and, in spite of careful selection and judgement, it is a statistical certainty that some of those ventures will fail (in the face of stronger competitors, contrary market behaviour, poor management decisions, technology failure and so on). Some other investments will only achieve mediocre performance. Investors thus make their profit on just a few highly successful investments, which compensate for the failures.

The entrepreneur's viewpoint. Understandably, entrepreneurs want to obtain as much finance as needed while giving up no more of their ownership than is absolutely necessary. Consequently, an entrepreneur's goal when planning to seek equity should be to:
   • keep as much value as possible;
   • by reducing risk as far as possible before taking investment.

A venture is much more likely to fail in its earliest stages, which is why investors will demand the highest ownership stake in the venture for their money, expressed as a low 'valuation' (price) for the shares, at this point. The more reliably you can demonstrate your venture's potential for growth and success, the lower the investor risk and the more value you can keep for yourself. Potential is demonstrated by compiling increasingly tangible evidence of feasibility, beyond an idea in your head or a plan on paper. Reaching objectives of this sort costs time and money. An investor may be attracted enough to invest 'seed' money to help you take early steps toward proof of concept, but will exact a high price for this high-risk investment.

Your aim as a founder (or group of founders) should therefore be to fund the earliest, riskiest development with the cheapest sources of capital you can find, and to take the venture as far as possible in this way before you seek equity investment. If you cannot reduce risk, your remaining option will be to cede a great deal of value to external investors at a very early stage in the process. This could nonetheless lead to a lucrative result for the entrepreneur if the company becomes hugely successful. However, because of the provisions that investors typically write into investment agreements to guarantee that, in the event of a sale or liquidation, they'll get their capital back before any remaining proceeds are distributed to founders and other shareholders, equity raised at a high cost may leave the entrepreneur with only a modest return or even a loss if the company is not a runaway success, resulting in a mediocre price for the company at best, or a fire sale of the office furniture at worst.

One of the arguments *for* raising early equity is that, if you have a truly attractive business proposition that can be rolled out quickly (without years of technological development) but you can't scrape together enough cheap cash and a high risk of competitors crowding you out of the market exists, an investor may help you get to market more quickly.

Taking the above into consideration, you should aim to think of your entrepreneurial journey in such a way that you foresee several stages of development, each of which achieves some tangible proof of the venture's ability to develop further and move a few steps closer to becoming a profitable growth business. The section below on milestone funding looks at this approach in more detail (see page 209).

Angel investors. As mentioned at the beginning of this chapter, much is made of venture capital as a source of funding for start-ups. However, 'angel investment' is increasingly seen as a first port of call for many early-stage ventures because many venture capital firms have retrenched in the past decade and now fund ventures at a later stage and with a lower level of risk. Furthermore, whereas venture capital funds seek investment opportunities requiring at least £1 million of investment (for reasons explained further on), angel investors may invest as little as £10,000 or as much as several hundred thousand in a new venture, depending on the company's capital needs and the angels' perception of the opportunity. Thus, angels are increasingly called upon to fill the equity gap between the funds that an entrepreneur can supply for himself and the larger amounts that could be provided at a later stage by a VC fund.

An angel investor is a high-net-worth individual who invests a portion of his personal wealth in a new venture. Most angels are experienced entrepreneurs who've cashed out of their own companies; though some aren't entrepreneurs but business people or professionals with significant experience of a particular industry. In addition to filling a funding gap, they frequently also fill a knowledge gap, providing valuable mentoring (and contacts) to the more junior entrepreneurs they back. While their primary reason for investing in a venture is to make a financial return, most of them also enjoy taking an active role in the development of the venture through frequent contact and communication, a role as chairperson or director on the board, or sometimes even an executive management position in the company. In part, this close involvement ensures that they can keep tabs on their investment, but it also affords them the fun of the entrepreneurial rollercoaster at one remove – in other words, without the long nights and sweat of earlier days spent building their own companies.

When a venture needs a large amount of money but is not yet ready for venture capital, several angels may invest together in a syndicate, each providing a portion of the total investment. In Europe, angel syndicates are known to invest as much as £1.5 million in a venture.

Angel investors are an appropriate source of capital when a venture:
• needs relatively moderate sums (less than £1 million) to help reach the point of launching on the market and making sales, if the founders cannot amass enough funds from cheaper sources. From then on, the company can begin to finance itself with a combination of revenues and debt.

• needs early funds to reach the point where larger sums can be raised from VCs. The backing of an experienced angel investor with a good track record also signals credibility to VCs who may consider investing at a later stage.

How to find and engage with an angel investor. Because they operate as individuals, angel investors are known to keep a lower public profile than VC firms, and tend to invest in businesses that are close to where they live so they can follow them closely. As a result, you may work hard to come across an angel but it also means that a few are probably located in your area, even if you're not based in a major entrepreneurial finance centre such as London, New York or Menlo Park in California.

Angel investment networks provide a useful forum for entrepreneurs and angels to meet more easily. These organisations, public or private, put on events and disseminate information to facilitate the matching of angel investors with investment opportunities. Some are set up under the aegis of a university alumni network and draw members from that specific pool of graduates; others are themed more simply by location.

An entrepreneur may submit an investment proposal to an angel network and, if it passes an initial screening, receive an opportunity to pitch the business idea directly to members of the network. Many angel networks now also offer consulting and coaching to selected entrepreneurs to help improve their proposals and pitches. The British Business Angels Association in the UK and the European Business Angel Network in the rest of Europe act as umbrella organisations, publishing directories of local angel networks within their catchment areas. Quite a few angels, however, don't belong to these networks or attend such events. You can also be introduced to angels by your own business contacts (even your lawyer or accountant may know one or two) or meet them at events held by local entrepreneurship networks.

Although they frequently mentor entrepreneurs, don't assume that an angel offers to fund and nurture every interesting new venture he encounters. A typical angel makes one or two investments in a three-year time span (although some invest a bit more frequently), and consequently takes very selective decisions. However, an angel might invite you to keep him informed about new developments in your venture, even if he doesn't back your business straightaway, and he may offer feedback and advice on your business proposal.

Angels typically look for:

- A capable founding team, with a good track record, skills and experience that fit the venture's needs. Although angels will sometimes back ventures started by novice entrepreneurs, they will still want to see some kind of industry experience or particular skill that suits the business proposition, in addition to passion and drive.
- A competitive and 'scalable' business proposition, capable of capturing a sizable market and achieving steep growth in value. Angels may invest fairly small amounts of money, but will still aim for a sizable return (of roughly seven to ten times their investment), so aren't interested in 'cottage industries'.
- An initial financial commitment from the venture's founders, signalling their genuine dedication to bringing their business idea to fruition. Angels want to see evidence that an entrepreneur won't quit mid-stream, and is willing to work all hours if that's what it takes to achieve the venture's goal.
- A business that can draw on the investor's own industry knowledge, experience and contacts. This allows the angel to both better assess the business opportunity and bring the added value needed to help the business succeed.
- Personal compatibility with the founders. In addition to hard business criteria, an angel investor will seek entrepreneurs with whom he thinks he can collaborate effectively.

An angel's investment horizon is typically three to five years for an individual venture. It could stretch further, but nonetheless you should factor in an opportunity for the angel to exit (sell) his investment to other investors for a good return in an acceptable timeframe in your company's growth plan and financing strategy.

Angel financing is often referred to as 'informal' venture investment. This is not to say that angels overlook formalities such as binding written agreements with the entrepreneurs they back, but the degree of formality and exactitude can vary a good deal from one angel to another, unlike venture capital investment that is subject to a broadly standardised, highly formal process.

Venture capital funds. Whereas angel investors operate individually or in syndicates of individuals, venture capitalists (or VCs) operate in small firms that manage pooled investment funds. In other words, a venture capital firm is an independent partnership that sets up one or more specialist funds drawn from investors (mostly large companies and financial institutions) to invest in entrepreneurial or technology ventures with high growth potential. Funds are constituted as limited liability partnerships, whose managers are referred to as general partners (GPs) and institutional investors as limited partners (LPs).

A VC fund has a fixed lifespan, typically of ten years, by the end of which all the investments must have been sold and cash proceeds returned to the fund's LPs. The GPs earn regular income by charging a fixed fee to manage the fund, (generally 2.5 per cent per year of the fund's life, used to pay for premises, salaries and administrative costs), but aim to realise a high return at the end of the fund's life by taking a 'carry interest' (usually pegged at 20 per cent) of the investment profits before distributing the rest to the LPs.

A venture capital fund generally expects to invest in each company it selects for five to seven years, although the period may be longer if extending it appears to promise a better return. A fund generally spends the first half of its life selecting and making investments, and the second half gradually divesting them.

Because the size of a fund can range from $20 million to $200 million (often expressed in dollars, reflecting the VC industry's US origins), a VC fund invests in a limited number of ventures (perhaps 20 to 25), each requiring substantial financing. Beyond such a limit, the fund's investment portfolio becomes too unwieldy to manage effectively with the level of active monitoring and involvement normally required. Thus, a fund will typically not consider investing in a venture that requires less than, say, $1 million (often the limit is even higher, at $1.5 or $2 million). The only exceptions to this rule may be public venture funds, sometimes called 'micro-funds', which are mentioned further on.

An important distinction to keep in mind is that, while angels are accountable only to themselves as individuals, VCs are accountable to their own investors, the LPs. These institutions, such as banks or pension funds, allocate a portion of their funds to high-risk venture capital investment and typically seek a return of two-and-a-half to three times the capital invested (excluding the management fee) once the fund sells its investments and cashes out. Thus, a GP in a VC firm – the person who'll probably take a seat on your board if you secure an investment from his fund – is under pressure not only to create a lucrative return for his firm through the 'carry' but also to generate enough proceeds to achieve the return demanded by the LPs. Underperformance will make it harder for the VC firm to raise its next fund. Just as your venture will compete with numerous other start-ups to secure investment, when a VC firm raises a fund it competes against its own peers to secure LPs.

Thanks to the uncertainties inherent in start-ups and new technologies, VCs expect as a rule of thumb that roughly one-third of the companies they invest in will fail and be booked as investment losses, another third will return little more than the initial capital invested and the final third, it is hoped, will generate spectacular returns to make up for the others and deliver the fund's profit. Some funds do better, and some do worse. However, when a fund first invests in an early-stage company, it is too early to know which third the investment will fall into. So if a VC drives a hard bargain, it's not just down to opportunism but also to the odds he's betting on.

VCs are often looked upon as a necessary evil by entrepreneurs but, by looking at the economics of a fund, you may understand the mechanism behind their apparently grandiose demands. In a simple example, if a fund amounts to $100 million and 2.5 per cent of this per year is set aside for management fees, $75 million is left for investment. Assume that one-third of investments fail, leading to a loss of $25 million and one third break-even, returning just $25 million. The remaining $25 million must generate proceeds of around $225 million, a return nine times the capital invested, to satisfy the LPs. That is the case because, if you add the $225 million to the $25 million breakeven to make $250 million, then subtract a 20 per cent carry interest of $50 million for the GPs, the LPs are left with $200 million, which is 2.66 times the capital invested, thus towards the bottom of the range LPs expect as a return. Consequently, to beat the odds, VCs look for investments that present a possibility of returning even more than ten times the capital invested because, on average, two-thirds of these will probably run aground.

It is also because of these difficult odds that an entrepreneur should not be fooled by an apparently friendly venture capital investor who is only looking for, say, a potential 5x return on an investment; that investor runs a high risk of going bust, leaving the investee companies stranded.

Public venture funds. Public venture funds, set up with government money, are formally mandated to apply the same commercial criteria as private funds to select investments, with the aim of realising a profitable return. However, they also have a social mission to stimulate business activity, innovation and economic development within their assigned territory. Consequently, they're usually permitted to take higher risks on early-stage technologies and ventures than most private sector VC firms, and are often willing to hold an investment for longer to accommodate the development time needed.

Public funds may provide early seed funding, but they're usually small in size (below $50 million), so as a rule co-invest alongside business angels or early-stage venture capital firms, thus encouraging private sector investment by sharing risk. A body of research[46] has indicated, however, that such public micro-funds often err on the side of spreading money too thinly across too many ventures, in a political effort to help as many entrepreneurs as possible. Consequently, ventures risk being too undercapitalised to achieve the near-term goals that would trigger further private finance. If you want to apply for finance from public venture funds, try to get a capable angel investor behind you to help you find a way through any potential financing gaps.

How to find and engage with a venture capital firm. Venture capital firms are fairly easy to find on the internet, and also through trade associations such as the British Private Equity and Venture Capital

Association (BVCA) or its counterparts in other countries.[47] VC firms tend to be physically located near financial or technology centres, with London boasting the highest concentration of VC capital in Europe. However, venture capitalists are more prepared than angels to invest further away from their home base, and to travel in order to scout and monitor investments.

Some VC funds specialise in a particular industry, such as biotechnology, engineering, ICT or media, so you must do your research. Don't waste effort approaching funds that have no interest in your sector. Experience is an even more important factor than interest: it is preferable to take investment from firms that have already made investments in your sector, and who understand how the sector works and how it is evolving, so that an entente over business strategy is more easily achieved, as the Siruna case study suggests.

Venture capital firms typically seek ventures with:

- A management team with considerable experience in the relevant industry. Venture capitalists don't invest in novice founder-entrepreneurs unless they have some experienced managers or angel investors on their team.
- A highly scalable and competitive business proposition, with perceived potential of returning 10–20 times the initial investment. This potential is signalled by such factors as strong intellectual property rights or possibly other solid forms of protection from imitation; a product that can command a price that will create gross margins (the profit left after the cost of production, expressed as a percentage of the sales price) of 70 per cent or more (hence the importance of value pricing, as described in Chapter 9); a business that could capture a sizable market, encountering little competition, make abundant sales and later expand into additional markets and/or follow-on products; the entrepreneurs' ambition to build a high-growth company, not a lifestyle company; some proof that the innovation or product works.
- The possibility of several alternative business models and routes to market. New ventures are subject to many uncertainties, and a turn of events could make a strategy

unfeasible. Entrepreneurs should be able to point to possible alternatives – such as addressing a different target market, developing a different application or taking a different position in the value chain – which may either replace an initial plan if setbacks arise or offer areas for future business expansion if the initial plan succeeds.

- An exit strategy. The existence of possible future buyers of the business, such as a large company with a likely interest in the relevant technology or market or the possibility of a stock market IPO, so that the VC can cash out and make a return on the investment.

Because of the strict financial and accountability requirements binding a VC fund, the venture capital funding process is more formal than its angel counterpart, with complex deal structures expressed in longer and more detailed 'term sheets' and shareholder agreements, a painstaking due diligence process and stringent requirements placed on entrepreneurs ('warranties'), all of which contribute to VCs' sometimes undeserved reputation for being arrogant and unreasonable.

If you think your venture needs the kind of sums typically invested by VCs, you need to determine how to reach a point where you have tangible proof of your venture's likeliness to fit the above criteria. Structure your business case to envision a development path that will meet specific targets to signal the venture's viability – such as concrete progress in the development of a working product through prototyping, successful technical trials, positive market testing, reputable partnerships or early customers, and the support of early-stage investors such as angels.

The equity funding journey. Equity investors, whether angels or VCs, typically see the venture development and funding process as divided into four stages, commonly referred to as:

- *Seed* – when a venture needs funds to develop and test a product, service or technology.
- *Early-stage or start-up* – when a venture has completed research and development, but needs finance and capacity to go to market and sell its offering.

- *Growth/expansion* – when a venture that has survived an initial period on the market now seeks finance to ramp up sales and expand into new or larger markets, or to grow substantially in headcount and technical capacity (if operating in the market for technology).
- *Mature/sustained growth* – when the now established small- to medium-sized enterprise makes stable, incremental increases in revenue, profit and size.

Investors in entrepreneurial ventures are usually specialised in financing one or more of the first three stages. They hope to sell or 'exit' their investment at a high point in the growth/expansion phase, usually through a trade sale or IPO, in order to realise a high financial return with respect to the period of time during which their money was invested (for example, an average compound return of 35–40 per cent annually for angels and 50–60 per cent for VCs).

Today, few VC funds are willing to invest in the seed stage of a venture, largely because of the risk and uncertainty involved (many VCs got sorely burned in the overly speculative dotcom bubble of the late 1990s), and in part because the investment amounts sought for early development tend to be smaller than a VC fund's floor limit. This phase is thus often financed by angel investors, incubators and other early sources. VCs usually back a venture that requires a large amount of capital, which may occur in the start-up or expansion phase.

Milestone funding. Experienced investors will never offer to invest in one lump sum all the funds that a venture will need to reach breakeven. An investment deal is typically divided into stages known as funding rounds, which are typically scheduled at intervals of 12 to 18 months. This arrangement keeps the entrepreneur focused on achieving set goals (milestones) as a condition for obtaining the next round of funding, and also allows the investors to back out from providing further funding if the venture runs into problems that seem to hail a bad end.

Evidence of a venture's likelihood to succeed comes from achieving concrete value-creating steps in the venture journey, such as (but not limited to):

- Creation of functioning prototypes
- Successful clinical or product trials and market tests
- Registration of strong intellectual property rights
- Partnerships with reputable firms or technical institutes
- Attainment of required licences or accreditation from government regulators
- Early sales or large customer orders

Consequently, depending on the type of venture and the strategy foreseen, an investor will structure a funding deal so that, at each round, the venture must achieve a set of objectives that move it closer to the probability of successful growth, thereby also increasing the expected value of the company and the likelihood of an attractive return on investment.

Novice entrepreneurs may understandably prefer the prospect of receiving all the investment in one lump sum and not having to await their investors' verdict every 18 months. While milestone funding may at first seem to work primarily in the interests of the investor, it is actually also useful to a venture's founders because, if all goes well, it makes for a lower rate of dilution of the founders' ownership stake, as explained in the next section.

Valuation controversy. Valuation – the monetary value attributed to a company – is a frequent point of contention between entrepreneurs and investors when trying to agree a deal.

Entrepreneurs want a high valuation: the higher the company's value, the fewer shares the investor will receive for the money she injects into the company; thus the founders keep a large ownership stake in the business in reward for their great idea and hard work, while also maintaining a higher degree of independence.

For their part, an investor wants a low valuation so she can buy more shares and take a sizable stake in the business to compensate for the high risk. If she has a larger stake, she also exerts greater influence as a shareholder over how the company is run, and thus has a better chance (she believes) of safeguarding her investment.

Ultimately, the valuation of an asset is down to what the buyer (investor) is willing to pay, which is usually based on accumulated past experience. Experienced investors can draw on past successes and failures, as well as examples of comparable companies in a similar line of business, and make fairly reliable estimates of a company's likely exit value in five to seven years if it achieves its value-creating milestones, and consequently what its going rate is likely to be today and in the intervening funding rounds. Keeping in mind that they hope for at least a 10x return on their investment at exit, they work backwards to calculate the ownership stake they'll demand for their £1 million investment today. (Chapter 12 has more on valuation and discounting.)

A novice entrepreneur will instinctively lean toward the investor (if she's lucky enough to have more than one) who offers the highest starting valuation for the lowest ownership stake. In truth, she should also consider later funding rounds when thinking about valuation. As the company moves into successive rounds of funding, new shares will be issued to the investors putting in new cash, increasing the total number of shares, while the founders will retain the same nominal number of shares as before. The founders' shares will thus account for a smaller slice of the pie, a process known as *ownership dilution*. At each round of funding, new shareholders may come in to dilute the ownership even more. If a company needs a lot of equity capital, the founders will inevitably end up with a minority share during the course of several funding rounds.

Figure 32 provides an example of funding rounds and dilution, based on the following information:
Round 1: £2m invested at £5m post-money[48] valuation at start of year 1
Round 2: £5m at £20m post-money at start of year 3
Round 3: £5m at £45m post-money at start of year 4

If the company makes good progress on its business goals and milestones, the perceived value of the company and its share price should increase at each funding round, making for milder dilution. If a founder were to receive all the money needed in a single round at the outset, when risk is highest, she would receive it at the lowest possible valuation and consequently have a lower stake than if she waits for the increase in valuation at each milestone.

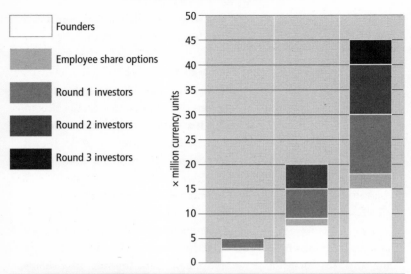

Shareholdings	Round 1	Round 2	Round 3
Founders	2.5	7.5	15
Employee share options	0.5	1.5	3
Round 1 investors	2	6	12
Round 2 investors		5	10
Round 3 investors			5
Total post-money valuation	**5**	**20**	**45**

Figure 32 **Example of funding rounds and shareholder dilution**

However, before you get too excited about milestone revaluations, remember that investors – especially VCs – will structure deals to limit their risk of losing money. They will also throw in clauses to allow lower valuations and other preventive measures ('ratchets', liquidation preferences and other technical devices to be found in term sheets or shareholders' statements) to limit the dilution of their shares if the company should not achieve its milestones.

Furthermore, the higher the stake demanded by an entrepreneur, the more challenging the milestones demanded by an investor will be. Ultimately, accepting a 30 per cent equity stake with achievable milestones and a good exit prospect will probably lead to a better result than taking a 40–50 per cent stake with very difficult milestones that could bring you up short in a future funding round.

STRATEGIC PARTNERSHIPS

Partnerships may offer another source of capital, as well as other potential benefits. Because strategic partnerships can take various forms, this topic does not fit neatly into Figure 31 but it may sit alongside other sources of capital or resources.

Defined broadly, a strategic partner could be another firm or organisation – large or small – that sees some benefit in collaborating with your venture, perhaps because of a similar interest in a technology or market.

The partner's viewpoint. Academic research and common wisdom concur that small firms are generally better at producing innovative ideas and products than large companies or institutions. Small firms are nimble and informal; their small, multi-skilled teams discuss problems and opportunities on a daily basis and adopt new solutions rapidly. Large organisations are set up to preserve the continuity of their existing business structure without disruption, through set procedures, structured reporting lines, established product families and business units, and long decision-making processes. The difference in the speed of their response to change resembles that between turning a large ocean liner or a small dinghy.

So, in a fast-changing world, large established firms seek partnerships with small firms that can give them access to new ideas, technologies and business opportunities of possible benefit. But small firms may also seek partnerships with other small firms, for mutual benefit.

Some large companies have dedicated 'corporate venturing' units, subsidiaries or divisions structured in a similar way to VC funds, with the fund's money provided by the parent company. Examples include energy group BP's AE Ventures in the UK, which invests in alternative energy technologies, and Germany's Robert Bosch Venture Capital, a division of the Bosch industrial group.

When considering a strategic partnership or innovation project, large companies like to deal with start-ups that have registered IP rights. Registered rights clearly define what is owned by whom at the start of the partnership, making it easier to draw up agreements with respect to further intellectual property that might be produced during the collaboration and avoid disputes at a later date.

The entrepreneur's viewpoint. A partnership with a prestigious company or research organisation can give a big boost to a start-up's legitimacy and credibility in the eyes of investors, customers and other potential partners. Corporate partners also tend to demand less ownership for their money than VCs, because their goals aren't purely financial, and may provide access to powerful distribution channels for the start-up.

At the same time, an entrepreneur should carefully analyse the other party's priorities and purpose in pursuing a partnership, and determine whether these are sufficiently aligned with the entrepreneur's own interests. For instance, a large firm may expect a partnership to boost sales of its own products, perhaps with some kind of exclusive agreement or a pledge to use the large firm's components and not deal with competitors. Such an arrangement may not always be advantageous for the start-up.

Types of partnership. A partnership between a start-up and another organisation may take a number of forms, including:

- Co-operation on R&D with the larger partner contributing both money and other resources (knowledge, people, premises and equipment). In these cases, the partner may be interested in a share of resulting intellectual property rights.
- Projects to co-develop a product (again, contributing cash and other resources, perhaps manufacturing expertise). This is especially likely if the partner is interested in using the product itself. Lead users (see Chapter 9 on market testing) may become strategic partners.
- Joint ventures (a third company part-owned by each partner). These may give the partner access to a novel technology or product, and the entrepreneur access to the partner's marketing and distribution networks.
- Buying shares in the start-up, either directly or through a corporate venturing unit. Corporate shareholders may cut simpler investment deals with an entrepreneur than a VC fund,

as they can tolerate lower financial returns and are often more interested in new technology, skills and markets (hence the term *strategic* partners) than in strictly financial outcomes. Venture capitalists often like to bring a minority strategic partner into a start-up's investor pool because corporate investors tend to demand softer terms than other financial investors. However, a corporate investor may restrict your exit possibilities – your corporate shareholder may be interested in buying your company at a future date if all goes well, but might also block it being sold to a competitor, even one that might offer a higher price.

A partnership agreement should be negotiated carefully so as not to prevent your venture from taking advantage of important growth opportunities outside the partnership. If a partnership offer is too restrictive, it may be best declined.

In summary...

Venture capital is the form of finance most popularly linked to entrepreneurial ventures, but should only be resorted to after cheaper sources of capital have been exhausted or are unavailable.

Even if you raise equity investment initially, debt will become a cheaper source of growth capital once you're able to achieve sales. Resorting to debt once possible, rather than raising further equity, also creates a greater return on the existing shareholders' money by avoiding further dilution of ownership.

Always picture your venture developing in a series of sensible stages that signpost your viability and can be matched to funding rounds. You'll probably have to change the plan over the months as circumstances change and you learn more about your environmental conditions, but the practice of thinking in this manner will allow you to engage on a common ground with your investors. Even more importantly, think of the actions that will add tangible value to your company by diminishing uncertainty in the eyes of an investor, and try to achieve as many of those steps as you are able to with cheaper means before raising equity from professional investors.

12. INTRODUCING THE VENTURE ROADMAP AND BASIC FINANCIALS

What?

Chapter 11 covers sources of capital and explains that investors divide venture funding into stages or 'funding rounds'. Entrepreneurs should also think of the development of a venture in terms of stages that group together a set of goals to increase the venture's perceived value. In other words, each stage of development should achieve a set of *milestones* that demonstrate an increased possibility of the venture succeeding.

Broadly, a roadmap is a description of these stages. It shows the different actions your venture must undertake on the journey to becoming operational and subsequently profitable or sellable, and the estimated and interrelated timing of these actions. We categorise these actions broadly into the areas of:

- *Product development and technology roadmaps* – which outline the development of the core asset you will sell.
- *Operational roadmaps* – which outline how you'll assemble the other assets required to put your offering on the market, and may include recruitment and hiring, securing premises and facilities, marketing and sales activities, maintenance and after-sales activities and administration.
- *Financial roadmaps* – which outline what you'll spend, how you'll pay for it and when you should break-even and move into positive cash flow and profit.

A milestone is a point on the journey that marks the completion of an important action or project, such as building a prototype, testing it, launching a product on the market, acquiring the first reference customers and so on.

In addition to estimating the time required to complete individual activities and projects, the timing of different activities in relation to one another is important. A roadmap should show how operational, technical and financial events or milestones will realistically interlink, so that hopefully one activity – such as technology development or hiring staff – will not be delayed because of unforeseen slowness of another activity, such as raising investment. A combination of activities or milestones that must be completed by a certain time could be called a stage or stepping stone.

Your venture roadmap is never static; it will change over time in response to internal and external events, such as changes in the market or technological developments, the rise and fall of competitors, the economic and financial climate, and anything else that might impinge on your business. Entrepreneurs are often overly optimistic about the timing of their venture's development, so roadmaps need to be readjusted at some point to reflect slower results than initially expected. Investors are said to typically look at an entrepreneur's development plan and assume that the time and money required will be double the amounts claimed in the plan.

Since a roadmap also includes financial events, this chapter outlines some basic financial concepts that affect a financial plan and of which an entrepreneur should have some understanding. However, for the detailed writing of a financial plan, if you're not experienced in this area, we recommend adding a finance expert to your venture's founding team or management, or at the very least appointing an accountant if you don't yet have the wherewithal to recruit a finance director. A number of service businesses exist in the UK that can provide part-time finance directors on a flexible or interim basis for small- and medium-sized enterprises.

Why?

A full, detailed roadmap is usually created at quite an advanced stage in the planning of a new venture, so may be outside the scope of this book about preparing an early business case. However, we think it is worth familiarising yourself with this topic at a basic level early on, while you think about the shape of your business, your market entry strategy and your likely sources of capital.

Understanding how the different elements of your business must coincide also allows you to more easily adjust your plans if new circumstances arise that are out of your control. A change in one area, such as a supplier problem or a longer-than-planned design process, will have a knock-on effect on other activities, such as production and marketing.

A roadmap can also be a diagnostic aid when you encounter a serious problem – you may be able to look back over your journey and determine how and where the problem originated, and how to adjust plans to address it.

How?

Of all the topics in this book, this one carries the largest disclaimer, because new ventures, technologies and markets are highly unpredictable. You should think of a roadmap as a living document, which can help you navigate the waters and adjust to changing conditions, rather than a firm prediction of future events.

Product development and technology

Your product and technology roadmaps may vary, depending on whether you intend to go into the market for products or to sell a technology outright, or both. In the first case, your roadmap may show how you will develop the product to meet the requirements of the target buyers of the technology. This may include trialling and adjusting the technology.

If your aim is to design a product or service using established technologies, your roadmap will describe the phases of product design and development including the incorporation of any technologies.

If your aim is to develop a product or service from your own technology, your roadmap will look at the process of enhancing the technology, adjusting it to specific applications and finally creating the product or service. It may be that your business also utilises technologies other than your own, so your roadmap should outline when and how these will be incorporated into your offering.

Figure 33 shows several possible product development paths for Siruna, the company described in Chapter 11. This roadmap provides a basic outline of the alternatives, and the lighter shaded boxes show the route ultimately taken by the company, based on its assessment of its industry environment and target markets.

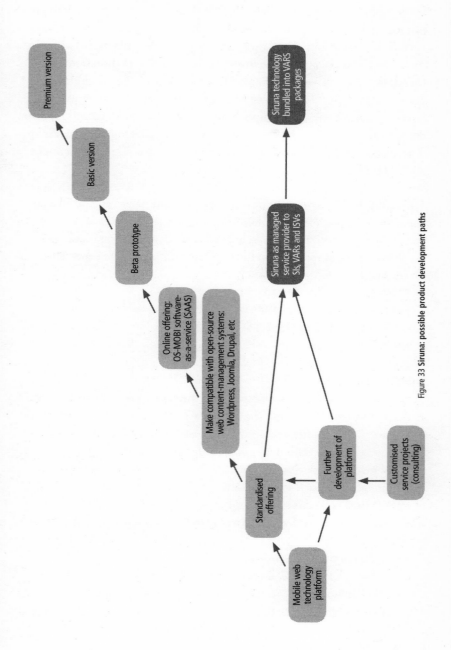

Figure 33 Siruna: possible product development paths

This product roadmap will be further elaborated for the development of more detailed features, such as those shown in Figure 34. A company such as Siruna, which has a proprietary technology platform, will also have a technology roadmap delineating possible future directions of the technology, as shown in Figure 35. In this case, the functionalities required for the OSMOBI service are confined to the lower left-hand quadrant of the graph, but possible future technological capabilities are shown in the other quadrants. A technology roadmap may also include plans for attracting funds for technology development, such as R&D grants.

For each possible development route, you should determine or estimate the answers to the following questions:
- What steps need to be taken to reach each development objective?
- How long will each step in the development process be expected to take?
- What testing activities are required?
- Which skills and how many people are needed to reach the objective within the expected time?
- What will the costs be?

Operational roadmap

An operational roadmap will depend on the type of business you intend to build, and may answer questions such as:
- When will you start operating? What sort of basic operations will you start with (technology/product design) and when will you add further functions such as marketing, sales, technical and after-sales support, administration and finance?
- When will you start to make sales?
- What functions will you perform in-house and what will you outsource?
- In terms of human resources:
  - When will you hire, for which areas of activity?
  - At what points in time will you need to increase the headcount?
  - How much will you pay people?
- What kinds of facilities, infrastructure and equipment will you use and when will you need them?

Feature	OSMOBI FREE	OSMOBI PREMIUM	OSMOBI PARTNER
Instant mobilisation Drupal sites on 99% of all devices	●	●	●
Instant mobilisation Joomla sites on 99% of all devices	●	●	●
CSS and content editing	●	●	●
Edit your mobile sites freely	●	●	●
Google analytics measurement	●	●	●
AdMOB mobile advertising platform		●	●
Different mobile themes		●	●
Native iPhone look and feel		●	●
iPhone webclip icon		●	●
Access and training SDK			●
Integration of OSMOBI in your technology			●
On-premise hosting of OSMOBI			●
Professional Services for complex mobilizations			●
Supported bandwidth	150 pageviews or 100 MB per day	up to 500 MB per day	customized
Mobile URL	www.yourURL.com	Any URL	Any URL
Service agreement	no SLA	SLA	customized SLA
Support	Forum support	E-mail support	Account management
Pricing	free	$45 or €30 / month	customized
Payment options	N/A	monthly by PayPal	customized

Figure 34 Siruna's OSMOBI service: detailed listing of product versions and features

THE SMART ENTREPRENEUR

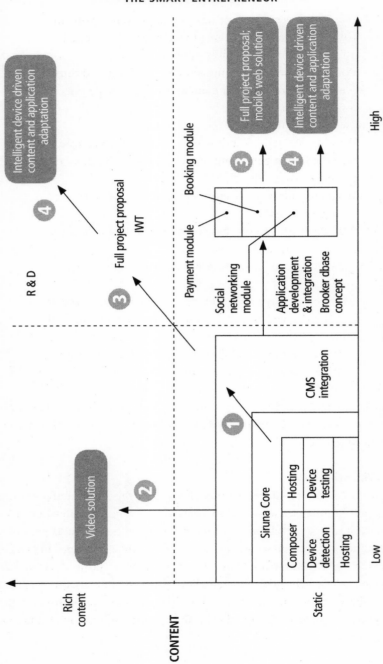

Figure 35 Siruna: technology roadmap (© Johan Thys)

- Facilities may evolve over time, perhaps even starting in your home and then moving to an incubator, serviced office, own company offices or building.
- Will production and manufacturing be performed through outsourcing, or will your company build or acquire its own facilities?
• For sales and marketing:
    - What marketing methods will you use? Will you create your own marketing operations and channels, or use those of a partner in your value chain?
    - What are your revenue targets for different periods, in monetary terms?
    - Reaching your revenue targets will depend on your sales process, for instance:
        - The number of customers and sales needed to achieve targets
        - The complexity of the sales process for a certain type of customer (see Chapter 7), and the consequent length of time and amount of effort required to make a sale
        - The number of sales calls needed to acquire a customer and likely success rates or conversion rates

Finally, as with the technology/product roadmap, you'll need to determine what all these operational activities will cost in order to inform your financial roadmap.

A BASIC ROADMAP

Figure 36 is an early-stage roadmap devised for the creation of a venture that will commercialise a novel software application for professional use. The technology is to be used in its initial unrefined form as part of a consulting service (top segment – 'operations'), while developed in parallel into a more refined version to be offered as a stand-alone product (middle segment – 'research and product development'). In addition, this roadmap also shows sales and marketing activities and, at the bottom of the diagram, the sources of capital expected to fund the venture at different stages in time.

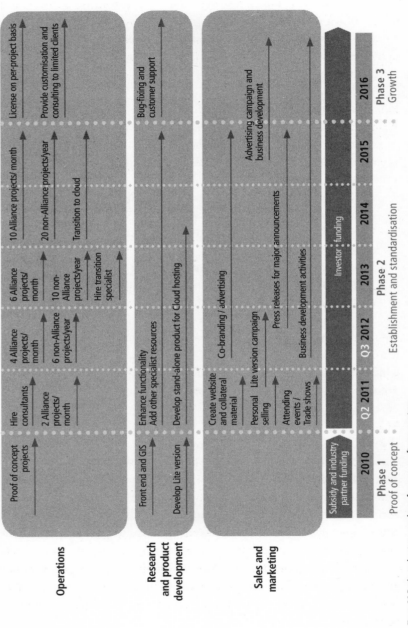

Figure 36 Basic early-stage roadmap for a new software venture

This plan will require more information and details to be added and corrections to be made over time as the venture evolves and additional needs are identified, but it demonstrates an initial endeavour to sketch out the shape of the venture and synchronise its various activities into logical stages, and may begin to form the basis of a milestone agreement.

Financial roadmap

A financial roadmap must ultimately answer several basic questions:

- How much will you need to spend on the activities listed on the operational roadmap described above (also known as 'cash burn')?
- How much of the money needed may be raised through activities that generate revenue, and from which point in time?
- How much money must be raised externally, from which sources of capital, and when?
- At what estimated point can the company's income from operations cover its spending (breakeven, followed by profitability and positive net cash flow)?

Figure 37 shows an early roadmap for a service business, which begins to factor in financial needs and set achievement targets ('customers', 'goals') which would demonstrate the increasing value of the business to a potential investor or partner (as recommended in Chapter 10).

BASIC FINANCIAL CONCEPTS FOR THE UNINITIATED

If you aren't well-versed in finance, you need to initially recruit someone with accounting and financial skills to prepare and manage a comprehensive financial plan. Later, you'll need to appoint an actual financial director. However, you shouldn't delegate financial matters entirely to others: investors like a founder or CEO to have a decent grasp of the company's financial situation and outlook, and the ability to present and discuss it.

While we recommend using a more in-depth book[49] to gain a proper grounding in financial matters, here we outline some basic financial concepts and describe their important effects on a company's financial position and development.

	2010	2011	2013	2014
Financials	Burn $520k	Revenue $650k Burn $290k	Revenue $1700k Burn $230k	Revenue $3454k Burn $230k
Operational	Team development Secure product partners	Mobilise sales team Staff recruitment	Fully national operation Secure new partners	Recruit expertise in other segments
Customers		300,000 people	600,000 (cumulative)	1,200,000 (cumulative)
Goal	Technology developed Seed funding raised	Sign up distribution partners Launch	Increase market coverage and product options Register repeat sales	Profitability Other market segments International roll-out

Figure 37 **An early roadmap including some financial estimates**

Different types of cost and their relation to profit. Costs are either *fixed*, which means that they remain the same no matter how much business your company is doing, or *variable*, which means that they'll vary according to the level of business activity.

Examples of fixed costs include monthly or periodic payments such as salaries, rent for premises, telephone line rental, internet access, loan interest payments and capital repayments, which essentially remain unchanged no matter how many product or service units you're selling. Fixed costs are often referred to as 'overhead' costs.

Variable costs fluctuate in relation to your level of business activity and sales. These could include fluctuations in administrative expenses such as telephone bills and also, more importantly, variations in costs directly related to making products. The latter are called *direct variable costs*, and may include the quantity of raw materials or purchased components needed to make each unit of product, the commissions or 'cut' on sales paid to distributors or retail partners, patent licensing fees paid to external owners of technologies that are incorporated in your product, or hourly wages that vary in line with the amount of work or production required.

Figures in £000s

	Column 1	Column 2	Column 3
Revenue from sales	100	100	150
Direct variable costs: 50% of sales	–50	–50	–75
Gross profit	50	50	75
Fixed costs	–50	–25	–25
Profit after fixed costs	0	25	50

Figure 38 **Profit after direct variable and fixed costs**

These distinctions between types of cost are important because fixed costs may have a strong impact on a company's overall profit, depending on its revenue levels.

Direct variable costs rise and fall in relation to the number of sales made, so they only affect gross profit, which can be expressed as the sale price of a product minus the cost of manufacture. For example, if a product is priced at £100 and costs £50 to make, the gross profit is £50 and the gross margin is 50 per cent of the sale price. This proportion never changes (unless you find and adopt cheaper ways to make the product).

Fixed costs, on the other hand, don't fluctuate. If revenues are low, fixed costs will eat up a larger proportion of whatever is left after variable costs are deducted, and thus will have a large impact on profits. As revenues rise, fixed costs will have a lower impact on profit.

For example, as shown in Figure 38, if a company's sales over the course of a year amount to £100,000 and direct variable costs equal 50 per cent of the sale price of a product, the gross profit will be £50,000. On top of that, if fixed costs amount to £50,000, the company will earn nil profit at the end of the day (column 1). If, however, fixed costs are only £25,000, the company will have £25,000 profit left (column 2). If, furthermore, sales go up to £150,000 and fixed costs stay low at £25,000, the company will have £50,000 profit after variable and fixed costs (column 3).

For this reason, most start-ups aim to keep fixed costs as low as possible in their early days. Potential investors inspecting a start-up's financial plan generally want to be reassured that it won't waste precious capital overspending on fixed costs. Hence the popular stories about companies which are started in a founder's garage or garden shed rather than a swank office. In addition, founders are typically expected to pay themselves low salaries – or none at all – until the company becomes profitable. As shareholders, founders are expected to receive their reward when they sell their shares, if the company achieves its business goals and the value of the shares increases exponentially.

An exception to this practice of thrift is made when a company needs to broadcast an image of opulence or of expensively backed competence to establish its brand or signal its legitimacy in an industry or market. This is the case with venture capital-backed companies in a highly technical and high-risk field such as biotechnology. Such a company will typically hire the best chief scientist available and a team of highly experienced, highly paid professional managers in order to signal the company's credibility and competence to the large pharmaceutical companies that it wants to become its partners, customers and/or potential acquirers.

For novel products and technology, the costs of product design and technical development – which consist primarily of the salaries of specialist technical and design teams – can be a high fixed cost at an early stage in the company. For this reason, early-stage venture capital investors in science and technology businesses also look for a product that commands a high value in the eyes of customers, so that it can be highly priced and realise very high gross margins (of, say, 70 per cent or more), in order to recover those development outlays, reach overall profitability and positive cash flow, and result in a rise in company value and an acceptable return on investment, all within a suitable timeframe for the investor. If you expect a more moderate gross margin from your product, you may find it difficult to raise venture capital unless your fixed costs are negligible or sales volumes are *very* high.

Timing differences and the relationship between revenue, profit and cash flow. Another important distinction that's often unclear to the financially uninitiated is the difference between profit and cash flow.

While real or expected profit affects how a company is valued at sale or at the moment of raising an investment, cash flow affects the company's ability to operate and, most importantly, the amount of money required from outside sources such as lenders and investors.

Profit is simply expressed as a business's revenue minus its costs. So, if a company sells £100,000 worth of product in a month and its costs (both fixed and variable) amount to £70,000, the company registers a profit of

£30,000. *Cash flow*, on the other hand, describes the amount of cash that a company receives or spends during a period of time.

This may seem a pointless distinction, until you take into account the fact that many businesses, like people, buy things on short-term credit. For instance, if an individual consumer makes a purchase with a credit card in January, and pays the credit card bill one month later, the *sale* has taken place in January, but the customer does not part with his *cash* until February. Similarly, when company A supplies a product to company B, a business customer, A typically has an agreement with B to pay the invoice some time later, say, one month or more. Company A will also have similar agreements with its own suppliers of raw materials to pay them a bit late. Consequently, a difference exists between *registering* a sale and *receiving* the cash payment, and between *incurring* a cost (or *buying* goods) and *paying out* the cash.

Assume, for the sake of simplicity, that B is A's only customer. If B buys £10,000 worth of goods in one month, but pays two months later, A will invoice sales of £10,000 in that month, will incur costs of £5,000 and earn £5,000 profit. However, the *net cash flow* and *treasury position* (cash in hand) at the end of the month will be nil. The following month, A will have negative net cash flow and a negative treasury position because it pays out to its suppliers one month before receiving payment from its customer. As the example shown in Figure 39 evolves, you see that it takes several

	January	February	March	April
PROFIT AND LOSS				
Sales (invoiced)	8,000	10,000	8,000	9,000
Costs (incurred	−5,000	−5,000	−4,000	−4,000
Profit for period	3,000	5,000	4,000	5,000
CASH FLOW				
Sales (receipts in)	0	0	8,000	10,000
Costs (paid out)	0	−5,000	−5,000	−4,000
OPENING CASH	0	0	-5,000	0
Net cash flow (S–C)	0	−5,000	3,000	6,000
Closing cash (Treasury position)	0	−5,000	−2,000	6,000

Figure 39 **Timing differences between profit and cash flow for company A**

months before A's cash position is in the black, even though the company books a profit on sales *every* month.

Companies often described as 'cash cows' are those that get paid by their customers *before* they have to pay their suppliers. Supermarkets, for example, receive cash from customers at the moment of sale (either in banknotes or via electronic payment), but they're typically able to negotiate to pay their suppliers several months after they receive delivery of the food and other products that go on their shelves.

Start-ups and small companies, on the other hand, typically find themselves in the inverse situation. Because they're seen as precarious and unestablished, suppliers tend to demand rapid payment terms. Early customers may also negotiate for more leeway in payment terms as a condition of their custom.

The significant point to bear in mind is that cash flow is more crucial to a firm's *survival* than profit, which is used to gauge its *value*. If a company is booking a profit on paper, but has no actual cash in hand to pay its bills, it is technically insolvent. New ventures often need to spend a lot of money in the early start-up phase, long before they can begin making revenue. Even when revenue begins to flow in as cash, it will take some time for accumulated cash flow to make up for that early cash burn. This is why new ventures often need to raise large amounts of capital, whether from the founders, from subsidies or from business sources, just to get off the ground.

Working capital. Working capital comprises the current liquidity (cash) and short-term assets[50] (such as inventory) that a company uses to conduct day-to-day operations (as opposed to capital that has been invested in equipment and other long-term assets).

However, as explained above, a company usually owes some short-term debt to its suppliers and has granted some short-term credit to its customers – and the timing of the two may be different. Thus, *net* working capital is calculated to see whether these differences result in a shortfall or in a surplus.

Net working capital for a specific period of time is calculated by adding up current (liquid and short-term) assets related to that period, including:

- *Cash* in hand
- *Stock*, including raw materials and work-in-progress (since it should be sold in the short term)
- *Receivables*, that is, money owed to you, usually by customers, due within one year, and subtracting from the above sum
  - *Payables*, that is, money you owe to suppliers that is due within one year
  - *Short-term loans* and *interest payments* due in the next 12 months

If the company has more current assets than liabilities, or if the two are equal, it means that the company can cover its short-term commitments and is said to occupy a positive or break-even net working capital position. But if current liabilities exceed current assets, the company has a shortfall and occupies a negative net working capital position.

Supermarkets, as described in the previous section on cash flow, tend to occupy *positive* net working capital positions because they receive cash more quickly than they disburse it.

Start-ups, on the other hand, typically pay out a lot of money during the period in which they set up operations, before receiving any cash from revenue. They may also have less advantageous payment terms with suppliers than supermarkets. Thus a start-up will need to have a pool of cash to cover the shortfall between payments in and payments out. This shortfall is called the *net working capital need* (NWCN).

So, to return to Figure 39, if company A had an extra £5,000 pounds cash in hand at the end of January, it would be able to register a cash breakeven in the month of February. Its net working capital need for that period is therefore £5,000, a sum that could be provided by a bank loan, an agreed bank overdraft or an equity investor. However, equity investors generally do not like to fund working capital once a company is making sales. Debt, such as a long-term bank loan, is a cheaper option for the company; it will avoid further dilution of shareholdings and thus ultimately lead to a higher return on the equity capital already invested by the founders and other shareholders.

Investment in fixed assets and depreciation as they affect profit and cash flow. When a company purchases a *fixed asset* such as a building or some expensive equipment used for operations, from a financial perspective this one-time outlay is accounted for in a different way from monthly costs such as production costs, salaries, office rental and the like, which are subtracted in full from revenue to calculate the company's profits.

A fixed asset purchase is an investment in an object that will be used to create the company's products, and is consequently expected to generate a return over time in the form of revenue. However, because equipment is usually subject to wear and tear, a fixed asset is also estimated to have a 'useful life', after which it must be either thrown away or sold second-hand and replaced by a new one. Consequently, its purchase is registered as a one-time event in the company's cash flow statement, but its gradual drop in value, known as *depreciation*, is registered over time in the company's profit statements. The rationale behind this accounting practice is that the asset's cost, set against revenue, is thus spread over the same time period as the asset's expected usefulness for generating that revenue from products.

Thus, as shown in Figure 40, a £10,000 piece of equipment expected to last four years will be depreciated in the company's profit statement by £2,500 pounds per year, although it has a one-time effect on the company's cash position in the first year.

	2010	2011	2013	2014
Effect on cash flow	−10,000	–	–	–
Depreciation effect on profit	−2,500	−2,500	−2,500	−2,500

Figure 40 **Example of a machine with a four-year useful life, purchased for £10,000**

The crucial point is that spending on fixed assets affects cash flow and profits at different times, so a large drop in cash as a result of a fixed asset purchase doesn't translate into an immediate drop in profits of the same degree. Since a company usually buys fixed assets at the start of its life, their purchase usually makes up a considerable portion of early cash burn before sales are even registered, but subsequently affects profit while *not* affecting cash flow in later periods.

Cash burn and funding need. By now it should be clear that your financial plan should focus as much on cash flow as on profit, especially at the outset when determining the amount of money that needs to be raised to fund the business at the seed and start-up phases. For a certain period, the company will be either spending cash only or spending more cash than it's receiving from conducting business. This cash will be spent on salaries, fixed assets and any other expenses essential to developing and launching the business and its products. Negative net cash flow is commonly referred to as cash burn.

As Figure 41 illustrates, the maximum anticipated cash burn before the company can reach breakeven is the amount of money that needs to be raised to fund the business, whether from the founder's own savings, debt

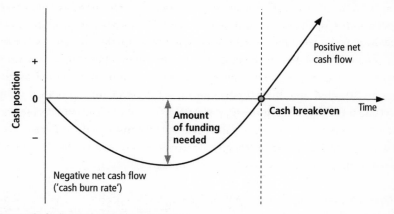

Figure 41 **The funding need created by early cash burn**

or equity investment. (It is actually a good idea to ask for a bit more than you expect to need to cover any contingencies.)

Cash burn should be kept as low as possible, on the one hand, yet cover the activities that are deemed essential to making the business successful, highly profitable and valuable, on the other. The less capital that needs to be raised, the higher the proportionate return on that capital in the long run.

The different effects of debt and equity on cash flow. In Chapter 11 on sources of capital, we explain that debt is cheaper than equity, and thus preferable for realising a greater return in the long run. A bank may grant a five-year loan and require a repayment of the loan plus 15 per cent per year in interest, whereas an early-stage equity investor will demand a share of the business that she hopes will entitle her to ten times her investment (1,000 per cent) when the business is sold in, say, five to seven years' time. Seeking equity investment at all may thus appear madness.

However, loans have an immediate effect on cash flow. Depending on the terms of the loan, a bank typically requires the borrower to start making monthly interest payments immediately, or to pay interest plus a portion of the loan repayment monthly. If a start-up venture is not yet selling product but is still in the phase of developing its offering, interest and loan repayments only contribute to cash burn. In theory, the company would have to borrow the amount of capital needed for its activities, *plus* the amount of interest and loan capital it would have to repay during the loan period. It is for this reason, and the risk involved, that banks generally don't make loans to pre-revenue start-ups. Government loan guarantee schemes in the UK allow for 'repayment holiday periods' to ease or avoid negative net cash flow, but this is still not a suitable option for long-term cash burn needs.

Equity investors in start-ups, on the other hand, do not expect to be repaid until they sell their shares at exit, so – in spite of the higher cost – equity investment is generally the more suitable source of capital for pre-revenue start-ups, if the founders cannot scrape enough money together from their own savings and those of friends and family.

Discounting and valuation. An aspiring entrepreneur may ask why investors make such low valuations of start-ups: if a promising new venture could be worth £100 million in several years, how can an investor demand a 40 per cent stake for a £2 million investment?

The answer is based on two factors: the *risk/reward ratio* and the *time value of money*.

In the first instance, it is an accepted business tenet that investors who take higher risks demand higher returns on their investments. In venture investing, this is especially the case because, out of a basket of high-risk investments, past experience shows that only a small portion will succeed, and the gains from these must make up for the losses elsewhere.

In the second instance, a nominal sum of money we expect to receive in the future is considered to be worth less than the same nominal sum if we are holding it in hand today. Apart from the expected erosion of buying power over time as a result of inflation, money in hand today is immediately useful to us, and therefore more valuable. If you lend one pound to someone for one year, the borrower will pay you interest at the end of the year to compensate you for tying up your money and foregoing other possible uses.

Therefore, a company expected to be worth £100 million in five years' time is worth considerably less today. Aside from the fact that the company's future value is still unproven and the investment consequently risky, investors demand compensation for tying up their money in a venture. The method by which they calculate that compensation is to *discount* the estimated future value of the company.

In purely financial terms, discounting is the opposite of compounding. Interest on a loan or bank deposit *compounds* or increases exponentially over time: £100 lent at a 5 per cent annual interest rate today will be worth £105 in one year (100 x 1.05) and £110.25 a further year on (100 x 1.05 x 1.05, also expressed as 100×1.05^2).

Discounting works in the inverse direction. If we again assume a 5 per cent interest rate, the present value of £100 that you will receive in two years' time is £90.70, or 100/1.05 /1.05, also expressed as $100/1.05^2$. If you have to wait three years to receive £100, the present value is $100/1.05^3$, or £86.38.

New venture investors are typically aiming for a potential tenfold or similar return on their investment to compensate for high risk (some angels may aim for a bit less and venture capitalists may even aim for more, for the reasons we explain in Chapter 11). So, a company that *could* be worth £100 million in five to seven years' time cannot be worth more than £10 million to the investor today, and the investor may discount the value even further for a margin of error, because there is a risk that the company could achieve a considerably lower value than £100 million in future, or even flop altogether. Hence the investor could potentially demand 40 per cent for a £2 million investment, valuing the company at £5 million today.

In practice, even this valuation would only be made for a company that's already achieved some milestones and proven some of its assumptions. Ventures at the seed stage, which are little more than a raw technology or product design and plan on paper, seldom get valued at more than £1 million when seeking a first round of investment of a few hundred thousand. The valuation remains low even if the business idea appears to have high growth potential, because the potential is largely unproven and the investment is consequently a very high risk. This is another reason why investments divided into tranches or rounds are beneficial to entrepreneurs as well as prudent for investors. If the company is able to prove its business assumptions by achieving its milestones and testing its offering, the company valuation will rise in the eyes of investors at each funding round.

In summary...

In short, a roadmap is a tool for planning and presenting a venture's interrelated activities and needs over time, but it is also a useful foundation for adjusting those plans in response to new events and changed circumstances.

We think of the components of a roadmap as falling into technical, operational and financial categories. In essence, we recommend that you:

- Map out alternative technology and product development and commercialisation paths, but determine which one you will prioritise and why. The reasons will usually lie in the characteristics of your industry environment and chosen market segments, as explained in Chapters 4, 5 and 6. The other possible development paths may however be kept in mind as fallback options, if environmental circumstances change and the preferred plan becomes unfeasible.
- Map out the likely operational development needed to achieve your chosen business goals, including types of business activity and the human resources needed to perform them.
- Cost these activities and determine or estimate the venture's likely financial development and funding needs, and preferable sources of capital. In most cases, it's important to aim to keep overhead costs as low as possible at an early stage, to limit cash burn and to synchronise activities so that increased value can be demonstrated at specific development stages, thus providing a rationale for follow-on funding rounds at increased valuations.

While assembling the above information may seem a tall order, don't wait until you have full information or certainty to create a roadmap. Start with a very basic map and then build it up or adjust it over time, as your venture's needs and prospects become clearer. You are likely to go back to the drawing board a number of times. Realise that potential investors will probably say that you need double the money and double the time you estimate!

EPILOGUE
THE ENTREPRENEURIAL BUSINESS CASE

In the introduction, we observe that many aspiring entrepreneurs get an idea for a business and instantly sit down to write a business plan, perhaps making use of templates available on the internet or in books on business planning. Rather than heading down that route, we recommend that you first do some serious research on your business *case*, and in this book we provide you with a staged approach to building a credible rationale.

The strength of your rationale depends on how astute your assumptions are regarding the product or service offering, the business, the market and the industry. The chapters in this book offer you some tools to help you test your own assumptions at an early stage, giving you the opportunity to adjust them and work out new strategies and business goals, or to entertain several possible strategies until your business landscape becomes clearer.

A business plan may take months to write and is often obsolete and needs to be rewritten by the time it's finished, because new venture environments change quickly in response to new technological, industrial and market developments.

Similarly, a venture business case is not a fixed story or a linear idea, but an evolving set of assumptions and intentions, much like the process of getting to know someone. It's likely to change over time as new information is unearthed and new developments emerge in your business and market environment, so you may find (or have found) yourself going through the thinking exercises in this book more than once, or in a different order to the one in which they're presented here, piecing together new assumptions and working out new strategies and business goals. Any new information you uncover should trigger the question: 'what does this mean for my intended business?'

Our model of a well-developed business case is one that can *explain* the following, in terms of:

- *Your product/service offering and its intrinsic value*:
  - A problem, need or opportunity and the product, service or technology you intend to commercialise as a solution or in response to the opportunity
  - How your solution addresses the need or opportunity, and why it is better than alternatives currently available
  - A range of possible applications for a technology, body of knowledge or idea, and why a certain application has been initially chosen over others

- *Your business's value and competitive position with respect to its environment*:
  - The chosen market segment, why it has been chosen as a first target over others, and how you can capture this segment
    - How the venture might expand to serve other segments subsequently
    - An understanding of the sales process required to address this segment
  - The industry environment for your chosen business idea, and the position your business will take in the industry value chain and why
  - Any steps you can take to protect your business from imitation
  - Your commercialisation strategy
  - Your route to a target market for products or technology, based on the environmental factors above and a chosen combination of technical, human, social and financial resources

- *Your direct understanding of your prospective customers and value chain partners*:
  - Ideally, you should be able to back up some of the assumptions outlined above based on preferred witness research and some basic, low-budget prototyping and market testing exercises
  - Industry and market reports published by research firms can offer a starting-point and some 'helicopter-view' information for further investigation, but they are no substitute for getting

the inside story from some real people, especially when your venture aims to target a niche market segment to start with or to create a new market altogether.

- *The resources you will need to implement the business*:
  - You understand the type of skills and team members required for your venture, and what sort of people you will need to find to complement your own knowledge and skills (including personal or 'soft' skills) or to fill any gaps
  - You have considered the type of funding path that will be most suitable for your venture
  - You have a basic view of the way the venture should develop technically, operationally and financially, and of possible alternative business strategies if your initial plans prove unfeasible

No book is a substitute for direct experience, and there's nothing wrong with trying and doing, and subsequently learning from the experience of success or failure. This book, however, describes some of the successes and pitfalls of previous entrepreneurs, and may help you to make sense of your own past experiences and results in order to take maximum advantage of any future opportunities.

The crucial point of a new business proposal, in whatever form, is your ability to justify your assumptions and intentions, based on the facts you know about your business environment and market, and to answer challenging questions that potential stakeholders (investors, partners and customers) are likely to ask. If you cannot answer such questions convincingly, it may be a sign that your business case needs more work.

When you come to write a business plan, there are certainly templates that you can adopt and guides you can consult.[51] Every business is different, however, and you should aim to create a document that does justice to your business rationale.

There's also a lot to be said for luck in entrepreneurship (being in the right place at the right time, meeting the right people and so on), as well as for initiative (adopting attitudes and taking actions that may help you find luck, such as an open mind, lots of networking and hard work).

When you meet your lucky moment, we hope this book helps you to be better prepared to seize it.

NOTES

INTRODUCTION

1. Anonymous quotation in 'Special report on entrepreneurship', *The Economist*, 12 March 2009
2. Office for National Statistics, Business demography, 2007
3. Department for Business, Innovation and Skills, SME statistics, 2007.

CHAPTER 1

4. Lumsdaine, E. and Binks, M. (2006) *Entrepreneurship from Creativity to Innovation: Effective Thinking Skills for a Changing World* (Oxford; Trafford Publishing).

CHAPTER 4

5. Ponnet, R. (2006) *Mijn Leven Aals Koppelaarster* (Netherlands: Standaard).
6. Miller, R.B. and Heiman, S.E. (2005) *The New Strategic Selling: The Unique Sales System Proven Successful by the World's Best Companies, Revised Edition* (New York: Business Plus). We also recommend that you read this book when you reach the stage of building a sales strategy.

CHAPTER 5

7. Porter, M.E. (1985) *Competitive advantage: Creating and Sustaining Superior Performance* (New York: Free Press).
8. Keller, K.L. (2008), 'Red Bull: Building Brand Equity in Non-traditional ways', *Best Practice Cases in Branding: Lessons From the World's Strongest Brands* (Upper Saddle River, NJ: Prentice Hall), pp. 73–99.

9. Teece, D.J. (1986) 'Profiting from Technological Innovation: Implications for Integration, Collaboration, Licensing and Public Policy', *Research Policy*, 15: 285–305.

CHAPTER 6

10. As first coined by Professor Henry William Chesbrough (2003) in *Open Innovation: The New Imperative for Creating and Profiting from Technology* (Cambridge, MA: Harvard Business School Press).

11. Garmin Ltd. and Garmin Corporation v. TomTom, Inc. [Case], 571 F. Supp. 2d 917 - Dist. Court, WD Wisconsin, 2007.

12. 'TomTom involved in several US patent lawsuits', Dow Jones Newswires, 28 April 2006.

13. 'The warning sound of TomTom', *ZDNet UK*, 27 February 2009.

14. 'TomTom settlement leaves key questions unanswered', *CNET*, 30 March 2009.

15. 'In our study of universities that own equity in start-up companies ... the average value of equity sold in 16 start-up companies is $1,384,242. ... In the U.S. about half of new businesses fail within five years ... If one assumes that half the start-ups will fail before they go public, the average value of equity at the time of sale is $692,121 ... A comparison we can make is to compare the average equity sale to the average income from a traditional license. In fiscal year 1996, ... U.S. universities received licensing income of $316,476,578 on a total of 4,958 licenses, for an average annual income per license of $63,832. The $692,121 average value of equity is therefore worth more than 10 years of income from the average license.' Cited in Bray, M.J. and Lee, J.N. (2000) 'University revenues from technology transfer: licensing fees vs. equity positions', *Journal of Business Venturing*, 15(5–6): 385–392.

16. Henkel, J. and Reitzig, M. (2008) 'Patent Sharks', *Harvard Business Review*, June; Fischer, T. and Henkel, J. 'Patent Trolls on Markets for Technology – An Empirical Analysis of Trolls' Patent Acquisitions', working paper, Technical University of Munich, 2009.

17. J. Henkel and Jell, F. (2009) 'Alternative Motives to File for Patents: Defensive Publishing in the Patent System', working paper, May.

CHAPTER 7

18. Clarysse, B., Bruneel, J. and Wright, M. (forthcoming 2011) 'Explaining Growth Paths of Young Technology Based Firms: Structuring Resource Portfolios in Different Competitive Environments', *Strategic Entrepreneurship Journal*; Bruneel, J. Clarysse, B. and Wright, M. (2010) 'Exploring the Commercial Strategies of Young Technology Based Firms: the Teece Framework Revisited', working paper, July.

19. Quotation and paraphrased story from Turpin, D. (2008) 'TomTom: building & marketing a new business concept' [case study], International Institute for Management Development, Lausanne.

20. A standardised service is one in which interaction with the customer is limited to specific, automated or scheduled operations, such as transportation services, banking and many online businesses. This is in contrast to customised services, such as a visit to a doctor or lawyer, where the service is produced on the spot in response to the client's immediate need, or semi-customised services, such as software consulting, whereby a starting set of software platforms or templates is customised for different clients. Companies offering standardised services function to a large extent like product companies.

21. Gans, J.S. and Stern, S. (2003) 'The Product Market and the Market for "Ideas": Commercialization Strategies for Technology Entrepreneurs', *Research Policy*, 32(2): 333–350.

22. Miller and Heiman, op. cit.

23. Tushman, M. and Anderson, P. (1986) 'Technological Discontinuities and Organizational environments', *Administrative Science Quarterly*, 31: 439–465).

24. Heirman, A. and Clarysse, B. (2004) 'How and Why do Research-based Start-ups Differ at Founding? A Resource-based Configurational Perspective', *Journal of Technology Transfer*, 29: 247–268.

25. Moore, G.A. (1999) *Crossing the Chasm: Marketing and Selling High-Tech Products to Mainstream Customers* (New York: HarperBusiness).

CHAPTER 8

26. Snyder, C. (2003) *Paper Prototyping: The Fast and Easy Way to Design and Refine User Interfaces* (Burlington, MA: Morgan Kaufmann).

27. Buchenau, M. and Suri, J.F. (2000) 'Experience Prototyping'; in Proceedings of the 3rd conference on designing interactive systems:

processes, practices, methods, and techniques, New York, pp. 424–433.

CHAPTER 9

28. Lohr, S. (2011) 'Can Apple Find More Hits Without its Tastemaker?', *New York Times*, 18 January.

29. www.fordcarz.com/henry-ford-quotes.

30. *Mad Men*, Season 4, Episode 4. Produced by Lionsgate Television, premiered on AMC, USA.

31. Zaltman, G. (2003) *How Customers Think: Essential Insights into the Mind of the Market* (Cambridge, MA: Harvard Business Press).

32. Malmsten, E., Portanger, E. and Drazin, C. (2001) *Boo Hoo: A Dot.com Story from Concept to Catastrophe*. (London: Random House).

33. Leonard, D. and Rayport, J.F. (1997) 'Spark Innovation through Empathic Design', *Harvard Business Review*, November–December.

34. Von Hippel, E. (1988/1994) *The Sources of Innovation*, first and second editions (Oxford: Oxford University Press).

35. Lilien, G.L., Morrison, P.D., Searls, K., Sonnack, M. and Von Hippel, E. (2002) 'Performance Assessment of the Lead User Idea-Generation Process for New Product Development', *Management Science*, 48(8): 1042–1059.

36. web.mit.edu/evhippel/www/

37. www.innocentdrinks.com

38. Lodish, L., Morgan, H. and Archambeau, S. (2007) *Marketing That Works: How Entrepreneurial Marketing Can Add Sustainable Value to Any Sized Company* (Upper Saddle River, NJ: Wharton School Publishing).

39. Such as Lodish et al., op. cit.

CHAPTER 10

40. Wright, M. and Vanaelst, I., eds. (2009) *Entrepreneurial Teams and New Business Creation* (Cheltenham: Edward Elgar Publishing Ltd).

CHAPTER 11

41. Two authoritative and accessible recent books by experienced European investors are: Berkery, D. (2008) *Raising Venture Capital for the Serious Entrepreneur* (New York: McGraw-Hill); Acland, S. (2011) Angels,

Dragons and Vultures: How to Tame Your Investors ... And Not Lose Your Company (London: Nicholas Brealey Publishing).

42. An animated video can be found on YouTube, at www.youtube.com/watch?v=0AMGqiVRAUA

43. Several demonstrations can be found on YouTube, starting with www.youtube.com/watch?v=NSiAmgtlbFo

44. www.mobify.me

45. www.businesslink.gov.uk

46. Murray, G. (1999) 'Early Stage Venture Capital Funds, Scale Economies and Public Support', *Venture Capital*, 1(4): 351–384.

47. A European directory can be obtained from the European Venture Capital Association (EVCA), www.evca.eu

48. The industry expression 'post-money valuation' means the value attributed to the company after the investors have provided funding. 'Pre-money' refers to a valuation before funding, eg the pre-money valuation at round one is €3m.

CHAPTER 12

49. For instance, Rice, A. (2011) *Accounts Demystified: The Astonishingly Simple Guide to Accounting* (Upper Saddle River, NJ: Prentice Hall); Berman, K., Knight, J. (2008) *Financial Intelligence for Entrepreneurs: What You Really Need to Know About the Numbers* (Cambridge, MA: Harvard Business School Press).

50. In accounting language, the terms current and short-term are used to refer to cash or any holdings (such as inventory) or commitments (such as outstanding invoices, bank overdrafts and loans) that are convertible into cash or due for repayment within 12 months. Money and goods held by the company are assets and monies owed are liabilities.

51. We recommend this succinct and reliable guide: Timmons, J.A., Zacharakis, A. and Spinelli, S. (2004) *Business Plans that Work: A Guide for Small Business.* (New York: McGraw-Hill).

INDEX